THE HANDBOOK OF
BRAND MANAGEMENT

THE
HANDBOOK
OF BRAND
MANAGEMENT

. . . . .

DAVID ARNOLD

The
Economist
Books

INTERNATIONAL MANAGEMENT SERIES

Addison-Wesley Publishing Company

Reading, Massachusetts   Menlo Park, California   New York
Don Mills, Ontario   Wokingham, England   Amsterdam
Bonn   Sydney   Singapore   Tokyo   Madrid   San Juan
Paris   Seoul   Milan   Mexico City   Taipei

Ashridge

Many of the designations used by manufacturers and sellers to distinguish their products are claimed as trademarks. Where those designations appear in this book and Addison-Wesley was aware of a trademark claim, the designations have been printed in initial capital letters (e.g., Gatorade).

The brand logos on the jacket of this book are registered trademarks used with the permission of the following companies: (clockwise from upper left) United Distillers, Pizza Hut, Inc Ocean Spray, Anheuser-Busch Companies, and Schering-Plough Corporation. These and other companies studied in this book did not necessarily participate in its preparation, and none of the companies warrant the accuracy of the representations contained herein.

LIBRARY OF CONGRESS CATALOGING-IN-PUBLICATION DATA

Arnold, David.
      The handbook of brand management/David Arnold.
         p.   cm. — (The Economist books) (International management series)
      Includes bibliographical references and index.
      ISBN 0-201-63279-9
      1. Brand name products—United States. 2. Brand name products—United States—Marketing. 3. Advertising—Brand name products—United States. I. Title. II. Series. III. Series: International management series.
      HD69.B7A76 1992
      658.8′27—dc20   92-31025
                                                                CIP

First published in Great Britain by Century Business, an imprint of Random Century Limited, in association with The Economist Books Ltd.

Jacket design by Richard Rossiter
Text design by Lloyd Lemna Design
Set in 10-point Palacio by ST Associates Inc., Wakefield, MA

3 4 5 6 7 8 9 10—MA—0201009998
Third printing, March 1998

Addison-Wesley books are available at special discounts for bulk purchases by corporations, institutions, and other organizations. For more information, please contact:

Special Markets Department
Addison-Wesley Publishing Company
Reading, MA 01867
(617) 944-3700 x 2431

Contents

List of Figures

List of Tables

Foreword

An understanding of brands and brand marketing is essential to an understanding of modern industrial society. Brands respond to the consumer's need for products that perform a clear function, perform it consistently, and offer something distinctive in open competition. Marketing starts with an understanding of the consumer's needs, functional and psychological. It encapsulates them in the brand and communicates them in the marketplace.

In doing so, marketing bridges the incredible range of production possibilities provided by modern technology, with the equally extensive range of consumer needs made possible by modern living standards. This is most obvious in highly advertised consumer goods, and to the service industries.

This book appears at a time when brand marketing is at a crucial stage in its development. More than ever, success depends on a sensitive response to the precise needs of specific markets and market sectors. At the same time, global trends in technology and lifestyle create markets for international brands, meeting similar needs in different countries. There are implications for every phase of marketing from product design to organization.

The coming generation of marketing practitioners and managers in general will live in an exciting and demanding world. They will, more than ever, need to understand every aspect of their business. This book will help them greatly in that task. It offers guidance at both the conceptual and practical levels. It is both timely and welcome.

Sir Michael Angus
Chairman, Unilever

Introduction

• • • • • • • • • • • • •

Brands—The Newest Assets

Branding hit the headlines in 1988, which *The Economist* dubbed "The Year of the Brand," and it has stayed there ever since. "What has made 1988 the year of the brand is the sudden discovery of the brand and brand-skill as things of capital worth. Until recently, few business people outside the big consumer-goods companies got excited about brands. . . . No longer."[1]

Two big company acquisitions in 1988 pushed brands into the limelight: Philip Morris's takeover of Kraft in the United States, and in Europe the takeover of the British confectioner Rowntree by the world's largest food company, Nestlé. What was newsworthy was the premium paid for the brand names owned by Kraft and Rowntree. Philip Morris paid four times the value of the "actual" or tangible assets, and Nestlé paid over five times. How could "names" be worth so much? The underlying cause of the sky-high valuation was that these brands were judged capable of delivering superior levels of profit over the long run.

The opening of a Moscow branch of McDonald's in 1990 illustrates how branding is now seen as a strategic issue. The media reported the event as the start of a new social order in the U.S.S.R. *The Economist* wrote that "the symbolism is irresistible: The epitome of capitalist consumerism comes to the citadel of world communism."[2] *The Times* of London described the opening: "A portion of the American dream came to Pushkin Square. . . . Contemplating what she described as 'this dazzling palace' one journalist said that the secret of McDonald's would be harder for Russians to penetrate than the B-2 bomber."[3]

The implication—that a fast food company could change the social values of a society—is staggering. Some reporters even argued that commercial brands like McDonald's, Levi's, and Coca-Cola were the only ambassadors capable of winning over the hearts and minds of former enemies.

Several factors make the power of brands more noticeable:

- The big brands are becoming more globally available, as their owners seek growth in new regions and as consumers travel more.
- The world is becoming more homogeneous in cultural terms as communications technology develops. Consumption patterns are therefore converging, and the big brands are the first to benefit.
- The big brands are increasingly used as entry tickets to new markets, as their owners look for growth outside their maturing home markets. Mars, with no experience in producing and distributing frozen products, has used its brand name to enter a mature European ice cream market and command a price premium. Within two years, it has forced an established player, Lyons, out of the market.
- Branding is no longer restricted to fast-moving consumer goods (FMCG) markets. Service companies are increasingly turning to branding as their competitive thrust. Even industrial companies are brand-building, perhaps inspired by the success of brand names in markets like computers and office equipment.

Underlying these trends is a new view of business strategy. After World War II, growth seemed guaranteed to any reasonably efficient management. Markets were growing, distribution was patchy, supply rarely exceeded demand, and consumers aspired to a common standard of well-being. Strategy was inevitably seen as the efficient expansion of capacity—hence the growth of diversified conglomerates in the 1950s and 1960s, and the development of strategy models based upon the relationship between investment in assets and returns.

In the 1990s, growth markets have become increasingly scarce and consumers, who are more discriminating and faced with greater choice, have the balance of power. Investment alone is not enough;

returns can be made only if the customer decides to buy, and buy again, from the choices offered. Research shows that attracting first-time buyers costs five to six times as much as selling to existing customers.[4] Companies like Philip Morris and Nestlé know that branding is the key to winning customer purchase decisions. The relationship with customers is increasingly seen as the central strategic issue for the long-term health of an organization. As a result, branding will long remain on the boardroom agenda.

REFERENCES

1. *The Economist* (December 24, 1988), p. 101.
2. *The Economist* (February 3, 1990).
3. *The Times* (February 1, 1990).
4. Tom Peters, *Thriving on Chaos*: *Handbook for a Management Revolution* (New York: Knopf, 1987), p. 321.

Acknowledgments

The original spur for writing this book was a request from a group of senior managers on an in-company development program at Ashridge Management College. They were increasingly finding decisions about brand-name products on the agenda at meetings but were confused by the details of an area previously left to marketing specialists. What they said they needed was an authoritative but concise guide to help them understand brands, something to refer to afterward. This book will, I hope, make life easier for them and the many other managers in the same situation in an increasingly brand-conscious business world. At the same time, I must acknowledge their contribution to my own understanding—all commentators or teachers learn a great deal from their "pupils," and the contribution of the managers from all types of brand companies and agencies with whom I have worked at Ashridge has proved immense.

Appropriately, many have contributed directly to the case history material in the book. I owe them all thanks for the time they have been prepared to devote to it.

In the United States and Canada:

> Jeffrey Bye, Gary van Deursen, Ann Jalbert, and Rob Pollack at Black & Decker
> Steve Dinsmore and John Moreton at Ocean Spray
> Larry Dykstra, Cindy Harris, and Paul McGochie at Quaker Oats
> Philippe Krakowsky, Richard Kronengold, Stacy Styles, and Jeff Williamson at BBDO
> Bob Kulin and Douglas Petkus at Schering-Plough
> Jeff Lawson and Roger Rydell at Pizza Hut
> Michael Lenzen at Fleishman Hillard

Donald Meyer at Anheuser-Busch
Gerald Schoenfeld at Schoenfeld Chapman & Pearl
Jan Soderstrom at Visa

In Europe:

David Baker at J. Walter Thompson
Carole Butler and Brent Gosling at Ogilvy & Mather
Gavin Chalcraft at Landor Associates
Carol Coutts at The Research Business International
Pat Dade at Applied Futures Ltd.
Keith Dilworth at Findus (Nestlé)
Stephen Gatfield, Brian Jacobs, and Glynne Jenkins at Leo Burnett
Terry Hanby and Philip Parnell at United Distillers
Kate Killeen and Jan Hall at Coley Porter Bell
Charlie Robertson at Bartle Bogle Hegarty
Michael Roe at Research International

All this research and consultation has required considerable effort and co-ordination. I should particularly like to thank Julie Gray (in the United Kingdom) and Miles Prescott (in the United States), who shared the research burden and provided a valuable sounding board to my ideas. Hubert Hennessy, of Babson College, and George Bickerstaffe also made valuable contributions to the research project. Thanks are due as well to all those who granted me permission to quote their material.

Finally, there are two organizations whose support has been my real source of inspiration. The Economist Books team of Sarah Child, Carolyn White, and Penny Butler have applied their encouragement and vision with great understanding to help me meet a tight schedule. My employer, Ashridge Management College, has provided a fertile ground for my ideas and, in a more practical way, support for the project of writing the book. I owe special thanks for the contribution of my colleagues Malcolm Schofield, who constantly challenges and sharpens my marketing thinking; Virginia Merritt, who turned an idea into a concrete project; and Sara Crowe and Lin Thompson, whose superb administrative skills were responsible for producing the manuscript.

THE HANDBOOK OF
BRAND MANAGEMENT

Understanding Brands

. . . .

The Power of the Brand

Table 1.1 is a ranking of the world's top brands carried out and published in 1990 by Interbrand, a British consulting firm.[1] These brands are leaders in their fields and represent between them billions in revenues and profits. Interestingly, this ranking was produced not from simple facts like sales, profit, or market share, but from a combination of qualitative criteria that give an idea of what a strong brand can deliver for a company: market leadership, a stable or sustainable competitive advantage, international reach, a platform from which to expand activities, and, of course, long-term profit.

What does it mean to say that these are "brands"? Some of them, after all, are corporations, whereas most people think of a brand as a well-known product.

Table 1.1 **The World's Top Ten Brands**

World ranking	Brand	World ranking	Brand
1	Coca-Cola	6	IBM
2	Kellogg's	7	American Express
3	McDonald's	8	Sony
4	Kodak	9	Mercedes-Benz
5	Marlboro	10	Nescafé

Source: Interbrand.

What Is a Brand?

The world's standard marketing textbook, written by Philip Kotler, defines a brand as "a name, term, symbol, or design, or a combination of them, which is intended to signify the goods or services of one seller or group of sellers and to differentiate them from those of competitors."[2] At one level this technical explanation is true. As improvements in manufacturing and distribution give consumers an ever greater choice, some form of supplier identification becomes a necessary piece of information in the purchase selection. However, the modern brand has outgrown the mechanical aspects of product differentiation. Today's great brands are personalities, as intrusive in our culture as film stars, sports heroes, or fictional characters. Clint Eastwood, Coca-Cola, Boris Becker, Kodak, Madonna, IBM, and Donald Duck are equally well known.

Ask consumers to describe a branded product, and they will not usually reply with descriptions of terms, symbols, and designs. They will reply with adjectives describing the qualities of the brand. Moreover, as any international market researcher will testify, consumers around the world are remarkably consistent. Brands are recognized and "understood" on an emotional level, in a way that most of their founders would find astonishing.

Ask the question of a brand's competitors and they will tell you that the biggest obstacle they face is the "name" or reputation of Sony, or Kellogg's, or whomever (just as audiences will flock to see a Clint Eastwood movie without knowing anything about it other than that he is in it). A brand, then, is a sort of prejudice, in the literal sense of a prejudgment. Like all prejudices, it will seem unfair to the people who are on the wrong end of it—in this case, the less well-known competitors of the big brands.

> *Branding, therefore, has to do with the way customers perceive and buy things; it is not simply a characteristic of certain industries.*

Principles of Brand Performance

Three important principles emerge from research into brand performance:

1. Market leaders and superior brand positions are interlinked. The top brands listed in Table 1.1 are virtually all leaders in their markets. This cannot be explained by the weight of their advertising, or some inherent product superiority, or the catchiness of their name, even though they all score well on these counts. The best research on the factors behind market performance, the ongoing PIMS (Profit Impact of Market Strategy) data base of the Strategic Planning Institute, suggests that the real key to market leadership is superior *perceived* quality.[3] Not inherent product quality; only the perception of the quality by the customer. Market leadership depends upon how the product meets the needs and wants of the consumer, and given that customers can sometimes want what seem like strange and irrational things, definitions of quality produced in the R&D laboratories or on the shop floor risk missing the point altogether. Because quality is driven by perception, branding is a key issue in attaining and keeping market leadership. The "market power" that simply comes from being a leader gives a brand all sorts of other advantages, from bargaining power with the distribution trade to a general aura of quality in the minds of many consumers. This does not mean that strong brands have to be big mass-market players; but that, even if they are niche products, they have a leading share of the part of the market they have chosen to serve or target (known as the "served market").

2. Market-leading brands tend to have higher profit margins. Traditional microeconomics suggests that lower prices are the key to higher sales, and yet all these top brands maintain their leadership positions in the face of cut-price alternatives. Research shows that market leaders command a price premium and therefore a higher rate of profitability. Recent surveys conclude that in the United States the market leader returns a margin four times that of the number two in the market, and in the United Kingdom over six times the margin.[4] Leading brands also demonstrate greater resilience during recessions or price wars. It used to be thought that this unfair advantage arose from economies of scale in manufacturing, but the PIMS research is demonstrating that brands become market leaders because superior perceived quality is reflected in consumers' willingness to pay more. Once brands have a leadership position, it is possible that economies of scale will follow; but it is important to understand that the quality is driving the scale. The "virtuous cycle" begins with superior perceived relative quality, leads on to higher sales, and delivers economies of scale as a symptom rather than a cause.

Table 1.2 **The Leading U.S. and U.K. Brands Since 1933, Selected Products**

U.S. Brands		U.K. Brands	
BRAND	MARKET	BRAND	MARKET
Eastman Kodak	Cameras/film	Hovis	Bread
Del Monte	Canned fruit	Stork	Margarine
Wrigley	Chewing gum	Kellogg's	Cornflakes
Nabisco	Baked goods	Gillette	Razors
Gillette	Razors	Schweppes	Mixers
Coca-Cola	Soft drinks	Colgate	Toothpaste
Campbells	Soup	Kodak	Film
Ivory	Soap	Hoover	Vacuum cleaners
Goodyear	Tires		

Source: Interbrand.

3. There is no such thing as a brand life cycle. Once a leading brand is established with a loyal customer base, it is more than likely that the position will be maintained for a long time. The brands listed in Table 1.2[5] (see above) have clearly defied the widely known product life cycle (explained on pages 99–101), by which all products are eventually superseded by superior alternatives. Brands are larger than products, large enough to be repeatedly updated and altered in almost any aspect to maintain their relevance to the market. Indeed, as long as the brand is kept up to date with evolving standards and values, there is no reason why it should not live forever; the actual contents of a can of Coca-Cola or a box of Bold may change, but the brand personality, if well managed, can remain the same. All purchase decisions involve an element of risk, and buying behavior shows that the drive for something well known and trusted is stronger than the drive for novelty.

> *A successful brand must offer the consumer superior perceived quality. It must be managed consistently over a long period, to develop a position or personality. Once this is achieved, market leadership and higher profitability may well follow.*

The New Emphasis on Customer Satisfaction

It is only in the last decade or so that companies (in the West in particular) have realized that the "softer" or less quantifiable elements of business, such as quality and brand image, are at the heart of business success. One of the most influential figures behind this shift in thinking, Tom Peters of "excellence" fame, has said: "All the evidence shows that if you look after long-term customer satisfaction, all the other stuff like profit and market share will be sure to follow—it doesn't work the other way round."[6] Most of our thinking on business in the West was until recently starting at the wrong end by dealing with the symptoms of business performance, such as rates of return on fixed assets, rather than with the causes of that performance, such as why people buy anything produced by those fixed assets in the first place.

Branding, because it deals with the mechanics of customer preference, is now seen as a powerhouse of profit rather than a selling gimmick. This view of branding is pushing it into the limelight and is also a symptom of a changing view of marketing in general in the 1990s.

Writing recently in the *Harvard Business Review*, Regis McKenna articulated an emerging view of how value is created for customers:

> Several decades ago there were sales-driven companies . . . practicing the "any color as long as it's black" school of marketing. [Later] companies expressed a new willingness to change their products to fit customers' requests—practicing the "tell us what color you want" school of marketing. In the 1990s, successful companies will practice "let's figure out together whether and how color matters to your larger goal" marketing.[7]

Marketing thinkers are increasingly stressing the need for a close relationship with customers, which will lead to a *total* understanding of what customers need. Marketing expert Stephen King describes contemporary customers as confident, mature, and affluent, which he argues will lead to "rampant individualism." He sees one of the symptoms of this as "a new concept of quality . . . increasingly based on what they feel are *real* values—not superficial styling."[8]

Brands as Equity

Companies with major brands have a major asset. The asset, of course, is no more than prejudice, even if it gets called goodwill, loyalty, reputation or preference. However, it is a powerful and lasting asset, and a company can make profits out of it for years, just as a film star or politician can live off a reputation for years. It is, in brand marketing terms, an equity. Some companies (see Chapter 10) now show these assets on their balance sheets in the same way that they account for tangible assets. (Until now they appeared in a company's accounts, as goodwill, only when the company was being valued for purchase.)

Companies without major brands are increasingly aware that merely supplying a product at the right time, place, and price is not enough to access customer loyalty. They are asking how brands are built, how they work, and how they should be managed. The answers to their questions go to the very heart of marketing.

Branding and the Principles of Marketing

Branding, properly understood, is virtually synonymous with marketing. The rest of this chapter deals with the principles of marketing in relation to branding.

Marketing is the management process responsible for creating and delivering customer satisfaction. This in turn should lead to the loyalty or prejudice that is the basis of repeat business, the foundation of nearly all great brands (see Figure 1.1 on page 7). A simplified view of marketing is that it is concerned with decisions in four areas, known widely as the "marketing mix" or the "Four P's": product, price, promotion, and place (or distribution). Decisions in these areas cannot be made without a clear idea of the benefits sought by customers and those offered by the company. Branding plays an important role in clarifying these points.

Some of the basic truths about the way people buy things help explain why branding exists:

1. **Customers never understand a product as well as the company selling it.** Suppliers understand everything that goes into a product and its various applications. A customer, by contrast, usually having only a fleeting and superficial relationship with the product, is relatively ignorant. Customers may not even be interested. Charles Revson, the founder of the cosmetic house Revlon, is often quoted as saying: "In the factories we make cosmetics; in the stores we sell hope." Unless people in the supplier company can put aside all their product knowledge, and put themselves in the shoes of their "ignorant" customers, they cannot claim to be market-oriented.

2. **Customers will perceive a product in their own terms.** Given their imperfect knowledge of the product, customers have to select some attribute relevant to them (the *salient* attribute) on which to

Figure 1.1. **The Marketing Chain**

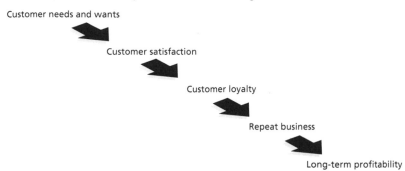

Customer needs and wants

Customer satisfaction

Customer loyalty

Repeat business

Long-term profitability

base their perception. This will usually be the attribute most obvious to the customer in the use of the product and the delivery of its benefits, even if it is actually peripheral. Tom Peters quotes Don Bird, the chairman of People's Express: "Customers think that if there are coffee stains on the flip-down tables, we don't do our engine maintenance right."[9] For an airline passenger, the flip-down tables are a salient attribute because they are right in front of them for the duration of the flight. The engines, arguably the most important factor in the delivery of the service of a flight, are not important to customer perception; they are out of sight, assumed to be in order, and largely out of mind. Similarly, we may judge a detergent by how it smells rather than how it washes; or a wine by the label design rather than the taste. Different customers will choose different salient attributes. There is no single way of perceiving a product or service; every customer has a personalized view. In most cases this is not based upon the attributes that the supplier would naturally use to describe the product or service.

3. Customer perception will focus on benefits, which are often intangible. Customer perception can seem almost irrational to people in supplier companies. This is because customers focus on what a product or service can do for them, rather than on what it actually is. Benefits, of course, are intangible—but that does not mean that they are not real. A gift may well carry extra benefits if it is manufactured by a top Parisian fashion house or a supplier to the British Royal Family. This is because an important benefit of a gift is the message that it sends from donor to recipient, and that message is enhanced by these "special" labels. Similarly, customers who declare that they will buy only cars made in their own country are seeking an intangible benefit.

4. Customer perception is not always at the conscious level. If we ask a customer why a product was chosen, we may get a rational answer, but it may not be the whole story. Feelings about products are not always easily articulated, because they are complex, emotional, and based upon a long-term relationship. We therefore need methods of probing into the subconscious to attempt to uncover what is driving the decisions.

In marketing, unlike other areas, these basic principles are of infinitely greater importance than all manner of specialist knowledge about technicalities. This is perhaps why marketing is often described as a "concept" or "philosophy" rather than a subject.

> *Customers rarely have detailed knowledge about products or services and judge them by any attribute that strikes them as important. The supplier may regard this attribute as peripheral. Customer perception may be based upon emotional responses, may involve intangible benefits, and may not always take place entirely on a rational and conscious level. The best evidence of the validity of these universal truths is the existence of brands.*

The Brand: The Means of Delivering Satisfaction

The Difference Between Brands and Products

Branding is about the way people perceive, and not about the products in isolation. A useful analogy is proposed by John Murphy in his book *Brand Strategy*, where he compares brands to the psychological concept of *gestalt*. This means:

> literally "form" or "shape" and the concept behind the *gestalt* is that nothing is simply the sum of its individual parts. . . . In psychology the process has been adopted to explain the process of perception. . . . A baby does not initially understand that the shapes it sees around it are people. Once it does, however, it is able to take scraps of information (a brief glimpse of a hand, or the smell of a particular fragrance) and conjure up . . . an overall form or *gestalt*. . . . A brand acts as a *gestalt* in that it is a concept which is more than the sum of its parts and which takes a long time to establish in the mind of consumers.[10]

A brand is then a form of mental shorthand. The main benefit is that it removes the need to shop around and devote effort to a serious analysis of the choices in the product category. Consumers simply cannot afford the time and energy to treat every purchase as a first-time buy. Choosing a brand is time-saving, giving a dependable and risk-free choice.

In some cases, there is very little difference between a product and a brand. A professional fuel scientist buying coal for a power station, for instance, is likely to be both knowledgeable and hard-headed about the commodity being purchased (although suppliers can still differentiate in areas like delivery and payment terms, after-sales service, and so on). Other consumers may not be able to tell the difference between products in a blind test and yet have very firm preferences when choosing between brands on a supermarket shelf. In such a case a very small piece of information, such as a logo or a particular shape of bottle, is enough to conjure up the brand personality.

> *It is clear that the starting point for brand management is to understand the satisfactions that the customer is paying for. This goes to the heart of marketing, the dynamics of demand.*

The vital first step is to be able to distinguish the two levels of demand: the need, concerned with market definition and strategic marketing; and the wants, the object of positioning and tactical marketing.

The Dynamics of Demand: Needs

Marketing-orientation means focusing on benefits rather than the products that deliver them. Thus a car is meaningless in itself but meets the need for transport, a benefit that makes it valuable to the large number of people who constitute the market. There is no market for cars, but there is a market for transport.

All organizations should understand the need met by their products. This is not always as straightforward as in the case of cars. A chocolate manufacturer, for instance, may be meeting the need for snacks with some products, and the need for gifts with others. Take a casual shirt and sew on a Lacoste or Dunhill logo and it soars in value, because it is moving from the clothing market to the fashion or status market. Is a light bulb manufacturer meeting the needs of lighting companies for an essential component, or the end users' need for an interior décor that improves the environment in which they live? Decisions like these will determine the way a company is managed.

"Need" is being used here not as an absolute survival need but as any enduring and widespread human motivation. This includes such ephemeral areas as information, entertainment, and status. Indeed, in developed countries where survival needs are taken for granted, these needs are far more motivating than the basic human needs of food and drink, clothing, and shelter. Try positioning a food product as something that the consumer needs to continue living, and you won't sell many. Position it as the food that film stars and royalty eat, and you have a chance.

Market definition (i.e., a market-oriented identification of the need) is a strategic necessity that will help a company in two ways. First, it will help the company see what it should do (or not do). Table 1.3 shows how the critical success factors for a Swiss watch manufacturer changed when it moved from the time-keeping market to the fashion accessory market after the advent of the digital quartz chip, which meant that accurate time-keeping could be virtually guaranteed at a relatively low price. A chocolate manufacturer may find that the key considerations in the snack market are all related to distribution and the taste of the product, whereas in the gift market for boxed chocolates the package is the most important consideration.

Second, a proper market definition will help a company identify its competition, understand its competitive arena, and formulate a competitive strategy. Swatch illustrates this well. Similarly, the competition for a chocolate bar is other food products, but for a box of chocolates it may be a gift, such as flowers, a book, a bottle of champagne, etc.

Despite these insights, the identification of the need for a product goes only some way toward building a brand. In many markets, the meeting of the need is a qualifying criterion for all competitors. All cars deliver the basic benefit of transport, so the customer will look at different attributes to differentiate between the alternatives offered. This is where customer preference is built, and this therefore is the platform for branding.

Table 1.3 **The Changing Challenge for the Swiss Watch Producer**

	Need	Appeal to consumer	Basic skill required	Critical success factors
Old market				
Watch	Information	Accuracy	Engineering/ craftsmanship	*Skilled workers *Product reliability *Quality of raw materials
New market				
Swatch	Fashion	Appearance	Design	*Frequent change of product range *Fashionable image *Widespread availability *Flexibility of production system

The Dynamics of Demand: Wants

In terms of consumer demand, wants are specific, vary much more between people than do needs, and change more frequently.

Wants are usually the basis of the selection of a product by a customer. All people in the transportation market share a need, but in choosing a car they differ significantly. Some want comfort, some safety, some better acceleration, and some a higher top speed. A cluster of people who share a want constitute a market segment.

A want may be neither tangible nor conscious. Plenty of brands are selected because their advertising creates a personality that consumers then transfer to the brand. It might be possible to make whiskey outside Scotland indistinguishable from Scotch whiskey in a blind test, yet millions of consumers would still want their whiskey to have been made in Scotland and would not even consider buying anything else.

These intangible wants of image or personality are becoming increasingly important, as the number of markets in which it is possible to boast a sustainable tangible superiority in the physical product decreases. Converging technologies, information that is more widely and speedily available—these and other forces conspire against simple product superiority in anything but the short term. However, products that are physically indistinguishable may be quite different in the eyes of consumers if they are presented or branded differently.

There are two reasons why intangible wants are so powerful in the creation of major brands. First, they are exceedingly difficult for competitors to copy. Competitors in Asia and other countries have shown how easy it is to copy IBM personal computers very accurately. Some customers will choose these "clones" because of their judgment on the relationship between physical specification and price. Yet it is clear that IBM's business remains strong because enough customers will not do business with anyone other than the industry leader and standard-setter.

Second, consumers get more involved in intangibles than physical products. In lay terms, consumers relate to a product with their brain, but to a brand with their heart. Customer loyalty, the essence of a brand, tends to come from the heart. Therefore the creation of a brand that offers values, or any image over and above the physical product, is more likely to elicit loyalty in a way that the simple product does not.

> *The need met by a product is vital for understanding the critical success factors facing a company, but brand differentiation is more usually driven by positioning to meet consumer wants. In particular, the intangible or emotional wants of consumers are the source of loyalty to a brand.*

SUMMARY

The last decade has seen a shift in the way we think about business strategy. In increasingly competitive markets, customer preference and loyalty are a key to success. Because branding can deliver these, it has moved up from a marketing concern to a general management issue.

Branding is, however, inextricably linked with the central principles of marketing. Marketing is about understanding two levels of demand: needs, which define the boundaries and the critical success factors of a market; and wants, the "extras" that are valued by customers and are used by them to differentiate between alternative products. Branding is concerned primarily with this second level, where customer perceptions form the basis of the relationship between customer and product. A brand is an expression of that relationship.

CHECKLIST

The management of a brand is only possible within truly market-focused organizations. The following questions must be addressed:

- What need defines the market?
- What salient attributes do customers judge to be the central benefits (and expect all products to offer)?
- What other benefits, tangible or intangible, are or might be valued by all or part of the market?
- What are the key dimensions of differentiation—that is, how do customers discriminate between products?
- How are the various products in the market perceived by customers and what are their brand personalities?

There is only one way to answer these questions—by asking customers. This must be done in a bias-free environment and the questions must probe beneath superficial, rational responses. A professional researcher is usually needed.

REFERENCES

1. Interbrand, *Brands: An International Review* (Mercury Business Books, 1990), p. 22.
2. Philip Kotler, *Marketing Management, Analysis, Planning, Implementation, and Control,* 5th ed. (Englewood Cliffs, N.J.: Prentice Hall, 1984), p. 482.
3. Robert D. Buzzell and Bradley T. Gale, *PIMS Principles, Linking Strategy to Performance* (New York: Free Press, 1987), p. 81.
4. Peter Doyle, "Building Successful Brands: The Strategic Options," *Journal of Consumer Marketing* 7, no. 2, and *Journal of Marketing Management* 5, no. 1 (1990).
5. Interbrand, *Brands,* p. 9.
6. Tom Peters, *A Passion for Excellence* (video), Melrose Video, 1986.
7. Regis McKenna, "Marketing Is Everything," *Harvard Business Review* (January/February 1991), p. 66.
8. Stephen King, "Brand Building in the 1990s," *Journal of Marketing Management* 7, no. 1 (1990), p. 5.
9. Peters, *A Passion for Excellence.*
10. John M. Murphy, *Brand Strategy* (Englewood Cliffs, N.J.: Prentice Hall, 1990), p. 45.

The Anatomy of a Brand

. . . .

Criteria of Success

Given the complexity of relationships between consumers and the things they buy, it follows that a successful brand is also complex. To be strong enough to deliver the superior perceived quality discussed in the previous chapter, a brand is going to have to address many elements of consumer perception and demand. Remembering that quality is not an inherent physical characteristic but a customer perception, we can arrive at the following criteria for a successful brand:

1. **On the product level, it must deliver functional benefits to meet the market need at least as well as the competition.** A brand is not merely the creation of advertising or packaging. Obviously, no product will thrive in the long term if it does not perform. To be the pioneering product in a particular area is a strong basis on which to build a brand, but it is not essential so long as the customer is satisfied with the product. A brand cannot be created by simply changing the name of a failing product and putting a large advertising budget behind it.

2. **A brand will offer intangible benefits over and above the product.** To elicit loyalty, a brand must offer some intangible benefits. These are usually referred to as values. The delight of watching Lendl play against Agassi at tennis is more than just watching the angle and pace of the shots. The contrast between characters, styles, and approaches to the game is what involves the crowd. It is the

same with products. Levi jeans offer the values of toughness, informality, and American-ness, whereas Gucci jeans offer style and a cosmopolitan image. These personalities are the stock in trade of branding. Personality is a benefit, as the price premium of leading brands over the decades demonstrates.

3. The various benefits of a brand must be consistent with each other and present a unified character or personality. The perception of brands is not based upon painstaking analysis; customers will often come to a quick and superficial conclusion, using their buying "shorthand." If the offer to the consumer is too complex, or different this year from last year, it may not be considered at all, not because consumers are stupid but because they may not be willing to take the necessary trouble to work out what is being offered. The brand must stand out from the crowd of its competitors. With Lendl and Agassi this is almost guaranteed; personalities do not change in the short term. With inanimate brands, a company must actively manage the personality to make it clear and consistent over time.

4. The values offered must be wanted by the consumer. No brand personality, however clear and consistent, is of any use unless it meets consumer wants. All purchases are judged on the basis of value. Value is not some intrinsic quality measurable on an absolute scale, but a consumer perception. If the brand can offer something that is valued and that customers judge that nobody else can offer as well, we have the basis of long-term preference. But wants change: In the 1990s brands can offer promises like "ozone friendly" or "low in cholesterol," which would not have added a penny of value in earlier decades.

The Balance Between a Brand's Tangible and Intangible Elements

In some markets, like cigarettes or certain drinks, it is still argued that advertising is the single most important element of the brand. Most definitions, however, suggest that a brand must have a basis in some form of product differentiation, however slight. Occasionally, a brand such as the Sony Walkman relies solely on product differences, but it is extremely hard to sustain this advantage. Sony is clearly well aware of the need to build intangible brand strengths to maintain the market position it has built up by perceived functional superiority.

With converging technologies, static markets, and increasingly affluent and discriminating consumers, everything points to the intangibles becoming ever more important in the brand equation.

The relative emphasis of these different characteristics in the
makeup of a brand is central to brand management. It governs decisions on the positioning strategy adopted to present the brand to the
market. The two extremes are brands based largely on image and
personality, and brands based primarily upon perceived functional
supremacy. In recent writings McWilliam and de Chernatony argue
that the balance between what they call "functionality" and "repre-
sentationality" is the basic variation between brands:

> A representational brand is a complex set of consistent beliefs and
> meanings held by its purchasers and users which are associated with the
> product or service but which exist over and above its obvious physical
> functioning. These beliefs . . . help them . . . in choosing the product
> which is best suited to their particular personalities, roles, set of needs,
> situation. . . . [Functional brands are] names developed by marketers to
> distinguish between competing offerings and to facilitate purchasers'
> and users' decision-making through rapid recall of consumer-relevant
> performance benefits. Their values are less to do with the purchasers'
> and/or users' personality and more to do with the product's functional
> capabilities and functional attributes.[1]

The idea of a representational brand is very much related to the
consumer's self-image and situational factors; McWilliam and de
Chernatony cite as examples Johnnie Walker Black Label and Audi.
Clearly functional brands are Teflon, Lycra, and Formica; these are
associated with performance characteristics rather than with particular values or "softer" aspects of personality.

This certainly goes to the heart of understanding the makeup of a
brand. A brand manager needs to go even further, however, and
understand the synthesis by which the component parts become the
whole unified personality that is perceived by the consumer.
Undoubtedly the best brands are those having a blend of appeals,
not relying solely on advertising or on functional benefits.

*A brand must be a blend of complementary physical, rational, and
emotional appeals. The blend must be distinctive and result in a
clear personality that will offer benefits of value to consumers.*

Figure 2.1. **The Relationship Between the Elements of a Brand**

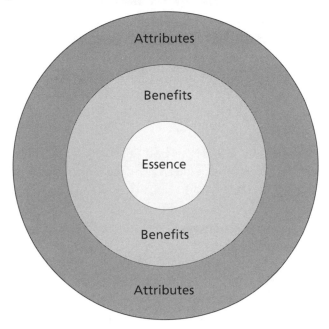

Brand Mapping

A useful framework for understanding the relationship between the various elements of a brand is to categorize and then map them on a chart.[2] The scheme in Figure 2.1 (see above) reflects the complex nature of the relationship between brand and consumer.

The "essence" of the brand is a single simple value, easily understood and valued by customers. It is the "personality" of the brand, and it is the element that should be distinctive within its market. This is what the consumer feels loyal to (even if not at the conscious level) and is therefore what is often referred to as the "brand equity." If we start here, we are capturing the elusive emotional element of the brand. We then move out to the obvious benefits that are delivered by the brand. By looking at a brand's use, we are forced to examine the wants and needs that it claims to meet. Only lastly do we examine the product's actual attributes.

Text continues on page 21, after the case study.

A Brand Is Born and Grows Up
Marlboro Cigarettes

•　　•　　•　　•　　•

The Marlboro cigarette brand is the best-selling packaged goods product in the world. Yet, as recently as the 1950s, it was an old, apparently dying tobacco brand in the United States.

A Decision to Relaunch

In 1954, after careful analysis of trends in the tobacco market, the management of Philip Morris made a number of key decisions to change the direction of the brand.

Old Marlboro	New Marlboro
Mild tar blend	Stronger blend
Less flavor	More flavor
Nonfilter	Filter
White pack design	Red and white design
Older image	More modern image
Aimed at women	Aimed at men
Product-based advertising	Imagery advertising

The relaunch was based on a product change. Although, at the time, 90% of U.S. smokers used unfiltered cigarettes, the company realized that the coming trend would be to filters, and this could help modernize the image. To appeal to young adult men, and offset perceptions of mildness created by the new filtration techniques, the strength and flavor of the smoking choroderivatives of the brand were enhanced. The filter was covered in tobacco-brown paper, indicating the strength and flavor. Lastly, the advertising was changed to reinforce the new smoking characteristics brought about by the product changes and to appeal to the young adult masculine target group.

A new advertising agency, Leo Burnett, developed a campaign to relaunch the brand using male role models in tough, rugged jobs. The first advertising featured men working in interesting, action-filled assignments such as a pilot, deep-sea fisherman, cowboy, or engineer. It was noticed that the cowboy was particularly popular with the target group. However, the campaign continued for some years to rotate cowboy subjects with other masculine jobs that matched the creative strategy.

Focusing on Marlboro Man

In 1963 research indicated that Marlboro needed a more clear-cut identity. The Marlboro Man, symbolized by the cowboy, was established.
    Campaign guidelines were laid down as follows:

- The cowboy must symbolize the type of man other men would like to be, and women would like to be with.
- He must be believable.
- Marlboro country must always be magnificent, never ordinary.
- Every ad in the campaign must be candid and have impact.
- Variety will be achieved by the rotation of cowboy portraits, smoking moments, and magnificent country material.

To the present day these guidelines have been maintained through all media.
    During the 1960s sales of the brand increased by more than 10% on average each year. By 1975 Marlboro had grown to U.S. brand leadership and continued to be rolled out to new markets around the world. With few exceptions, the U.S. strategy and cowboy campaign have been strictly adhered to. In most of the 150 countries in which the brand is sold, the consumer is invited to "Come to Marlboro country ... where the flavor is." Where it has not been used, it is for cultural, political, or legislative reasons.
    All campaign material is produced by Philip Morris and its agency on location in the western United States. Thus management can maintain strategic consistency and ensure the highest quality control. Whatever flexibility the headquarters allows local companies, the positioning of the Marlboro brand remains the same *in detail* throughout the world.

Consistency in the Marketing Mix

Another consistent feature of Marlboro's advertising is the use in marketing communications of the red roof graphic from the pack. Thus pack recognition is reinforced. It has also allowed the company to utilize creative opportunities in some countries where legislation restricts the use of some media, such as TV advertising.

In the 1980s and 1990s there have been major investments in motor racing (particularly Formula 1), popular music, and other activities. In all of these promotions the existence of a brand "property" in the form of the red chevron allows Marlboro to give clear visual messages without using words or names. Indeed, in many countries Marlboro is associated today with a wide range of masculine sports.

Diversification activities have increased enormously, and the trademark has been taken into clothing, books, motor accessories, and design.

CONCLUSION

The history of Marlboro shows the importance of a clear brand identity as the basis for strategy.

- When it was decided to rejuvenate Marlboro in the early 1950s, every part of the product and its packaging and marketing was looked at and brought into line. No element was asked to turn the brand around alone.
- In a product category where competitive physical differences are negligible, image values become very important. Brands in this product category are international, so a trademark needs consistency of image across frontiers and boundaries. The highly successful Marlboro campaign has not been allowed to fragment.
- It can take a long time for great campaigns to settle down. It took from 1954 to 1963 before the cowboy in Marlboro country was brought clearly into focus, to the exclusion of all other masculine role models and symbols.
- Having found a "big idea," it has been consistently applied in all media and across all aspects of the marketing communication.
- The psychological aspects of the young adult, rugged, independent, masculine positioning symbolized by the cowboy have a universal relevance, applying across frontiers and cultures.
- To achieve a consistent campaign over the long term, firm management is needed at the center, issuing clearly understood guidelines and controlling creative execution. Temptations to change things to cater to minor local variations in taste, or when new managers arrive, must be resisted.

- All aspects of the marketing communication carry identical or similar imagery, or are aimed at the correct target group.
- Long-term consistency has helped many markets to overcome the loss of broadcast media and to maintain momentum when legislation drastically dilutes campaign values.

Text continued from p. 17.

To ensure that we have a unified proposition, we can scan from the essence to the outer ring of the circle. It is important that the product attributes do not clash with the brand essence; indeed, they should reinforce it. Furthermore, we must make sure that all the attributes deliver relevant benefits. Are any of the attributes working against the basic brand personality? Are any benefits being delivered that are not attracting the attention of the consumer because they are not linked to a characteristic or attribute that would get them noticed?

The Marlboro case study is a perfect example of a company that understood the relationship between physical and emotional attributes and combined them into a simple, motivating personality that united all the elements of the brand.

Brand Personality

A graphic representation of how brand anatomy applies to the Marlboro brand is shown in Figure 2.2.

Brand Property

The Marlboro cowboy and the red chevron pack sum up the brand personality and become what is often known as the "brand property." The principle is the same as that of the corporate logo: The brand property must be something by which the consumer can identify the brand immediately. Ideally, it will also be a "big idea," something that not only identifies the brand but also says something about it. The brand property will usually be one of the physical attributes from the outer ring of the brand anatomy framework (in the case of both Coca-Cola and Perrier, the bottle shape is a brand

Figure 2.2. **Marlboro: The Anatomy of a Brand**

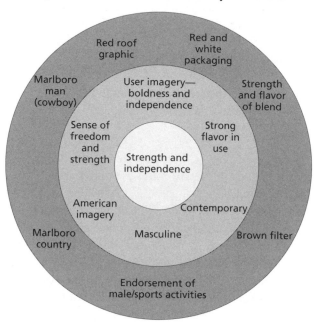

property) but could equally be a slogan or a figure from advertising (such as Colonel Sanders or the Jolly Green Giant). Historically, many of these have arisen by accident but are now so inextricably linked with the brand that they are jealously guarded.

USPs

Another idea that emphasizes the need to make the personality tangible is the USP (Unique Selling Point or Proposition), a term with a long heritage from the world of advertising. It was originally devised as a guide to communicating with consumers through advertisements, but it is now used more widely. It stresses the need to offer something that is clear, simple, different, and motivating.

Like the idea of the brand property, the USP is a useful way of looking at the brand from the consumer's point of view. A decade or two ago, it would have been fairly widely accepted in FMCG markets that the one thing a brand needed above all else was a "property," and huge resources were channeled into coming up with a catchy name, or an appealing figure to star in the advertising.

While it may be true that a mistake in these areas may doom a brand to failure, modern brand management tends to take a wider view of the brand proposition, placing more emphasis on the range of satisfactions offered by the brand and the balance between rational and emotional appeals. This view is more appropriate to the advertising-literate and value-driven consumers of the 1990s, and it also guards against the risk of becoming "gimmicky," something these consumers would be quick to react against. Above all, it encourages management to manage the whole brand, rather than just pushing the proposition from one aspect. The result is the development of a more powerful asset.

Changing Consumer Attitudes and the Functionally Driven Brand

Much current writing stresses the increasing importance of integrity in marketing. One of the practical consequences of this may be greater antagonism among some consumers to messages about intangibles (in particular an aversion to image-building advertising), and a consequently increasing need to stress the functional aspects of the brand. At the moment this would seem to favor the Asian and European big brands, which are generally in more functionally driven markets. The obvious counterargument is that the American skill in brand marketing will ensure that if it becomes necessary, the American super-brands will reposition themselves to meet changing market wants. There is also a view that as more economies drift toward service economies, we shall see the continued growth of the service brands, such as McDonald's, which have emerged only relatively recently; these of course are much more intangible in their character. What does seem certain is that with an increasing focus on building brands in all markets, the previous dominance of a few mainly American companies will be challenged in the years to come. It will almost certainly demand a high order of management skill to understand and develop a fully rounded brand personality.

How Brands Behave

It is only in recent years that much research has been done to verify whether customer loyalty is indeed the reward for successful brands. It is now possible to discern common patterns in the sales of brands over long periods, and the research is producing some surprises.

Research into Consumer Buying Behavior

There are two major areas of learning. The first concerns the surprising degree of regularity in consumer buying behavior across product markets and in different countries. The second deals with repeat buyers.

Stephen King, a doyen of brand thinking based at the J. Walter Thompson agency, was perhaps the first to articulate outside academic circles the importance of certain patterns, which were becoming clear from analysis of sales patterns of FMCG brands.[3] He noticed that it takes only a relatively short period for new brands to reach their peak in terms of penetration of the market—that is, the proportion of the target population who have tried the product by buying it at least once. The average is probably around the third or fourth purchase of the brand, known as the "buying cycle," which will vary between product categories. Thereafter, sales tend to decline fairly quickly to a level that remains relatively stable, often for years. The level at which a brand settles is usually around 80% of its peak penetration. What is remarkable is that the "drop factor" (the percentage decline from the peak to the stable level) is often virtually the same even though the peak level of market penetration is very different. The pattern is stable enough to provide a platform for predicting long-term performance from initial results with some confidence.

From these and other studies of repeat buying rates it became clear that consumers likely to be interested in the brand try it out fairly quickly, and, while some drop out, the core of the brand's eventual market are usually in this group. Other consumers with a less strong interest may try the brand later, but their repeat purchase rate is likely to be lower.

As years pass, more consumers drift in and out of the brand franchise with generally fairly light purchase rates. The core of consumers buying the brand frequently remains relatively small.

The dynamic between these two variables of penetration and repeat purchase rate is demonstrated in the case study on Ocean Spray's Mauna La'i guava drink (featured in Chapter 4). This new brand achieved satisfactory "trial" rates (first usage) but the repeat purchase rate was poor in most cases. The company understood that, unless it acted quickly to establish the drink in the repertoire of a wider segment of the market, it would not survive.

The main learning point from this is that a brand's success is very much related to its initial appeal to the consumer. Once it has reached its natural level of sales and market share, it will take an enormous amount of promotional activity to effect major changes in its standing. This is indeed reassuring for the owners of success-ful established brands. Success will be decided early on during trial, and will be determined by the total package of value satisfac-tions, rather than being the product of the cumulative expenditures behind a brand, or a catchy name or package.

The spotlight then moves on to repeat buying behavior. Here too there are remarkably consistent patterns. In the words of Andrew Ehrenberg, the most prominent researcher in this field, "The funda-mental finding is that despite all the apparent complexities of the buying situation . . . the same empirical results hold for different brand and product-fields." This might sound encouraging at first, but there is a surprise—brand loyalty turns out to be something of an illusion. "In general, the observed patterns of repeat-buying do not depend on the brand or product itself, nor on what else buyers of the brand buy as well, nor yet on external factors such as adver-tising, pricing, distribution, etc. Instead, repeat-buying patterns depend only on buyer behavior as such."[4]

Ehrenberg's research found that brand loyalty was rarely exclusive. The majority of consumers included the brand in their "repertoire" of acceptable brands, and they bought it occasionally but did not let it dominate their purchase patterns. In very few cases indeed did Ehrenberg find that one brand dominated the repertoire, although there were certain categories (the most notable was cigarettes) where the repertoire was not so important. So the "80/20 rule," or Pareto Principle, whereby 80% of economic activity is accounted for by 20% of participants in an industry, holds good for most brands: A minority of customers accounts for the majority of sales. Ehrenberg also found that initial penetration was the key variable, rather than repeat pur-chase rates, although there was a slight tendency for repeat purchase rates to be higher where penetration was higher.

Lessons for Brand Management

These relatively recent findings call into question two previously widely accepted principles of how people buy brands: first, the "high-involvement" model, which assumes that purchase decisions are the output of a conscious information-processing sequence where con-sumers become aware of the brand, gather information, develop an attitude, and then purchase it; second, the idea that brand loyalty is a monogamous relationship. The best that can be hoped for in most situations is priority from among a group of acceptable substitutes.

It is important to note that Ehrenberg's research was restricted to FMCG markets—that is, where total sales of the product category were not changing. Subsequent research, however, suggests that the patterns he uncovered are common in other markets. A survey by the *Wall Street Journal* suggested that brand loyalty was equally rare in other markets (see Figure 2.3 on page 27). So although this research is restricted to FMCG products (because they are the only product fields with the extensive base of statistical data necessary for the analysis), the conclusions involve key concepts that can be applied to many markets:

1. The distinction between heavy and light users. Buying patterns are usually skewed between a minority of very loyal buyers and a majority of occasional buyers with little loyalty. Clearly it is vital to maintain the favor of the loyal minority. Any attempts to woo the majority that risk antagonizing the loyal core of a brand's customer base will probably damage the brand in the long run, even if the short-term result is to boost purchase rates among the long "tail" of the market.

2. The importance of market penetration. All the evidence indicates that it is market penetration that can be influenced, and that repeat purchase rates are much more difficult to shift in the long run. This tends to reinforce the conclusion, discussed earlier, that market share is of prime importance as a measure of consumer acceptance and therefore long-run success. If the brand does not have a positive initial reaction from the market in the form of good penetration, it is unlikely to prosper in the long run.

3. The importance of the "repertoire." It is clear that the majority of consumers see different brands in a given product field as complementary rather than as competitive. This has important implications for brand management. In particular, it warns against positioning a brand by claiming superiority over another. It also suggests that the consumer looks at the product field first and only then considers the individual brands within it; if this applies, it is important for the brand clearly to offer the general benefits or need of the category, as well as to differentiate within it. It might be said that all brandy should offer mellow and smooth values, rather than the glittering and lively values associated with vermouths or white rum. Whatever

Figure 2.3. **Users Who Are Loyal to One Brand, Selected Products (%)**

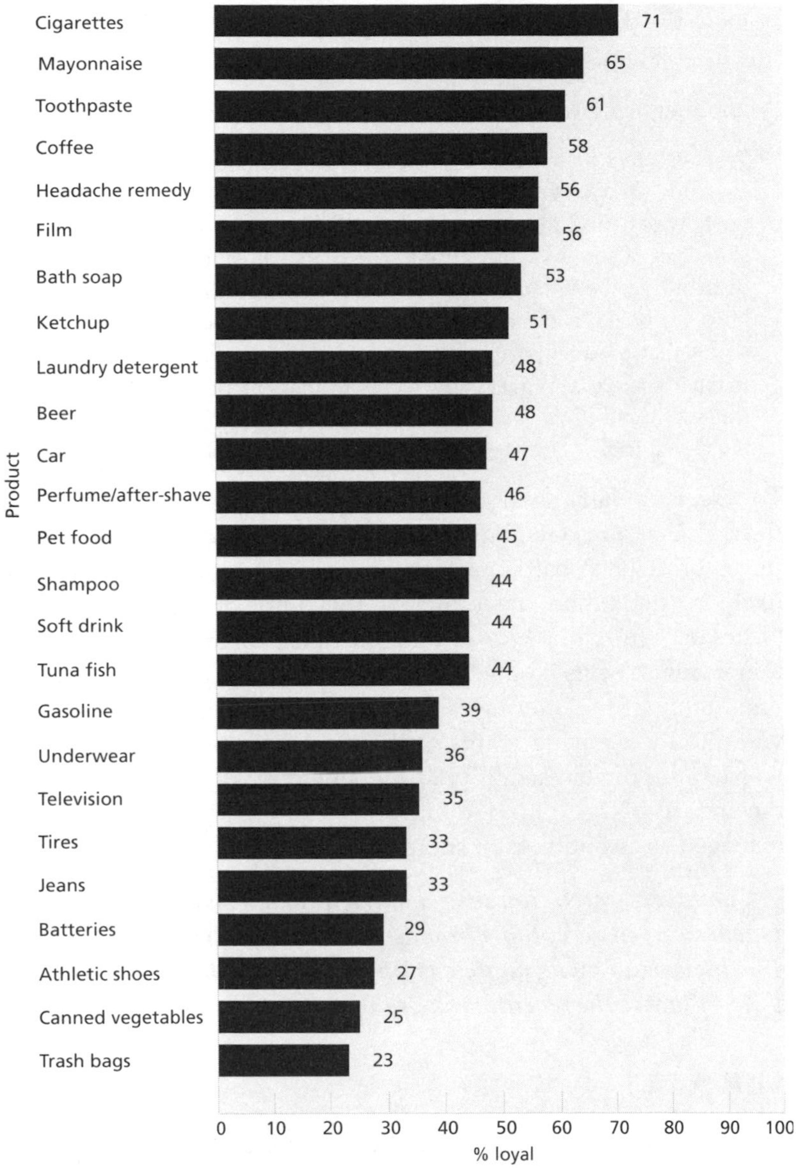
Cigarettes 71
Mayonnaise 65
Toothpaste 61
Coffee 58
Headache remedy 56
Film 56
Bath soap 53
Ketchup 51
Laundry detergent 48
Beer 48
Car 47
Perfume/after-shave 46
Pet food 45
Shampoo 44
Soft drink 44
Tuna fish 44
Gasoline 39
Underwear 36
Television 35
Tires 33
Jeans 33
Batteries 29
Athletic shoes 27
Canned vegetables 25
Trash bags 23
Product
0 10 20 30 40 50 60 70 80 90 100
% loyal

Source: Wall Street Journal (October 19, 1989), p. B1.

the sector, it is generally important to identify what the consumer sees as the core values for the entire product field, and not to isolate a brand from these in an attempt to differentiate it.

4. The importance of managing the whole brand. Most important of all, these specific characteristics of brand buying behavior point to the danger of managing separate elements of the marketing mix in isolation.

As Stephen King wrote in his 1973 book *Developing New Brands*:

> What matters for success is the *nature of the brand*. . . . At first sight, it may not seem very startling to conclude that success or failure depends on how satisfied the customer is with the brand in use. But in fact it shows us where to concentrate. The actual business of launching and distributing the brand can, if it is badly done, make the brand fail; but however well it is done, it cannot by itself make the brand succeed . . . it seems that product parity or minor product improvement is not enough to ensure success. What really seems to matter in the marketplace is the *total range of satisfactions* that the new brand offers its early and most interested triers.[5]

To use a military analogy, the battle is essentially won or lost through decisions taken away from the front line. The nature of the forces brought to battle, and their position at the outset, are more likely to determine the outcome than any amount of changing tactics once the battle has started. This does not mean, of course, that minor adjustments to the brand are not required; on the contrary, fine-tuning of the offering is essential to maintain the brand's relevance to the evolving wants of the market. But significant changes will require drastic action, and the single most significant factor is the nature of the brand offering. If this is not understood and managed as an entity, then success is unlikely.

Customers, rarely loyal to a single brand, usually choose from a repertoire of acceptable brands. It is vital for a brand's success to achieve trial by as many customers as possible, since it is harder to influence the repeat purchase rate.

SUMMARY

A brand must present a clear, unified proposition to the market. The summary personality must be instantly recognizable to consumers through the consistent use of a symbol or "property," such as the red chevron for Marlboro or the green Perrier bottle and logo.

Behind this apparent simplicity, however, a brand always consists of a blend of physical, rational, and emotional attributes. The balance of these aspects of the brand personality will vary according to the standards of the particular market and the brand's position within that market. In many consumer markets in the 1990s, customers are shifting away from emotional "image" appeals to a concern with functional aspects such as the materials used in a brand's production or the environmental qualities of its packaging.

The overall brand proposition, and its initial appeal, are the key factors determining its market success. Research into brand behavior shows that peak sales often occur early in a brand's life as consumers try it out, and that it then settles at a lower level. Exclusive brand loyalty is rare. A product is usually incorporated into a consumer's repertoire of acceptable brands.

CHECKLIST

An understanding of brand anatomy is critical if an effective proposition is to be put to the market.

- What are the physical attributes of the product or service, and how do these complement the intangible benefits?
- Do the various levels of the brand complement each other and reinforce the essence of the brand proposition?
- Is the balance between tangible and intangible elements understood and consistently managed?
- Can management describe the anatomy of the brand, and is this used as a guide to managerial decision making?

In monitoring market performance, the following facts need to be understood:

- The brand's penetration of the market
- The identity of the customer base
- The repeat purchase rates of heavy and light purchasers
- The relationship between the brand and its competitors in the consumer repertoire

REFERENCES

1. Gil McWilliam and Leslie de Chernatony, "Appreciating Brands as Assets Through Using a Two-Dimensional Model," *International Journal of Advertising* 9, no. 2 (1990).

2. The idea of "levels" of product and the usefulness of mapping them recurs in much marketing writing. I have developed this simple model from a composite of sources. For a good commentary on the idea see Theodore Levitt, *The Marketing Imagination*, 2nd ed. (New York: Free Press, 1986), p. 79.

3. Stephen King, *Developing New Brands* (London: Pitman, 1973), p. 16.

4. Andrew S. Ehrenberg, *Repeat Buying: Facts, Theories, and Applications*, 2nd ed. (New York: Oxford University Press, 1988), p. vii.

5. King, *Developing New Brands*, p. 22.

The Brand Management Process

· · · · · · · · · · · · ·

Brand management is above all about balancing a variety of inputs. Companies have traditionally organized themselves by functions—R&D, sales, production, and accounting. A brand, however, while drawing on all management functions for support, is a distinct aspect of the company, and it is defined by the consumer's perception, not the company's. Brand management therefore stands at the junction of company and customer, and it must integrate the totally different decision dynamics of the two worlds.

This is the rationale for the organization structure common in most brand marketing companies, where one manager (usually called the brand manager or product manager) has overall responsibility for a given brand. The brand manager's role is to look after the brand, and to prevent the immediate concerns of the company from getting in the way of that duty. Brand managers need not be expert in any functional area, so long as they have the management competence to get the best from the functional inputs involved, and to integrate them into a single brand proposition that can be taken to market and make sense to the consumers. Because it is the *raison d'être* of marketing to deal with customers, brand manager appointments are virtually always made from people qualified in marketing. This makes sense but should not obscure the fact that anyone with general management ability and a commitment to the idea of the brand can make a good brand manager.

Brand management is essentially a balancing act. Balances have to be struck between the external market and the internal capabilities of the company; between the company's inputs into the product and the influences on the consumer perception; between the short-term need to maximize profit and the long-term need to invest and develop. It is difficult because of the obvious imbalance between the complex process by which companies produce products and the apparent simplicity with which consumers choose brands.

Brand Management—An Incremental Process

The process by which the inputs are merged is a sequence of marketing decisions. Brands develop over long periods and are constantly being refined by a huge variety of stimuli. The brand management process has to start with the background context of a brand; it cannot look at purchase decisions in isolation in order to reach valid conclusions.

Brand management is therefore an incremental process. Isolated decisions are dangerous. What perhaps most distinguishes good brand marketing practice from bad is when every decision is taken at its proper time, in the context of previous learning, and with a clear understanding of how this will shape future decisions and, ultimately, the brand's market performance. A decision on an advertising budget, for example, needs, first, a firm understanding of who the target customers are and, second, what they already know and think of the brand. Without these pieces of information, any advertising activity is likely at best to be ineffectual, and at worst to change the character of the brand and its market franchise.

Which needs and wants are met by a brand, and the precise nature of its competitive advantage, must inform every other decision. These questions, although they are the most fundamental, are also the most difficult to tackle, because the answers lie deep within the customer's mind. They are therefore often ignored, and this is the most common reason for bad marketing decisions. The area of advertising and promotion in particular, is plagued by decisions taken without the informing basis of a defined strategy for the brand, specific objectives for the promotion, and predetermined evaluation mechanisms. The best brand managers keep going back to basics; the worst make decisions in isolation, relying on their own experience and knowledge of the market rather than the cumulative learning gleaned from analysis of the consumer perception.

Management has to try to organize the information that it possesses about a brand so that it can distinguish between symptoms and causes. Figure 3.1 (see page 33) is an attempt to map that decision sequence.

Figure 3.1 **The Brand Management Process**

The Sequence of Marketing Decisions

Step 1: Market Analysis

The starting point is the market, not the company. The key to a successful strategy involves the scope of the desired brand position. No army would venture into battle having considered its own strengths and weaknesses but without having conducted a reconnaissance of the terrain. In the business world, however, this happens all the time. Companies often begin their planning with their own history, and from that moment on they are restricted in their vision.

The importance of starting the planning process with an objective and comprehensive assessment of the external market has gained credence since the publication in 1989 of Gary Hamel and C. K. Prahalad's seminal essay on strategic intent. This offered a valuable idea for brand management—"loose bricks," the uncontested corners of a market that can act as launch pads for a stronger position:

> The search for loose bricks begins with a careful analysis of the competitor's conventional wisdom. How does the company define its "served market"?. . . The objective is not to find a corner of the industry (or niche)

where competitors seldom tread but to build a base of attack just outside the market territory that industry leaders currently occupy. . . . When Honda took on leaders in the motorcycle industry, for example, it began with products which were just outside the conventional definition of the leaders' product-market domains. . . . Honda's progress in creating a core competence in engines should have warned competitors that it might enter a series of seemingly unrelated industries—automobiles, lawn mowers, marine engines, generators. . . . Changing the terms of engagement—refusing to accept the front runner's definition of industry and segment boundaries—represents another form of competitive innovation. . . . Competitive innovation works on the premise that a successful competitor is likely to be wedded to a "recipe" for success. That's why the most effective weapon new competitors possess is probably a clean sheet of paper. And why the incumbent's greatest vulnerability is its belief in accepted practice.[1]

The close links between business strategy, which this essay deals with, and the strategies of brand positioning have already been noted. All companies, whether leaders or followers, should begin their brand planning with a detailed map of the market, and repeatedly update it. If marketing management does not have such a map in its collective understanding, then it cannot possibly understand its own target market or the dynamics of competition. The brand management team should be performing the same function as the military control rooms familiar to us from the movies, with the room dominated by a huge map of the battlefield, constantly updated as new intelligence comes in. From this we should know not only the boundaries of the market but also its structure, which will be determined by any segmentation patterns.

Segments of a market are essentially clusters of customers with similar wants, and the "loose bricks" discussed by Hamel and Prahalad are segments that are either not noticed or ignored by competitors. At one point, for instance, the large food multinationals made the decision that the segment demanding health foods was no longer a "fringe" or "specialist" corner of the market but was going to grow to a size that would attract them.

This important area may at times become technical, especially when dealing with market research. It may also involve the spending of budgets and the setting up of market intelligence systems. Chapters 8 and 9 deal with the decisions to be made in this area.

Step 2: Brand Situation Analysis

Only secondly, then, should management examine the strengths and weaknesses of its own position, to get behind the simple quantitative data gathered in step 1 ("Where are we?") to examine the brand perception in full detail ("Why are we there?"). At this stage, an assessment must be made of which brand management decisions are contributing to which effects. Is advertising, for instance, giving the brand an ultra-modern image? Is the packaging too aggressive? Is it time the product itself was updated to reflect changing wants among consumers? It is clearly in this particular phase that information and views from other functions within the company will be needed. Building links between causes and effects, between company practices, brand attributes, and the brand's market position, is the main objective. The focus will be initially on the company's own brand(s), but it is possible at this stage to give much of the work an overall market focus and gain a greater understanding of the competitor brands that feature in the consumers' comparative judgments about the product category.

Some of the case studies in this book demonstrate how the revitalization of a brand starts with a fundamental examination of its character. Marlboro and Johnnie Walker are two of the world's most successful brands because they have revisited the basic components of their brand personality, assessed the need for refreshment, and implemented fine-tuning to balance the need for continuity with the need to keep the brand relevant to changing wants in the market. This heritage will be best understood by investigating the essence of a brand, teasing out the values it conveys to consumers. Special market research techniques have to be used to penetrate to this deep level. The company should then have a clear picture of the anatomy of the brand, and an idea of the relationships between its essential values, overall personality, and specific attributes.

The biggest danger facing management at this stage is that of overconfidence. Because a company's management knows its industry fairly well, it often assumes that it knows how consumers think and feel about the products on the market. Given that research at this stage is difficult, and qualitative rather than scientific, many managers will be tempted to shortcut independent consumer research. In practice, however, the dynamics of brand perception cannot always be understood through mere familiarity with a market. Even consumers are often unaware of the full nature of their relationship with a brand, some of it being at a subconscious level. Very often it turns out that the brand is not what management thought it was; it has taken on what seems like a life of its own. Many companies have discovered, and it is a salutary lesson, that their brands are not entirely within their own control, and that the influences on the consumer include such "random" factors as the comparative perception of all the other brands on the market, fashion, changing social values, and even standards imported from another product area altogether.

Step 3: Targeting Future Positions

With a clear understanding of the current position, the brand manager is now in a position to define a target for the future. All marketing managers have a duty to promote corporate change. It is a cliché to say that the one certain factor in a market is that it will change, and like most clichés it is true. Any brand strategy should incorporate what has been learned in steps 1 and 2 into a view of how the market will evolve and what strategic response is most appropriate. There are useful models of "common wisdom" in this area of market life cycles, and these are discussed in Chapter 6.

At this stage the tools for analysis and strategy formulation familiar from more general approaches to strategic planning will be needed. The company's situation, in areas as varied as its financial resources and its political background, defines the parameters within which it can act (often referred to as its strategic degrees of freedom). The heritage of its brands is another aspect of this. Levi Strauss, for instance, overestimated its degree of freedom in its well-publicized venture into "Tailored Classics" men's suits. The brand personality of Levi's, to do with informality, toughness, and outdoors, could not be leveraged that far, even though the company undoubtedly had the skills to produce a perfectly good product.

The future position can now be targeted. This will involve two principal elements. First, will the market be more or less fragmented, requiring new decisions about coverage of segments? Second, will the response necessitate changes to the brand proposition (such as the incorporation of new extra benefits) or the brand scope (such as the introduction of line extensions)?

Step 4: Testing New Offers

Most current writing on strategy stresses that the most common failure is in the area of implementation. While many companies find that they have relatively effective processes for the generation and articulation of strategies (perhaps because most academic thinking has been in this area), they find it more difficult to turn them into action. Brand management, interestingly, has comparatively well-developed practices for testing the marketing mix by which strategies are implemented. Indeed, the most common failing is a lack not of implementation skills but of a clear vision of the brand's future target position. Best practice has long been to make no major strategic decisions or sizeable investments without testing them first. The reasons for this are not clear, although they perhaps have something to do with the tradition of agencies or consultants being employed to work exclusively on individual elements of the marketing mix. Only in recent years has anybody questioned the value of testing everything in advance, on the grounds that it can make a company unduly reactive.

Tests of marketing programs are conducted in two ways. First, individual elements of the marketing mix can be tested on their own: Advertisements are usually pretested, as would be a change to the formulation of the product. Other elements, such as price or packaging, can also be tested. The important point here is that individual elements should be tested to see not simply whether consumers like them but whether they contribute to the overall strategy. It is no use at all having an exciting and attention-grabbing package design if some other element of the mix is going to give out a different message when the whole brand proposition eventually goes to the market.

Second, it is common practice to test the whole offer (the marketing program as it will eventually be) in a limited area before trying to cover the market as a whole. Clearly this is most necessary when developing a new brand, but a test may still be desirable if changes are being made to an existing brand that may influence its position. Such a test will obviously have value only if it replicates the eventual market conditions, so the full marketing program will be rolled out, with wide distribution and promotional campaigns.

In attacking a market as large as the United States, some sort of regional test market is usual to reassure management that the total offer is sound. By this time, brand management is a long way down the line, so such a test should not result in major surprises—if it does, it suggests that previous steps have been either skipped or done badly. (A test market is in itself a considerable investment, so the drawbacks of using it as a substitute for the earlier phases of brand management should be self-evident.) It is quite feasible, however, that small refinements will be made to the offer as a result of a test. Most importantly, it should be possible to make informed estimates of the volume and nature of business that will be gained, and these are the basis for planning the company's future operations.

Step 5: Planning and Evaluating Performance

The marketing program necessary to implement the strategy will unfortunately not be obvious from steps 1 through 4. In particular, there will be continuing debate on the level of expenditure needed.

If the brand management process has been conducted logically, we should nevertheless have very clear and well-understood objectives for our marketing activity. These will not just be simple goals, such as "sell x units" or "achieve $x\%$ market share," but they will address the intermediate stages through which consumers go before the purchase decision. Objectives can then include awareness, understanding of the brand's benefits, availability, etc. In summary, we can direct our activity at consumer motivations. Once we have such objectives, the role of each marketing activity is clearer and becomes easier to manage: advertisements can have a single clear message, media budgets can be calculated to reach the people we want to influence, and so on. Expenditure, then, can be more accurately estimated and controlled.

Objectives are only half of the equation—they are useless without evaluation mechanisms. One area in which market research has certainly advanced in recent decades is that of market analysis, and in particular of tracking consumers' attitudes and motivations as well as their behavior. It is now possible to get information quickly that will feed back to a company an idea of the impact of almost any sizeable marketing activity that it or its competitors may undertake. It is possible to argue that without this information the whole brand management process will be a waste of time. It is certainly true that, as in other areas of management, a company will never get far with brand marketing unless there is clear evidence of the effect of its past activity. Just as the whole brand management process is a learning relationship with the consumer, so a company should not even consider itself an effective manager of brands unless it has proven processes for setting objectives and evaluating performance against those objectives.

SUMMARY

Brand management has come full circle. The information gathered in the tracking of performance is exactly the sort that is needed for market analysis. In this sense it is not a process with a discrete beginning and end, but a continuing round of activity. A company may enter the loop and make a small decision on specific activities within the program at any time, but, unless it has a full understanding of the context in which that decision is made, it risks getting results it never bargained for.

CHECKLIST

Step 1: Basic market analysis is above all the tracking of trends. Information must be gathered continuously, like military intelligence. A company must understand the following aspects of its territory:

- The size and scope of the market
- The segments in the market
- The players in the market and their positions
- The trends in all these areas

Step 2: Brand situation analysis should produce

- An in-depth understanding of the brand personality and values
- A picture of the brand anatomy, and how its attributes are contributing to its overall position
- The same information for competitor brands

Step 3: The strategy formulation phase should produce

- A view on the future character of the market (i.e., step 1 projected into the future)

- A strategy outlining the future targeted brand position:
  - benefits offered
  - brand personality development
  - scope of brand
  - target segments

Step 4: The practice of advance testing is designed to do the following:

- Gain understanding of the contribution of individual brand attributes to the overall position
- Assess how changes to any element of the brand will influence its position
- Test the total brand proposition when attacking new markets or after fundamental change

Step 5: Planning and tracking activities are designed to provide the following:

- A clear plan for the timing and objectives (in consumer terms) of marketing activity
- A basis for judging the level of activity and in particular the level of expenditure necessary to achieve those objectives
- A program of evaluation mechanisms to monitor progress
- A basis for continuing market analysis

REFERENCE

1. Gary Hamel and C.K. Prahalad, "Strategic Intent," *Harvard Business Review* (May/June 1989).

Using Research to
Understand Markets

· · · · · · · · · · · · · · ·

Information: The Brand Battleground
of the Future

The basis of marketing is information gathering—to bring the customer's point of view into the organization. Branding, which is the marketing concept in concentrated form, begins and ends with the perception of the customer. Good brand management means good information on customer needs, wants, and brand perceptions.

In an essay entitled "What the Hell is Market-oriented?" Harvard professor Benson Shapiro lists as the first criterion that "information on all important buying influences permeates every business function." He comments further:

> A company can be market-oriented only if it completely understands its markets and the people who decide whether to buy its products and services. . . . To be of greatest use, customer information must move beyond the market research, sales, and marketing function and permeate every corporate function—the R&D scientists and engineers, the manufacturing people, and the field-service specialists. . . . Corporate officers and functions should have access to all useful market research reports.[1]

In other words, in a market-oriented company, the analysis of market research is a general management function.

It used to be easier to run a business on the basis of simple intuition. As long as markets were essentially mass markets, customers had to make do with the nearest thing to what they wanted. The balance of power is now firmly with the customer, and markets are fragmenting. Increasingly, a company has to provide *exactly* what a customer wants, or lose the business. Modern technology enables forward-thinking companies to do this; it both helps them understand better what customers want and enables them to be ever more flexible in delivering it. Management guru Tom Peters places information at the heart of all marketing activity:

> Basically, every market . . . is in the process of being fragmented, sliced, resliced, and micronized. . . . Fuelling the process of customization is the addition of intelligence to every aspect of product and service: smart marketing, design, service, and distribution relative to the outside world; smart functional and network integration within the firm and between its customers and suppliers. A McGraw-Hill division can now deliver individualized class textbooks virtually to order, containing easier or harder material for slow or fast learners, supplemented with selections from a vast database of documentation or illustration. Printed in the book will be the teacher's name, the student's name, and the class number. The order lead time for all the above is 48 hours. This is the new nature of markets. For all practical purposes, if you cannot customize it, if you cannot add unique value, and if you cannot do it by noon tomorrow, do not bother.[2]

At the same time as the new appreciation of information is offering the potential for competitive advantage, the market research industry is itself maturing. As in so many marketing fields, the large FMCG companies have been the pioneers in driving forward the research industry. But the use of market research is widening all the time. With its statistical and methodological complexities, market research can seem a relatively technical area of marketing, and an intimidating one. Increasingly, however, general managers are being drawn into marketing decisions, and need research evidence to support arguments. This chapter will not delve into technicalities; it will instead try to give an overview of what should be understood by a general manager in a company concerned with building brands.

The Role of Market Research: Help or Hindrance?

A Note of Caution

Marketing information is not the answer to all marketing problems. Indeed, the 1990s have begun with several commentators claiming that market research has been overused in certain industries, to the extent of reducing the competitiveness of some companies, especially in the field of innovation. The debate is heating up.

There are two principal attacks on market research. The first objection is that it simply does not deliver the goods: Customers' real motives for purchase are so deeply embedded in the subconscious that they are unresearchable. To some extent this is clearly true. The customer point of view can be ill-defined, complex, unpredictable, and impossible to capture—much too insubstantial a base for management decisions, perhaps. The formulation of a motivating offer will always involve a degree of subjectivity and therefore of risk. But the marketing-oriented organization will argue that the greater risk lies in not even attempting to gather information on customer perceptions. If market research is viewed as a way of reducing risk, rather than as a philosopher's stone providing absolute answers, then it will not seem a waste of time.

The second objection is perhaps more important: that reliance on market research leads to a reactive (as opposed to a proactive) approach, limited by the imagination of the consumers being researched. According to this line of argument, it is possible to get so bogged down in researching consumers and markets that the company will never manage to do anything different and better:

> Competitive advantages won this way tend to be short-lived, simply turning into endless games of strategic leap-frog. Enduringly successful firms focus on being creative, not reactive. . . . This will be tough for firms nurtured on reactive strategies like market research, the usual method western firms use to find out what customers want. Car-makers are among market research's biggest fans, as the dull similarity of modern cars testifies. But the most creative ones try instead to produce their vision of what the customer might want. The result: everything from Nissan's quirky minivan to four-wheel-drive "leisure vehicles" like Suzuki's Vitara.[3]

Exponents of this argument start from the premise that genuine innovation is the best bet for long-term advantage. They contentiously suggest that it is therefore better to encourage innovation unfettered by market considerations (in the belief that this creates a more innovative environment in the firm), and then go to the market and let the customers decide. This way, they claim, a firm may occasionally produce a brand that will genuinely change the market. Market research is seen as incremental at best; radical action is necessary to achieve major improvements in market standing.

This, interestingly, is a view propounded in the main by academics and observers rather than practitioners; most managers when discussing the issue are quite clear that there are different segments of the market that can be understood and targeted. Nevertheless, it may lead some companies to question their approach to marketing if it continues to gather momentum during the 1990s.

A Note of Optimism

The two approaches are not in fact incompatible. The fact that most new brand launches have failed in the past should not mean giving up on market research altogether. The challenge is to use research in new ways or to develop new research methods that are more effective at predicting market reaction. The ability to investigate strategic branding forces, like the segments of a market, is improving as the market research industry develops beyond the crude demographic measures with which it began. Research is also becoming more proficient at projecting the imagination of consumers, rather than merely reporting their superficial responses.

It is also vital to remember, again, the distinction between a product and a brand. When we are developing a new product, it may well be that the level of invention is beyond the imagination of the current market. Research, in other words, will merely play back consumers' perceptions of existing products. But when we are developing a new brand, we are trying to position ourselves not on technology but on consumer attitude and perception, areas in which consumers are the experts, full of imagination and possibilities. Consumers, rather than the R&D labs, are the source of brand innovations.

Market research is just one of the many tools that are available to management, and its output will reflect the quality of its input—that is, how it is managed. The following guidelines will help the management process:

1. Don't confuse market information gathering with management decision-making. Only where research is expected to provide complete answers is it doomed to fail. Market research, even though parts of it are managed scientifically, is not a science. Its functions are to reduce (not remove) risk, and to aid (not replace) management insight in marketing.

2. Use research creatively—never assume or guess. There is an apparently in-built tendency among many managers to assume that they know what customers need and want. This is quite understandable; many of them have worked in the industry for years.

Nevertheless, comments like "What people like is. . ." must never go unchallenged. Such a view is bound to be at best subjective, and at worst company-oriented. Informed opinion and customer intelligence are valuable, but they are quite different from objective and independent research of the whole market. Remember also that research can be used for investigating as well as reporting—the imagination of consumers is almost boundless, and skilled researchers can tap consumer creativity.

3. Understand the trade-offs in gathering information. The management of marketing information will always involve trade-offs. The truly valuable "gold nugget" of information, the makeup of the customer's perception of the brand, is buried deep. To get even close to what the consumer really wants is at the limit of market research potential. It requires enormous resources of time and money. Along the way, however, there are various points at which more easily gathered information will help skilled managers to make inferences with reasonable confidence. Eventually, managers have to decide that there is enough information on which to base decisions, and that the benefits of further research will not justify the extra effort. The understanding of the segmentation pattern of a market is a perfect example of this (see Chapter 5).

4. Use independent professional researchers. It is fairly common practice to use company personnel for market research, especially in industrial or business-to-business markets. The main reason is that the company's own personnel of course come free, at least in cash flow terms. Their use is more often justified by the argument that, with the limited range of customers common in industrial markets, the company knows how to relate to them individually. It is also tempting to believe that external researchers who do not work in the industry will not even begin to understand the customers or the "industry language." This is a dangerous trap. The relationship between a sales representative and a customer is certain to introduce bias into any information, no matter how skilled the salesperson. Without devaluing the customer intelligence that any good sales force feeds back to the company on a constant basis, it must be recognized that objective professional research will produce different information on customer perceptions of the market, which can only improve marketing decisions.

> *Market research is an aid to decision-making, not a science producing "correct" answers. It is invaluable in making the customer the starting point of brand strategy and will also provide a potential source of competitive advantage.*

The Process of Managing Market Analysis

As in so many other areas of marketing, the sequence of decisions and activities in market analysis is vital. The main dynamic is the relationship between two levels of information:

WHAT is happening?
WHY is it happening?

There is little purpose in launching a qualitative study of brand images and customer motivations ("why?") if basic data on relative performance ("what?") have not been gathered. Conversely, testing possible modifications to the marketing mix is a waste of time if the customer motivations that determine the current situation are not properly understood. An ideal cycle of research activities would look something like Table 4.1 on page 47.

The two basic research tasks are to measure what is happening and then to try to explain it. Actions are easier to identify, so more accurate, quantitative answers can be given on what is happening. Trying to infer motivations from behavior is more difficult, as judgments and opinions are involved; the answers are not usually capable of high levels of statistical reliability, and so the research is usually qualitative.

Many companies base their marketing activity on analysis of observed behavior because they measure some behaviors (such as purchase amounts) in any case for other purposes such as accounting. This has traditionally proved a sufficient basis for marketing decisions—it was enough to know market shares and growth rates. Advances in the technology of data gathering are increasing the sophistication of market research systems for observing consumer behavior. With a greater emphasis on targeting and branding, many companies are for the first time attempting to understand how they are perceived by customers and what motivates their purchase decisions.

Because the two types of research are quite different, they rarely overlap in a single research activity. The two are nevertheless interdependent. Quantitative research will be the starting point in

Table 4.1 **Cycle of Market Research Activities**

Activity	Output
Market measurement	Performance data
Motivation research	Market map of segments and brand positions
Testing new offers	Assessment of probable customer acceptance of changes to marketing mix
Test markets	Quantitative forecasts of probable performance of new offers
Evaluation of marketing activity	Understanding of how marketing mix elements contribute to brand performance

gathering essential market facts, but these facts will also be the basis for assessing marketing activity at the end of the cycle—for example, what happened to sales volumes when the price was increased? Qualitative research, traditionally used mainly to generate new ideas and pretest new packages or advertising campaigns, is now gaining importance in the evaluation phase as it becomes possible to track attitude and image shifts and to map markets.

At any one time a serious brand marketing company will be conducting several research projects on various issues. Occasionally, it is necessary to get a complete picture of a market, going through the whole cycle as one project. This is often known as a U&A (Usage and Attitude) study. Because of the time and expense required to produce such a full report on an ad hoc basis, it is usually commissioned only when a new market is being approached or a major strategic review is necessary.

The case study on the European computer market that follows shows how rigorous survey techniques can establish the "wants" of consumers in a market and can measure the way competing brands match those purchase criteria. If a clear need for marketing action, such as a competitive disadvantage in brand awareness, is perceived at an early stage in such a study, then tactical action may be taken quickly to remedy this. In order to understand the brand positions fully, however, more exhaustive and demanding qualitative research will be required.

Text continues on page 57, after the case study.

Market Analysis: The European Computer Market

· · · · ·

The Western European market for business computers and information technology is huge. Price Waterhouse estimated the world computer market at $649 billion in 1992, of which Europe accounts for 31.5%. This is a fairly rapid and significant advance on the mid-1980s, when Europe's share was estimated at 25%.

Companies within this buoyant market must know their competitive positions. A pan-European survey carried out in 1990 by Research International set out to discover these. RI carried out 2,049 15-minute telephone interviews in eight leading European countries. The samples were just over 300 in the "large" markets of France, Germany, Italy, and the United Kingdom and just over 200 in the "medium to small" markets of the Netherlands, Spain, Sweden, and Switzerland. Within each country, the interviews were divided equally between large and medium to small companies. The interviews were also split between technical and nontechnical managers, though all were at a senior level and all had some responsibility for choice of computer equipment in purchasing decisions.

The RI survey revealed that IBM, Digital, and Hewlett Packard were the three top brands in Europe. However, to state that certain brands are "top" is almost meaningless. Market-driven strategies must direct effort at customers' motivation rather than the outcome of those motivations—sales and usage.

The Components of Demand

The survey aimed to break down demand into several component elements:

- A model of *buyer behavior* that progresses from awareness of the brand, through considerations for purchase, to actual usage. This model covered all eight markets and was also broken down by country.

Table 4.2 **Buyer Behavior**

Computer Brand	Awareness		Considered for purchase		Usage
	SPONTANEOUS	TOTAL SPONTANEOUS AND PROMPTED	FIRST SPONTANEOUS	ALL SPONTANEOUS	
IBM	94	99	66	83	82
Digital	47	91	8	29	37
HP	35	90	3	15	36
Bull	28	82	4	11	15
Siemens	24	82	2	8	15
Olivetti	22	90	1	8	25
Unisys	21	76	2	7	12
Compaq	20	–	2	11	33
Nisdorf	20	84	1	5	12
Apple	17	–	1	7	24
NCR	14	78	2	6	11
ICL	13	67			
Wang	10	–			10
Philips	8	84			12
Datagen	7	–			
Ittnokia	6	64			
Toshiba	5	–			
Fujitsu	5	56			
Sun	4	44			

- Measurement of *purchase criteria*—that is, the "wants" in the market.
- A ranking of vendors against these wants to arrive at a picture of *consumer perception* or brand image broken down by country, users of the brand versus nonusers, and technical users versus non-technical users.

Table 4.2 (see above) shows the awareness, consideration, and usage rates for 19 computer vendors across the eight markets. Table 4.3 (see page 50) shows the preferences of consumers for various attributes of computer and information technology systems. The right-hand column shows the markets that rank these attributes differently from the overall average.

Table 4.3 **The Importance of Various Factors in the Choice of Computer Equipment**

Purchase criteria	Europe score	Europe rank	Country differences
Reliable systems	126	1	2 France, Switzerland
Reliable service and support	123	2	1 France, Netherlands, Switzerland, 4 Germany, 2 Sweden, Spain
Provides high-quality systems	113	3	5 France, Switzerland, 4 Germany, 2 Sweden, Spain
Offers good value	111	4	3 United Kingdom, France, Germany, Switzerland, 5 Italy, 6 Spain
Offers flexible systems	105	5	4 France, Italy, Switzerland, Spain
State of the art/ most advanced systems	91	6	7 France, Switzerland, Sweden, 5 Spain, 8 Netherlands
Leads the field in networking	89	7	6 France, Netherlands, Switzerland, 8 Italy, Spain
Wide range of systems	85	8	7 Italy, Netherlands, Spain, 6 Sweden

In order to compare computer suppliers with these wants, respondents were asked how companies rated against a list of 16 attributes, including the wants ranked in Table 4.3. The attributes were as follows:

- Provides high-quality systems
- Wide range of systems
- Reliable systems
- Forward-looking
- Reliable service and support
- Offers flexible systems
- State-of-the-art systems
- I feel I know a lot about them
- Leads the field in networking
- Approachable
- I think I would enjoy dealing with their staff
- Offers good value
- Rigid in dealing with customers

- Sympathetic
- Academic rather than practical
- Overspecialized

The results of this analysis for three key markets are considered in detail later.

Summary of Pan-European Results

In terms of *buyer behavior* patterns, IBM, Digital, and Hewlett Packard emerged as the top three brands in all eight markets by a significant margin, though only IBM was almost universally mentioned spontaneously. (Awareness was measured by the total number of times a brand was mentioned both spontaneously and after prompting.)

These three brands also topped the table of considerations for purchase, though Compaq also featured in this area. Again, IBM was the company always mentioned first. There were, however, variations in the types of applications for which each was considered. Digital, for example, was "on the shopping list" for networking, scientific and engineering, and business and administration applications. IBM tended to be considered for networking, business and administration, office information, and desktop applications, but not for science and engineering uses.

The survey shows, perhaps not surprisingly, that IBM is the most widely used computer vendor across the European markets surveyed, followed by Digital and Hewlett Packard, though this did not hold in every country.

It is apparent that reliability and quality are the key *purchase criteria* in consumers' minds and that these aspects of user friendliness far outweigh whether a system is advanced or whether a supplier is offering a wide range of systems.

Differences in *consumer perceptions* of the top three companies were mainly by country. And, perhaps a little surprisingly, few key differences related to whether the user was technical or nontechnical. Only Digital had a noticeably stronger image among technical users.

- IBM was particularly strongly associated with three attributes: wide range of systems; reliable service and support; and "I feel I know a lot about them." Its image was weaker on "I think I would enjoy dealing with their staff"; and offers good value.
- Digital got strong rankings on leads the field in networking; and offers good value. It received weaker ones on reliable service and support; and academic rather than practical.

Figure 4.1 **Consumer Perceptions: Total Europe (based on total sample)**

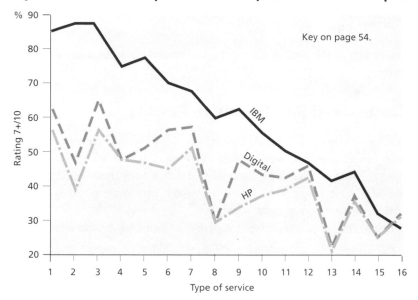

- Hewlett Packard was associated with reliable service and support; and offers good value.

The profiles of the three companies across the eight markets are summarized in Figure 4.1 (see above).

Based on overall preference, the ranking is IBM, Digital, and Hewlett Packard, followed by the rest. Across the eight markets, IBM is preferred to Digital by 66% and to Hewlett Packard by 78%. Digital is preferred to IBM by 34% and to Hewlett Packard by 64%. Hewlett Packard is preferred to Digital by 36% and to IBM by 22%.

Summary of Key Country Results

Although positioning an image across the major European markets taken together is important for developing an overall international strategy, local or national markets are the areas where most brand managers find themselves challenged. Local conditions can vary greatly from aggregated norms and demand highly focused strategies and responses—for example, to deal with local players who may have low pan-European penetration but who can command a significant share of a national market. The results of the survey, and particularly the brand image analysis, in three key markets—France, Italy, and the UK—are therefore considered below.

France

In this market a significant local player, Bull, influences *buyer behavior.* Both Bull and Apple are more widely used than in the rest of Europe, and Compaq, rather than Digital, is the second most-used supplier after IBM. Bull also appears among considerations of purchase, behind Digital but ahead of Hewlett Packard.

Good value and flexible systems are rated as more important *purchase criteria* than high-quality systems.

Consumer Perceptions.

- IBM has a strong brand image on wide range of systems; "I feel I know a lot about them"; and rigid in dealing with customers; its image is weak on overspecialized; and offers good value.
- Digital has a strong image on forward-looking; leads the field in networking; and sympathetic; it is weaker on reliable service and support.
- Hewlett Packard has a strong image on state-of-the-art systems; and sympathetic.
- Bull is rated as strong on wide range of systems.

The profiles of the four companies against the 16 attributes are summarized in Figure 4.2 (see page 54).

Italy

As in France, a strong local player, in this case Olivetti, has an impact on *buyer behavior.* Olivetti is the second most-used make after IBM, with Hewlett Packard third and Digital and Compaq a joint fourth. IBM is even more strongly established than in the rest of Europe, but Digital is less often considered for business and administration and desktop applications.

Italian *purchase criteria* put flexible systems ahead of good value.

Consumer Perceptions.

- Olivetti has a strong image on offers good value; and "I feel I know a lot about them"; it is weaker on state-of-the-art systems.
- IBM is seen as having a wide range of systems; and reliable service and support; but it is also viewed as rigid in dealing with customers.

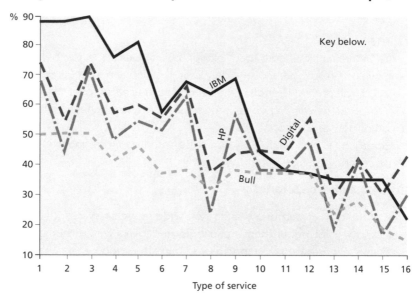

Figure 4.2 **Consumer Perceptions: France (based on total sample)**

Type of service

Key to Figures 4.1–4.4 on pages 52–56:

Type of service
1. Provides high-quality systems
2. Wide range of systems
3. Reliable systems
4. Forward-looking
5. Reliable service and support
6. Offers flexible systems
7. State-of-the-art (advanced) systems
8. I feel I know a lot about them
9. Leads the field in networking
10. Approachable
11. I think I would enjoy dealing with their staff
12. Offers good value
13. Rigid in dealing with customers
14. Sympathetic
15. Academic rather than practical
16. Overspecialized

- Digital has strong rankings on networking; and offers good value; but it is also seen as overspecialized, and weak on reliable service and support.
- Hewlett Packard is viewed as overspecialized.

The profiles of the four companies against the 16 attributes are summarized in Figure 4.3 (see page 55).

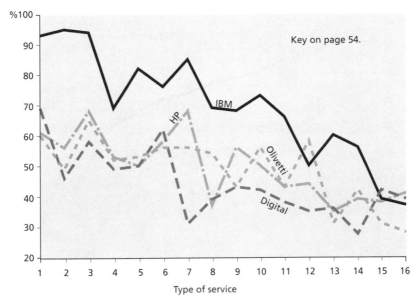

Figure 4.3 **Consumer Perceptions: Italy (based on total sample)**

United Kingdom

The local U.K. player, ICL, does not appear to be a major influence on *buyer behavior* in the British market. As in France, Compaq rather than Digital is the second most widely used supplier after IBM. Apple, Wang, and Hewlett Packard are also more widely used than in the rest of the markets that were surveyed.

IBM is less widely considered than in other markets, though it is still ahead of the other two leading companies. Digital is lower on the list for scientific and engineering applications than in other markets.

U.K. *purchase criteria* rank good value as being as important as high quality in choice of computer systems.

Consumer Perceptions.

- IBM is ranked strongly on wide range of systems; reliable service and support; and "I feel I know a lot about them."
- Digital's image is strongest on leads the field in networking; and offers good value.
- Hewlett Packard is most highly rated on reliable service and support; and offers good value.

Figure 4.4 **Consumer Perceptions: United Kingdom
(based on total sample)**

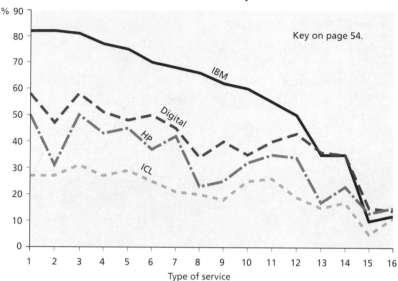

The profiles of the four companies (the three leaders plus local player ICL) against the 16 attributes are summarized in Figure 4.4 (see above).

CONCLUSION

The mass of data in the RI survey give guidance to current competitive positions and can be used as a basis to formulate future strategies.

IBM emerges as the clear leader because it scores highest on the key purchase criterion, reliability—of both systems and service and support. IBM's strategy can only be to continue to build on this strength. There is little it can do to improve its near-100% awareness rating.

Digital is seen as a relatively "technical" brand and is popular with the technical user sector. This sector is likely to mature earlier than the mass market, so a central element of Digital's strategy should be to reposition itself with the general buyer. Its lower awareness rating could allow it to do this.

However, although IBM could be vulnerable in the general market because of its relatively low ranking on friendliness and flexibility, as a technical brand the Digital name might not be capable of taking on IBM in this sector. Indeed, such a ploy could ruin the strengths the brand currently has. One solution might be to create a new brand rather than go through a repositioning exercise.

Hewlett Packard is perhaps the weakest of the leading trio. Its brand proposition is not strong, as evidenced by the way its image varies from country to country. It is also the brand that appears to suffer most from the influence of strong local players.

––––––––––––

Text continued from page 47.

Using Quantitative Research

A company should be in touch with what is happening in its market by constantly gathering market-wide quantitative data. Marketing managers in FMCG companies are in industries with systems such as audits and panels set up to deliver this type of information. In other industries where these systems do not exist, continuous quantitative information will be more expensive to gather and may involve specially commissioned studies. Such companies will however be gathering information that their competitors may not have.

Quantitative research is about measurement, and it relies heavily on statistics. Statistically validated results can be used with confidence. Key considerations will be the size and composition of the sample; robustness of the questions (i.e., will all respondents interpret the question the same way?); and effectiveness of the systems for gathering and sorting the data. This all points to the importance of the initial design of the survey; the execution is often left to unskilled workers or machines.

While these surveys deliver breadth in their picture of the market, they are not designed for depth and should be used for only superficial observations. Bill Blyth of the research firm AGB suggests that only a few questions are behind all quantitative market analysis:

Who are you?
What do you buy?
Where do you buy?
How much?

At what price?

When?

What else could you have bought?

Where else could you have bought it?[4]

Many firms outside the FMCG world (and even some within it) do not have these most basic data about their market. In industrial markets, a good deal could be obtained from the company's own internal information systems, but often the data are divided between departments, and no effort is made to bring them together to form an accurate market picture. Simple though the data may seem, they are invaluable at more than one level. They will certainly enable the company to make tactical adjustments to its marketing effort to make best use of its resources, and they will also give insights into the evolution of consumer motivations.

The development of a marketing information system should start here, mainly because this type of information is as reliable (statistically) as any market data can be, covering a wide part of the market more cost-effectively than qualitative research.

The main types of survey available are as follows:

- **Industry data**. In some industries sales data are available from trade associations or from government or regulatory sources. Often these have been obtained with the co-operation of the suppliers in the industry. Although such information may be inexpensive or even free, it may appear late and at irregular intervals. In industries where there is no established audit system, this may be the only option.

- **Audits**. Also known as retail audits (or even "Nielsens" after the best-known company providing the service), audits are simple measurements of goods at a specific point in the supply chain, usually the retail outlet. By measuring stock levels against known delivery details, researchers deduce sales levels. From there, audits are able to provide data on market size and shares, stock levels and consumer take-off rates, details of display and merchandising, and information on the performance of brands at various prices, package sizes, etc. Traditionally, audits have been carried out by research companies for a syndicate of suppliers in the same sector, and the data have been gathered by researchers visiting the stores and counting items on the shelves. The data usually cover one- or two-month periods. The development of EPOS scanning systems will drive major changes in audit practice, with the potential to provide snapshots at more frequent intervals (or almost continuously) and enable measurements to be made even at individual shopping basket level. This should enhance the other role of audits: special add-on surveys can be used to monitor brand performance when an experiment such as a special promotion is being carried out. This increasing level of detail will make audits even more powerful in suggesting hypotheses about what is driving a brand's performance. The drawbacks are the lack of named-source data and the lack of consumer detail to relate to sales levels.

- **Panels and diaries**. These surveys are based upon representative samples of the consumer population ("panels") recording their purchases over time. Although never able to provide the comprehensive detail available from audits, panels and diaries do make it possible to obtain a portrait of each consumer involved, and therefore to attempt to relate brand performance to market segments. This form of survey will also prove useful in analyzing consumer purchase patterns such as penetration levels, the make-up of a repertoire, repeat purchase rates, loyalty, and brand switching. The most common method of data gathering has always been self-completion diaries, with a minority based upon interviewing, and data have been structured from weekly surveys into monthly reports. Again, new technology will improve panel data. New features include scanning equipment at home, and even smart cards that consumers present at the point of sale in the store to identify themselves.

- **Omnibus surveys**. Like panels, omnibus surveys are conducted with representative samples of a population at regular intervals. Unlike panels, the questions vary with each survey and are usually divided between different industries or product types, because the survey has been syndicated to various clients of the market research company. Thus a research company might advertise that it asks ten questions every week to a sample of, say, nurses, and anybody can buy the facility of asking a few of those ten questions. The survey will thus be cost-

effective if only a few simple (probably behavioral) questions
need to be asked and are not wanted on a continuous basis.

- **Audience research**. The biggest single sector of the market
research industry is audience or media research. The objective
is to measure the size and character of the audiences for all
media—television, press, radio, movies, posters, etc.—in order
to sell and measure advertising in those media. Information is
gathered through interviews, diaries, or, where possible, electronic means such as meters in TV sets, which record when the
set is on and on which channel. The main problems in this area
are those of measurement—does being in the same room
count as watching a TV program? Does reading the front and
back page of a newspaper count as an opportunity to see an
advertisement inside? Despite these problems, these data, usually available sorted into some sort of demographic profile of
the audience, are essential in monitoring any expenditure on
promotion through these media.

- **Tracking studies**. Of relatively recent origin, tracking studies
are usually employed to measure the results of promotional
activity. They measure variables such as awareness and also
ratings against certain attributes or attitudinal statements.
Norms are now being built up that allow models to be drawn
up for what might be expected from a burst of promotion in a
given market (see Chapter 9).

The value of good quantitative market data is demonstrated in the
case history of Ocean Spray's Mauna La'i guava drink. The use of
sophisticated electronic systems to track repeat purchases showed
that the real customer target was different from that predicted by
the brand company.

Text continues on page 65, after the case study.

Finding the Real Market for a New Product
Mauna La'i Guava Drink

•   •   •   •   •

In 1984 Ocean Spray Cranberries had many popular fruit beverage brands in the U.S. market. Experiencing rapid growth, the company wanted to expand the fruit beverage market with flavors that would broaden its brand name appeal. Its answer was Mauna La'i guava drink.

The company described this new drink as "different in color, taste, and aroma from any other fruit drink on the market." Its greatest worry was that the product might not conform to the mainstream tastes of the American consumer. It also departed from the conservative, traditional roots of Ocean Spray. The risk involved in introducing Mauna La'i required a lot more test marketing than usual line extensions.

Testing with BehaviorScan

In view of the special risk of introducing this nontraditional product, the market research manager of Ocean Spray recommended BehaviorScan —a high-tech electronic data system in which consumers identify themselves with a "smart card" at the store when they buy their groceries.

This quantitative measurement system allowed Ocean Spray to determine the number of purchases each week and the percentage of repeaters. On the basis of these results, adjustments in the mix of marketing expenditure could be made. BehaviorScan was also chosen as the means of measuring performance, as the tropical beverage segment was so small that market share figures were meaningless.

Test market support included the following:

- **Packaging**: 48-ounce glass bottles with a Hawaiian scene on the front label and on the back label a short story about the type of guava and its origin.
- **Advertising and promotion**: The majority of the advertising budget was on TV ads featuring typical Hawaiian scenes, such as Hawaiian dancers, exotic birds, and misty mountains.

- **Target market:** The target range was the company's cranberry drink users, from older children through older adults of average income and education.

Prior to test marketing with BehaviorScan, Ocean Spray used in-home market research extensively. This allowed it to determine case volume projections, based on the number of households in a given market. Using the trial and repeat purchase rates seen in the in-home product test, the following objectives were set for Mauna La'i:

- **Trial purchase numbers:** The average trial rate for this type of beverage product was 1.1—that is, a household trying out the brand bought 1.1 bottles on average.
- **Repeat purchase numbers:** To be regarded as successful, a minimum of 40% of consumers had to make repeat purchases of the brand, with an average of 1.3 purchases for each repeat user. (This was known in the company as the "Minimum Buying Proposition".) A great product was considered to reach 50% or greater, with an average repeat number of 1.5.
- **Return on investment (ROI) criteria:** Ocean Spray would normally have set a minimum ROI target of 25% (i.e., the ROI must equal 25% when the market performance is at Minimum Buying Proposition level). However, Mauna La'i was more a marketing investment than a new capital investment, as the only additional processing was of the unique guava ingredient. As the corporate ROI average was 15%, a cushion was allowed with the Minimum Buying Proposition of 20%.

An additional cushion was the selection of Texas and Wisconsin as the two test markets. These conservative regions were less likely to be aware of guava as a fruit, so success here would mean success nationwide.

Right Product, Wrong Target

After six months, halfway through the test marketing, results showed as follows:

- **Trial numbers:** rated good, with numbers exceeding the 1.1 minimum.
- **Repeat numbers:** below the minimum 40% needed for profitability.

Previously, these results would have meant a withdrawal of the product, since it is not a good sign when the number of repeat purchasers is low.

However, with BehaviorScan, Ocean Spray was able to look more closely at the data.

Through the 2,500 panel in each test market whose purchases were recorded with BehaviorScan at grocery stores, not only was demographic information such as age and income provided but also repeat purchase rate.

The data revealed that the buyer base for Mauna La'i was very concentrated and made purchases more frequently than expected. Moreover, this buyer base was more upmarket than the average-income consumer targeted; that is, the product was being bought by "Yuppies." Ocean Spray decided to target these consumers to broaden the number of repeat purchasers in this demographic segment.

Most importantly, the BehaviorScan system provided hard data on the phenomenon of depth of repeat. Live test markets that gather attitudinal data do not provide this concrete information. Ocean Spray was able to use BehaviorScan to overlook the lower than expected rate of repeat purchase in favor of the potential market that was extremely attracted to the guava concept.

Lastly, by tracking a large panel for a long period BehaviorScan allowed comparisons in repeat purchases between past Ocean Spray consumers and new users. Product management could see exactly how Mauna La'i was expanding Ocean Spray's reach outside its normal user base.

Thus, BehaviorScan allowed Ocean Spray to readjust its media plan and avoid the failure that would have occurred if it had continued to target average-income users who seldom purchased the product. The advertising itself did not need to be altered to target the most frequent purchasers of Mauna La'i either. What needed to be changed was the mix of TV shows that featured the product so that the commercials received optimal visibility by the new target.

Success

The upscale group continued to drink Mauna La'i heavily in the final six months of the test market, and Ocean Spray decided to launch the product nationally immediately after the test.

Only a few months after introduction, inventories of Mauna La'i were so low that Ocean Spray had to introduce a larger 64-ounce size to keep

Figure 4.5 **Growth in Cumulative Trial of Mauna La'i:**
16 Months After Introduction

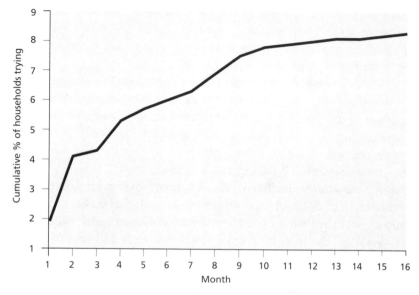

Source: Company data, March 1991.

Figure 4.6 **Growth in Cumulative Repeat of Mauni La'i:**
16 Months After Introduction

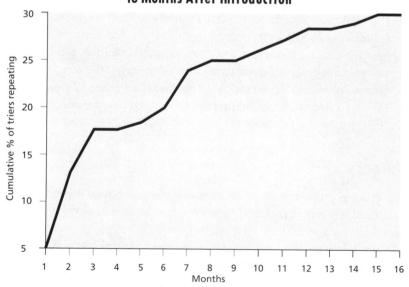

Source: Company data, March 1991.

up with demand. First-year sales were far in excess of one million cases. In fact, they exceeded BehaviorScan estimates by 300,000 to 400,000 cases.

Sixteen months after introduction, the product was 20% above sales forecasts. Its growth is displayed in Figures 4.5 and 4.6. Later that year, Mauna La'i was selected by *Consumer Network* as one of the best new products of the year. Its success also paved the way for consumer acceptance of many other Ocean Spray exotic drink flavors.

By 1991 Mauna La'i was a well-established business, with sales exceeding four million cases a year and with several line extensions.

———

Text continued from page 60.

Using Qualitative Research

Quantitative research is concerned with observing what happens and measuring it. Qualitative research exists to help marketing managers to explore and explain the reason for observed behavior. Just as human motivations cannot be boxed and numbered, so qualitative research is relatively unstructured, and the commissioning and using of it require rather more skill than simply buying into well-established systems. The research relies for its value not so much upon the accurate design of the survey but upon the skill of the researcher at the interview and in the subsequent interpretation of the results. The output of qualitative research consists of hypotheses and also perhaps recommendations from the researchers—the client company can either accept them at face value or use quantitative research to test the hypotheses.

From a management point of view, qualitative research is a difficult but powerful weapon. It deals with the forces that drive branding and may therefore open up real possibilities for building a competitive advantage, yet there are almost no rules or set procedures for managing it. Because it can be used to explore the possible reasons for almost any marketing question, the key is the interaction with quantitative research. Very rarely does qualitative research explore completely virgin territory; even if no quantitative survey has been commissioned, desk research will usually uncover a few facts that form a context for any exploratory research (managers will know which brands are growing or fading in a market, for instance).

If a company does embark on a qualitative survey before knowing any facts about the market area, it is quite likely that the research results will make no sense. When properly managed, the output of qualitative research is often a clear roadmap for a piece of quantitative research: "Now that we have a clearer idea of what we *think* is happening, we shall test whether it's true and if so to what extent."

The main areas in which this type of research is used are as follows:

1. **Explanatory research**. If a company has discovered a specific issue on a brand from quantitative or continuous research, such as a sudden surge of brand switching to a well-established competitor, it may as a result commission qualitative surveys to generate possible explanations.

2. **Monitoring market attitudes**. If a company wants to understand the positions of the various players in its market, it cannot conduct quantitative surveys to measure attitudes until it knows the correct questions to ask—that is, what variables the attitudes will fix upon. Qualitative research can discover the driving forces behind consumer perceptions of the market, using projective techniques (see below) to explore beneath the superficial rational responses. A company might discover, for instance, that it needs to measure attitudes to whiskey on the basis not of its strength, but of its "suitability for mixing" and its "heritage." This would be useful for the subsequent ability to rate attitudes and construct a market map, and at the same time it could well generate new ideas about brand positioning.

3. **Generating new ideas for brand positions**. An extension of the previous type of research is to use qualitative sessions for what managers usually know as "brainstorming"—that is, encouraging participants to think of new ideas for products, positions, etc.

4. **Testing new ideas**. A possible change to any element of the marketing mix can be tested with target consumers to explore their reactions to it at a deeper level than simply rating it. Consumers are provided with some stimulus material such as storyboards of advertisements or new packs, and they are asked to explain the reasons for their preferences.

Methods Used in Qualitative Research

Qualitative research is much more dynamic and much less reliant upon established procedures for data gathering. The creativity of the researchers in employing innovative methods for getting to customer motivations should be encouraged.

The key distinction is between one-to-one interviews, known as "depths," and group discussions, known as "focus groups." A depth will produce a detailed picture of the consumer, whereas focus groups will produce less information on the individual but more on the topic being discussed. This is because in a group the various contributors (usually six to eight) will spark off in each other ideas that would not be teased out in the less creative and more intense environment of a depth.

The methods used vary from the relatively straightforward to the highly creative. At one end of the scale, the interviewer may be working from a standard set of questions that form the skeleton for a discussion on a given subject. At the other extreme are, for instance, projective techniques, which are methods designed to bring to the surface ("project") feelings that the respondent normally stores at an emotional, subconscious level. Such methods may appear almost like games: the role-playing of brands in minidramas; the drawing of pictures to represent certain brands or users; word association exercises.

Another common approach is to use "repertory-grid" or "cluster analysis" techniques; the consumer sorts a set of alternatives into those that are alike and those that are not. A variety of stimuli, such as models, pictures or even audiocassettes of music or words, may be used to help. In attempting to understand how different brands of car are perceived, for instance, a group of consumers might be given a set of model cars and asked to park them in groups. This would tease out the dimensions of difference between cars. Eventually such research should lead to an understanding of the important differentiators that drive consumer preference and brand images.

SUMMARY

Market research has grown in importance as brand companies seek to understand their customers better and as information is increasingly seen as a potential source of competitive advantage. Good management of the research effort is vital; market research can stifle innovation.

The roles of different research tools, and how they relate to the overall marketing process, must be understood. Distinctions should be made between quantitative and qualitative research, and between continuous and ad hoc research. Finally, the various data outputs are combined into a summary picture of the brand positions in a market.

CHECKLIST

Watch for the following in managing market research:

- Use independent professional researchers.
- Don't confuse market information with management decision making.
- Use research creatively.
- Don't assume or guess; start research with an open mind.
- Examine the trade-offs between the effort of getting the information and its likely value.

REFERENCES

1. Benson P. Shapiro, "What the Hell Is Market-Oriented?" *Harvard Business Review* (November/December 1988), p. 121.

2. Tom Peters, *Time, Information Technology and the Slicing of Markets*, Economist Management Briefings, Economist Special Report No. 1202 (April 1990), pp. 69–70.

3. *The Economist* (December 1, 1990), p. 107.

4. In Birn, Hague and Vangelder, eds., *A Handbook of Market Research Techniques* (London: Kogan Page, 1990), p. 192.

Identifying Target Customers— Understanding Segmentation

. . . .

The purpose of market analysis is to identify and understand the target group of customers. The true target—a full understanding of consumer motivations for purchase—is virtually impossible to hit, and different companies will see the target market in different ways. As long as these differences exist, there will be potential for one company to gain competitive advantage through the way it targets its brands, which in turn is determined by the way it interprets market data.

Understanding the Segmentation Pattern of a Market

It might be thought that an understanding of market segments would emerge naturally from any properly managed research activity. This may be true, but if the segmentation is fairly self-evident, then it is likely that competitors will be able to see the same targets, and so the probability of a winning position is diminished.

Segmentation actually offers considerable scope for creativity. However static an overall market in terms of size, customer wants will usually be changing. It is like a deceiving stillness on a summer day: the air appears still but there are always thermal updrafts of hot air that birds or gliders use to fly higher. A company that can spot a new want, or can address wants in a new way, can find a thermal of growth in even a static market.

How can this be creative if it is merely an uncovering of what exists already? It is, after all, a principle of all marketing that demand is not created by suppliers. The answer lies in the dynamics of consumer perception. Although consumers are often largely unaware of wants until they are explicitly addressed, this does not mean that the wants do not exist; it is within the power of creative marketing managers or researchers to uncover them. For instance, the gradual shift of consumers away from suntan-worship to being sun-cautious (see the case study on Water Babies sunblock in Chapter 7) had to be uncovered by the researchers and the brand managers had to judge the correct time to address this emerging segment with a new offer. Those who get this right will be the only people addressing a newly emerging segment. The chief criteria of the segment in such situations are as follows:

- It is different from other segments.
- It is sufficiently homogeneous as a group.
- It is large enough to sustain the proposed brand offer financially.

Note that this is different from creating a fashion or "hyping up demand." If the want is not real, it will not last, and the segment will be too transitory to be financially attractive.

The increasing importance of segmentation as a basis for target or "niche" marketing has led to a growing sophistication in approaches to describing market segments, and a more proactive approach to using market information to find advantageous positioning possibilities. This requires an understanding of what segments really are. Using the needs and wants framework employed earlier, segments are clusters of customers who share a particular want as their first consideration in purchase. Segmentation is thus a market characteristic, and as such it must be distinguished from a company's response to it, which is best described as differentiation.

Too often, managers even in brand-oriented companies make the mistake, largely through habit, of assuming that segments are people who share some demographic characteristic such as age or family status. Such characteristics are of use only if they are accurate substitute measures of different wants. Whereas a division into age bands was once sufficient to distinguish between customer groups, many companies will now take the view that age is an insufficiently

Figure 5.1 **Getting to the Heart of Segmentation**

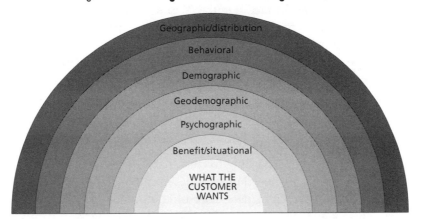

discriminating indicator of customer wants, and a more penetrating variable must be used, such as personality type. Hence the emergence of such consumer typologies as "Yuppies," "aspirers," etc.

Segmentation offers a perfect example of the trade-off inherent in the management of market information and analysis. In theory, there exists an absolutely true picture of the makeup of customer wants. In practice, this is never obtainable because it is embedded deep in the personality of the customer; to get anywhere near it will be resource-intensive and at some point will produce diminishing returns. The brand company therefore has to decide how far it will go in its efforts to understand customer motivations.

The basis of the trade-off is illustrated in Figure 5.1 (see above). The "nested" approach to segmentation variables was first propounded by Bonoma and Shapiro when discussing industrial markets (see below), but it is clearly applicable to all types of markets. Each layer out from the heart of the nest is further from what the customer actually wants, but it includes information that is easier to gather.

Geographic/Distribution Segmentation
The simplest approach is to choose areas of the market, such as regions or certain distribution channels, and operate on the basis that variations in wants coincide with this division. This must not be confused with a company organizing itself into geographic units

(for perfectly good reasons) and then assuming that each region is a different "market." In fact, genuine segmentation by geography is not as common as might be supposed, and it is probably becoming less so as global segments emerge. It will obviously be more common in large countries such as the United States rather than small countries such as Britain. Where it does exist, it tends to be fairly obvious and offers little scope for competitive advantage—probably forcing a company to go deeper to gain a unique position.

Behavioral Segmentation

Dividing the market according to customers' behavioral status relative to the brand in question would typically produce categories such as heavy user, light user, user of competitor brands, or non-user. This is valuable in many cases—different marketing mixes may well be appropriate for the different segments. The main drawback of such a scheme, however, is that it indicates only what is happening, and not why. Different heavy users may be buying on the basis of quite different perceptions. Any changes would therefore be addressed to changing behavior and are unlikely to be fundamentally different brand positionings.

Demographic Segmentation

This category covers all the standard population statistics available to marketers, such as age, sex, income bracket, household composition, occupation, ethnic group, and social class. These are by far the most popular bases for understanding segments. They are used almost invariably in quantitative research and are a reasonable halfway house in the trade-off. When simple distinctions in the market structure explain differences in consumer behavior, demographics work well, as in the case of selling drinks or snacks to children as opposed to adults. In more subtle cases, they can reflect finer distinctions in consumer wants, especially in the more sophisticated demographic schemes such as the famous "lifestages" scheme of Wells and Gubar, based upon family composition:

Bachelor stage (young singles living away from parents)
Newly married, no children
Full nest I (youngest child under 6)
Full nest II (youngest child 6 or over)
Full nest III (couple with older dependent children)

Empty nest I (couple still earning, children left home)
Empty nest II (couple retired, children left home)
Solitary survivor (still earning)
Solitary survivor (retired)

This scheme would be ideal for the financial services market, where family composition matters particularly. Other schemes are imaginative combinations of several demographic variables—for example, the Sagacity scheme, which combines lifestage, income, and social class.

There are problems with demographic segmentations. The first is the definition; with the more complex schemes, it is common for allocation of customers to categories to vary between researchers or surveys. The second problem is the undiscriminating and all-pervasive way in which they are often used: The lifestage scheme would be of little relevance in analyzing the market for anything where requirements are constant throughout life, such as shoes, clothes, or soft drinks. Because demographic data are readily available, there is a tendency to fall back on them and look for meanings that are not there. Like geographic segmentations, the distinctions are in many cases obvious and necessary but they are unlikely to lead to a winning position in themselves; what is important is not that a breakfast cereal brand is targeted at children, for instance, but exactly *how* it is positioned for them. The general problems already identified also apply here—consumers are tending to vary more within demographic categories, and, because the information is widely available, it is seldom the source of competitive advantage.

Geodemographic Segmentation

A modern variant of demographic schemes is the geodemographic approach. As the name implies, this divides up the population on the basis of where they live. In typical schemes, such as PRIZM in the United States or ACORN in the United Kingdom, consumers are put into small clusters of homes, and each neighborhood is given one of several labels. Marketers can then access only homes of selected types, such as "urban apartment blocks higher than six storeys" or "detached suburban homes with more than three separate bedrooms." The principle that "birds of a feather stick together" holds good in areas such as the United States and the United Kingdom (but not France), where (a) people tend to invest as much as they can in their homes, and (b) the population is relatively stable (which is not true of large cities). In these areas, geodemographic schemes are especially suited to direct mail promotions, as the addresses can be accessed direct from computers at the push of a few buttons. Such schemes are also widely used to assess the make-up of a neighborhood prior to siting a new retail outlet, medical practice, etc.

Psychographic Segmentation

Increasingly, brand companies are digging deep down to the psychological types into which their target customers fall.

As the basis of these models is the psychology or personality of the consumer, they are quite close to the wants that then manifest themselves in brand preferences. The drawback is that customers can be characterized only after extensive research. Any company that is prepared to commit the resources to this research, however, is likely to gain a competitive edge at this stage by understanding the market structure better than anybody else, and thus being able to target the offering better.

Psychographic segmentation schemes will usually produce labels for each type, relating to their general motivation. One scheme, produced by the advertising agency Young & Rubicam, divides the population into four broad types:

Segment	Central motivation
Mainstreamers	Security
Aspirers	Esteem
Succeeders	Control
Reformers	Self-fulfillment

Also well known is the VALS (Values and Lifestyles) scheme, which is based on whether individuals are outer-directed (i.e., take their standards and tastes from those prevalent in society) or inner-directed (i.e., develop their own individual standards). The case study on the U.K. convenience food market (see pages 83–88) uses this scheme. Some other schemes are known as "lifestyle" segmentations and may be based upon activity patterns such as leisure activities, or "AIO" segmentations (Attitudes, Interest, and Opinion).

These segmentation schemes allow brand companies to aim their offers directly at motivations. There is a double benefit: first, the motivation will be a better predictor of what the consumer is likely to buy; second, the segment is likely to be more homogeneous. It is a guiding principle of such schemes that they cut across "cruder" measures such as demographic descriptors. The "innovators" in a market, for instance, might be found scattered across various age, income, or social class groups—the only thing they have in common is the description of "innovator."

The problems with this type of scheme are twofold. First, in some markets there is no evidence of a link between "general" personality type and brand preferences. This may be overcome as research gets better at handling this type of variable. In any case, any general scheme must be understood to be just that—a first point of contact rather than the whole picture. The second problem is that, if targets are identified, they may be hard to access; a valid objection, although the situation will surely improve with the fragmentation of the media and the increasing sophistication of direct marketing methods.

The general psychographic schemes should be looked at as replacements for or enhancements of the old general demographic schemes. In that they address consumer motivations rather than external characteristics, they must represent a step forward.

Benefit/Situational Segmentation

It is possible to apply psychographic schemes not at the general level but in a market-specific way. Customers are divided up on the basis of their attitudes and usage patterns in a particular market. This amounts to a segmentation by the benefits sought by consumers in that particular market. Such a scheme has to be produced by a specially commissioned research study (whereas some general psychographic schemes are available on the open market); it could be syndicated among members of an industry, but such is the scope for providing a competitive edge that it is more usual for a company to undertake the research on a solo basis.

The customer profiles that emerge can in fact be a mixture of behavioral, psychographic, and demographic information. This gives an in-depth picture of the dynamics of demand in the market, which is by definition the basis of properly informed marketing management, and it can be used to aid any marketing decision. Such studies are carried out only periodically (say, every three to five years), partly because of the resources needed, and partly because they deal with fundamentals of demand that may evolve only slowly. They are generally commissioned to gain a picture of the overall market when a major strategic decision is being considered, such as a new brand launch or a repositioning. The case study on Schering-Plough's Water Babies sunblock in Chapter 7 is an example of such a study.

Industrial Market Segmentation

Although branding is less common in industrial markets, the need to understand market segments is possibly even more urgent, as customers tend to have far less in common.

The idea of a hierarchy of segmentation variables still applies. In Bonoma and Shapiro's "nested" approach (see Figure 5.2 on page 77)[1] the outer ring is the most easily perceived but it is the least likely to lead to a competitive advantage. Organizational demographics include variables such as the industry, size, or location of the customer companies. Operating variables, such as the technological system used by the target company or the product application, will cut across industries and will therefore offer a better base for segmentation.

The purchasing approach is critical in industrial markets, partly because industrial purchases are so often group decisions. The approach may be determined by the organization of the company (is purchasing centralized or not?), but it is more likely to be explained by the structure of the decision-making unit.

The best way of looking at group purchasing activity is to attempt to identify the role being played by each participant. The simplest situation is where there is a buyer and a user—an organization's professional procurement manager, for instance, or a parent buying something for a child. But often the group is larger still. The group as a whole is known as the decision-making unit (DMU) or buying center. A useful way of highlighting the roles is the BUILD acronym (see Table 5.1).

Each member of the buying center has different wants. The case study on the European computer market in Chapter 4 demonstrates how an industrial market can be understood on this basis. One of the world's biggest brands, IBM, has been built largely on its appeal to deciders, who tend to be senior general management authorizing capital expenditure on computers. Though few would admit it

Figure 5.2 **The Hierarchy of Segmentation Variables in Industrial Markets**

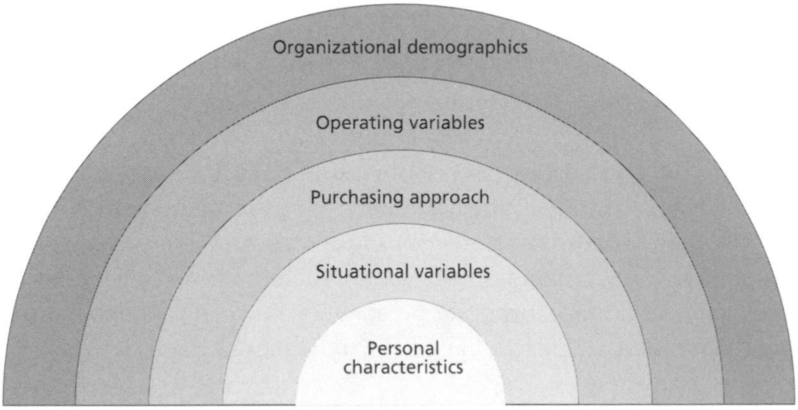

Organizational demographics

Operating variables

Purchasing approach

Situational variables

Personal characteristics

Source: Adapted from Thomas Bonoma and Benson Shapiro, *Segmenting the Industrial Market* (New York: Free Press, 1983).

Table 5.1 **Typical Roles in the Decision-Making Unit**

	Name	Role	Typical motivation
B	Buyer	Executes purchase	Price
U	User	Operates/consumes product	Performance
I	Influencer	Provides criteria to influence selection	Technical or opinion
L	Lodgekeeper	Controls access and information flow to others	Personal
D	Decider	Formally authorizes purchase	Policy issues or internal criteria

openly, many of this group are not computer literate and are even a little intimidated by the whole area; they value the feeling of security, care, and solidity that is the IBM brand. The second brand in that market, Digital, has traditionally focused more on technically minded users, stressing product characteristics. Indeed, it could be said that IBM's leadership is based upon the fact that for a long time it was the only supplier in the market that thought in branding terms.

At the center of this nest are two close-up variables. The first is the type of order: Is the situation demanding an order that is large or small, desperately urgent or more planned, routine or customized? Beyond this is the level of the personal characteristics of the customer. It might not seem possible to apply personal "types" to companies, but industrial clients are after all made up of people. If this variable can be unearthed, it is a powerful segmentation descriptor.

One key area where industrial customers can be classified into "types" is their *attitude* toward innovation, whatever their stated policy. Any good salesperson in an industrial sales force will probably be able to predict quite accurately which of their customers will be the first to buy into a new product. Research by Axel Johne of London's City University suggests that industrial buyers can be segmented by their corporate personality into "innovators," "early adopters," and "laggards," just as in consumer markets.[2]

Market Mapping

When all these stages of market analysis are complete, the results, converted into a simple description of the market structure, provide the basis for management decisions. The relatively recent emergence of *perceptual maps* has contributed enormously to bringing brand positioning decisions into the boardroom. The benefits of a perceptual map are twofold:

1. It maps the consumers' perceptions and so provides a real picture of the brand rather than the product.
2. It encourages managers to think in terms of strategy and positioning in a way that tables of numbers never can.

A market map should show both the division of the market into segments, and the position of leading brands relative to those segments. From the customer's point of view, the segmentation variable is the benefit sought or perceived, which is at the heart of the hierarchy. This has only become possible in recent years with the advent of software that can perform sophisticated clustering analysis on consumer ratings of attributes. Typically, the research process necessary to arrive at a market map is as follows:

- Quantitative research (continuous, ad hoc, or desk research) gives an idea of the size and growth of the market, and brand shares.

- Qualitative research groups then establish the consumer values in the market as a whole and identify the salient attributes used in choosing between the alternative brands offered. As many as 30 to 50 attributes may be used at this stage.
- Consumers are asked to rate various brands against the same list of attributes.
- Researchers then feed the raw data into a computer program, which clusters attributes into similar groupings until a few key discriminators remain. The position of various brands relative to these dimensions of difference is then plotted.

The resulting map can be used as the basis of research for some time because it is based upon customer perception, which generally evolves slowly. If a company were considering a new offer, for instance, it could ask consumers to rate the new concept alongside the existing brands in the market, and an idea could be gained of the influence of the new brand on the market as a whole as well as its likely position and acceptability.

Two main types of map are offered by the research companies: correspondence mapping and point vector mapping.

Correspondence Mapping

Here brands and attributes are associated if they appear close together on the map. If they are some distance apart, then it is reasonable to assume that they are distinctive offerings.

An example of the use of such mapping is the work carried out by a U.K. research company, shown below in the case study on the U.K. convenience food market and the battle for the emerging health-conscious segments.

This form of mapping charts deep-rooted values that will be reflected in all markets. This is a general psychographic segmentation of the entire population, classified into "types" on the basis of different value systems. Such core beliefs are highly relevant to a market like food, and the framework can be applied to brand positions by examining the category into which a brand's users typically fall. Because of the research company's detailed knowledge about the psychological makeup of the "types" it uses as the basis for much of its research, it is possible to get a good idea of the brand's position from its changing customer base.

The research company's model is based originally on Abraham Maslow's well-known work on individual psychological development. This quantifies the deep-seated individual values, beliefs, and motivations of entire national populations. Although these value structures alter relatively slowly in individuals, they can cause radical changes in long-established societies and markets.

Initial work on the model was begun by the consulting firm SRI in the early 1960s. Additional work, based on the psychological trends created in society by the changing values of individuals, was pioneered by Daniel Yankolovich in the late 1960s. In the United Kingdom, these two approaches were merged into the single model. This approach is based on a social values survey called "Monitor," run annually in 23 countries and consisting of several hundred attitudinal and behavioral questions.

The scheme divides society into psychographic or attitudinal "types." There are three major groupings, the discriminating variable being their basic value orientation.

- **Sustenance-driven**. This group's values are essentially concerned with survival. It consists of the more conservative members of society, who tend to view life as uncertain, difficult, and sometimes threatening; therefore individuals in this group value tradition and security. Their outlook is localized and family-oriented, and their cultural life tends toward escapism. Formerly the bulk of the population, this group is now shrinking.
- **Outer-directed**. This group takes its values from society, rather than from internal motivations. They are therefore materialistic, status-conscious, and inclined "to move with the times." They are avid followers of fashion and their consumption pattern tends toward status symbols.
- **Inner-directed.** The values of the so-called "new consumer" are personal and derive from individual motivations for quality of life. This group will be concerned with self-fulfillment and individualism, and will be socially aware, in the vanguard of environmental and health concerns. They dislike the idea of being part of a mass grouping.

The differences between them can be illustrated by the following real statements explaining why people are eating less these days:

Figure 5.3 **Overall Values Trend Map in U.K. Society**

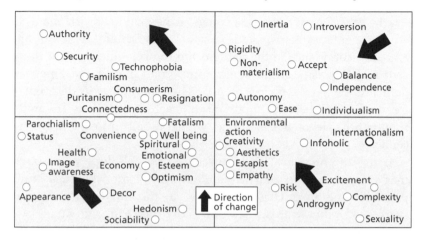

Trends in the lower right quadrant are "leading edge" trends. They will move toward the center over time. Trends in the bottom upper right will also move toward the center over time. These trends will become more important in tomorrow's society.

Trends on the left-hand side will tend to move up and away from the center. These trends will be less important in tomorrow's society.

Sustenance-driven: "I'm eating less these days because food is getting so expensive."

Outer-directed: "I'm eating less these days because I want to wear a bikini on my vacation."

Inner-directed: "I'm eating less these days because I feel so much better for it."

The key attitude areas from which these types are drawn can be plotted on an overall values trend map. This is the result of a complex computer program that clusters attitudes on specific issues so that similar attitudes appear together—a "type" will therefore be very likely to hold all the attitudes that appear together on the map. This level of detail means that there is a good in-depth knowledge of consumers and their basic motivations.

Figure 5.3 (see above) shows the current trends in consumer thought in U.K. society, the dynamics that *previously* molded the market and the likely direction of future value changes. It shows that values based around the traditional nuclear family, needs for economic and political security, needs for certainty (fear of change), and fatalism about the future are declining as determinants of behavior as they move toward the top left-hand corner of the map. On the other hand, feelings of connectedness and concern about the environment, needs to experience new behaviors and thoughts, and a greater confidence in the self and the future, which appear in the center of the map, are now more important and are making new demands on products and brands. The emerging, "leading edge" trends that will become important in *tomorrow's* markets are on the right-hand side of the map and will gradually move toward the center.

Using the analytical tools developed by this type of research, marketers are able to understand the historical appeal of their brand positions and their current "equity" in the minds of their consumers. In other words, they can know which of the values of a brand coincide with the values of consumers.

More significantly, they can identify psychological trends in society that today may be almost indiscernible but in the future will become highly significant. Establishing a brand proposition that appeals to "growing" values (mainly those in the right-hand half of the map), and by definition to groups of people who hold those values, positions the brand as being in tune with real changes that are happening in society.

Point Vector Mapping

The other main type of map is point vector mapping, where all attribute axes radiate out from the center of the chart. Once again, the closer together the brands and attributes are, the closer they are linked in consumer perceptions; the further away from the center of the map a brand is positioned, the more closely it is associated with one particular attribute—that is, the more one-dimensional is its image in the market.

Text continues on page 88, after the case study.

Mapping the Changing Battleground of the Frozen Food Market

• • • • •

The U.K. food market in the 1980s was a classic example of a mature market undergoing radical restructuring through fragmentation. While the market remained more or less static in terms of volume, the emergence of new "wants" provided thermals for growth in the form of almost brand-new market segments. The mass-market branding that had held sway for almost a century was being forced to give way to niche marketing as a tool to help marketers understand the dynamics of a rapidly changing marketplace.

The new character of demand was driven by three new "wants":

- A new awareness of nutrition and its contribution to health.
- A new demand for convenience food, driven by changing social patterns and the decline of the family meal.
- A new interest in exotic foreign dishes, driven by increased foreign travel.

Initially, many of the new segments were regarded by the large food companies as highly specialized niches, too far outside their definitions of their served markets. However, the rapid growth of these segments and their origin in changing social values (which suggested that they were long-term trends rather than sudden "fashions") meant that the larger companies had to make strategic moves to cover them.

This case study charts the battle between two of the food industry's giants as they attempted to adapt their brands to this new market structure. The repositionings of MenuMaster and Healthy Options (brands belonging to Unilever through its Birds Eye subsidiary) and Lean Cuisine (from Findus, part of Nestlé) are monitored using maps of social values of the type described in the previous pages.

Figure 5.4 **Applied Values Trend Map: Initial Positions of MenuMaster and Lean Cuisine**

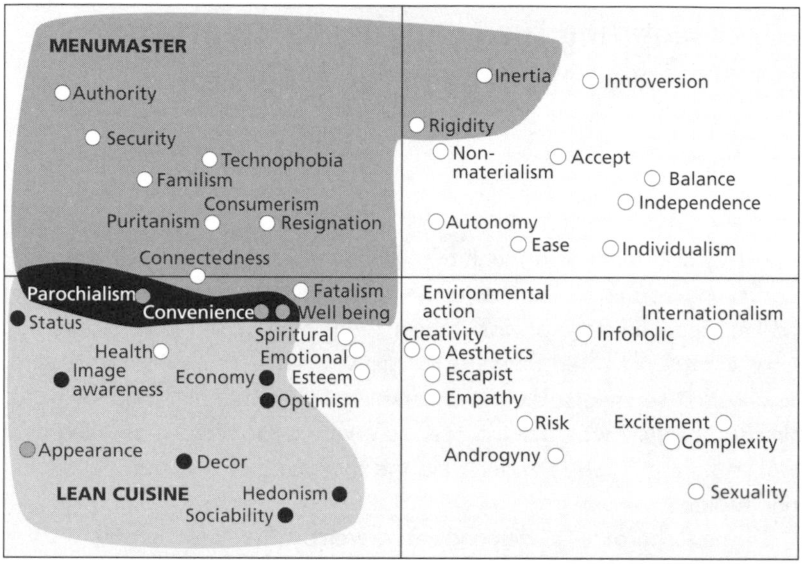

MenuMaster—A Heritage in Mature Segments

MenuMaster was a brand experiencing declining market share. When researchers studied its position in terms of the dominant values of its typical consumers, using the values trend mapping technique, it was clear that the core position was in cultural segments of society that were declining in terms of market importance. In fact, the researchers were able to correlate closely the fall in overall market share of the MenuMaster brand with the rapid decline in the number of people in this cluster (which, as we have seen, is almost exactly the sustenance-driven segment), from 40% of the U.K. population in 1973 to only 27% in 1989. This was a real problem for the brand because it had strong equity with the value systems of past and present consumers.

The classic brand management response to such a situation is gradually to move the center of gravity of the dominant brand values toward "growth" values; in other words, to reposition the brand for growth rather than defend the existing safe but declining market. This response would have moved MenuMaster toward the center and lower-left quadrant of the map, the outer-directed segment where values are all about looking nice for others, looking healthy, having "nice" things, and flaunting them.

Unfortunately, this option was not open to MenuMaster. This territory was already fully occupied by the brand's main competitor and source of lost market share, the Lean Cuisine brand (see Figure 5.4). Going for the same market could only mean expensive head-on confrontation with no certainty of success.

Lean Cuisine—A New Entrant

The Lean Cuisine brand was a response by Swiss food giant Nestlé to the value changes in the 1980s discussed above. The concept had proved successful in the United States, and it was introduced into the United Kingdom via the Findus frozen food brand.

Lean Cuisine as a product was formulated to meet demands for healthy and nutritional convenience foods featuring exotic recipes. The concept was clearly defined: "Lean Cuisine is a new range of really delicious frozen recipe dishes proving that food can be appetizing and satisfying without being high in calories." Each serving contained fewer than 300 calories and the range included such dishes as Glazed Chicken, Cod Florentine, and Chicken Chow Mein. Lean Cuisine therefore neatly encapsulated all the values that MenuMaster was failing to address.

Repositioning MenuMaster

Unable or unwilling to confront Lean Cuisine head-on, Birds Eye decided to develop the MenuMaster brand for a completely new segment of the market. Unfortunately, this required a radical repositioning that almost destroyed all the equity that had been built up in the brand over several decades.

The only new position available to MenuMaster was in the lower-right quadrant (see Figure 5.5 on page 86), a position occupied by the leading edge values of the inner-directeds. Repositioning the brand required major changes to the product in order to meet the food-related values of this group. Predictably, consumers experienced dissonance when they tried to reconcile the new positioning of the brand with its traditional value set.

Such dissonance need not directly harm a brand, but it can dramatically affect the impact of market communications. This happened to

Figure 5.5 **Applied Values Trend Map: Repositioning of MenuMaster**

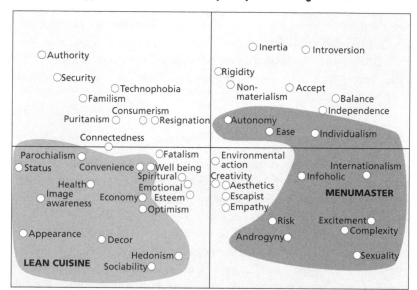

MenuMaster. Tracking studies showed that the new target market of inner-directeds, who are light TV viewers, couldn't recall even seeing the repositioning campaign for the brand. On the other hand, the brand's traditional supporters, the sustenance-driven, who *are* heavy TV viewers, could recall the campaign but did not associate the images with MenuMaster and thus did not recognize it as "their" brand. Analyzed by social value researchers, the new position of MenuMaster could be explained as too radical a shift in its brand values from its heritage or equity.

The repositioning campaign was a failure and Birds Eye was left with two major headaches:

- Lean Cuisine was too strong to attack.
- MenuMaster was too strong to reposition radically.

A New Brand for a New Market

The dynamics of social change that had made MenuMaster such a successful brand in the past were now in danger of destroying it. Birds Eye was forced to take radical and courageous action in response. On the assumption that even major players now had to be adept at niche

Figure 5.6 **Applied Values Trend Map: Eventual Positions Within Market**

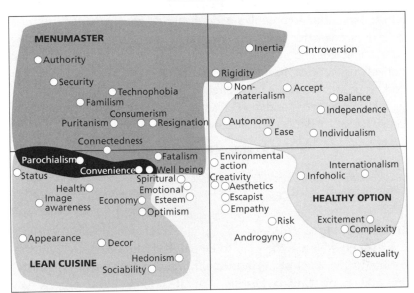

marketing in this fast-moving market, it decided to create a completely new brand.

Since MenuMaster could not be repositioned and appeared inevitably linked to the declining value systems of the sustenance-driven group, the range was pared down to the products consumed primarily by this group. It was also given only defensive market support, allowing a much lower level of advertising expenditure. This strategy allowed the brand to maintain its reduced market share at a greatly reduced cost.

The rest of the original MenuMaster product range was then augmented with other more adventurous and health-oriented food to create a new niche brand, called Healthy Option. This brand was built on the value systems of the inner-directed group, which had not been targeted by either the original MenuMaster brand or the competing Lean Cuisine.

Healthy Option became a successful brand, without cannibalizing the reduced MenuMaster products range. More significantly, however, the creation of Healthy Option and the retention of MenuMaster gave Birds Eye a strategic position on the cultural trend map that suggests it would be very difficult for the Lean Cuisine to be repositioned (see Figure 5.6). In effect, Birds Eye had closed off virtually three-quarters of the map.

CONCLUSION

When deep-seated social value trends influence the development of a market, brands have to evolve accordingly. Relatively modern research techniques can offer brand management new ways of understanding market structure and segmentation patterns in terms of the values and motivations that dictate brand preference. This is especially relevant in markets based upon core human needs, such as food. The monitoring of the U.K. convenience food market in this case study explains the reasons for the success and failure of different brand positionings.

━━━━━━━━━━

Text continued from page 82.

Brand Mapping

It is also possible for the map to be based not upon the whole market but at the level of an individual brand. The "essence analysis" undertaken by United Distillers on its Johnnie Walker whiskey brand (see the case study in Chapter 11), is an exemplary "brand map" exercise. This is an exposition of the personality of the brand, covering how the consumer sees the brand, user imagery, preferred usage occasion, etc. Everything is still described as the consumer sees it, and the basis of the segmentation is still at the deepest level—benefit sought or drinking situation. In this case, the only segment shown is the one addressed by the individual brand; the others may be implied, but the competitor brands are not shown. This type of analysis enables a management team to make an in-depth assessment of targeting and positioning strategies.

These methods of reducing a mass of data to a clear picture of the structure of consumer perception are powerful aids to brand management. They may not be scientifically accurate, but they do map consumers' perceptions rather than physical product reality and in doing so go to the heart of a brand personality.

SUMMARY

Segmentation is a market characteristic, to be distinguished from differentiation, which is a company's response to it. A segment must be homogeneous in its market wants, and different from other segments. Since every consumer is slightly different, the identification of the boundaries between segments has to allow for interpretation and even offers scope for creativity.

Marketers use increasingly sophisticated techniques to get closer to the motivations of customers. Where simple measures such as age groups or social class would previously have sufficed, brand management now has to probe behind consumer behavior in order to understand attitudes. If this is successful, the company may be able to perceive a target that its competitors cannot and gain a competitive edge.

REFERENCES

1. Thomas V. Bonoma and Benson Shapiro, *Segmenting the Industrial Market* (New York: Free Press, 1983).

2. F.A. Johne, "Segmenting Buyers on the Basis of Their Business Strategies," *International Journal of Research in Marketing* 1 (1984), pp. 183–98.

Brand Positioning

• • • • • • • • • • • • • •

Positioning: The Key to Strategy

Branding is a strategic issue. The most brilliant tactical decisions will build a real brand equity only if a strategic view underlies all activity. A brand evolves far too slowly to shift in response to uncoordinated short-term stimuli. The brand strategy *is* the brand.

If an organization is committed to the concept of branding, it accepts certain ideas about the nature of strategy:

- **Strategy starts with customer satisfaction**. The satisfaction of customers is the *raison d'être* of any organization.
- **Strategy is long-term**. A company needs to be confident of its ability to continue delivering this satisfaction, so that it can plan its investment in order to achieve growth.
- **Strategy is competitive.** The aim of a strategy is to differentiate a company from its competitors, so that customers perceive a clear choice and develop a repeated preference.

These ideas are now part of the general acceptance that effective strategy must be market-oriented. They will therefore inform not only brand decisions but the way the company approaches everything else it does.

The relationship between brand strategy and corporate strategy is very close: The ultimate objective in both fields is to develop a *sustainable competitive advantage*. Corporate strategy will cover the means by which that advantage is created and delivered, such as management of the corporate culture or the production capacity; brand strategy is one part of corporate strategy, concerned solely with the positioning of the organization's outputs in the minds of its target customers. The market is the ultimate judge of any organization's work. That judgment will draw on the basic dynamics of customer perception. It may be irrational and ill-informed, but it is made from a position of power.

If customer perception is at the heart of strategy, then clearly the challenge facing any organization is to *position* the offering in a way that will appeal most to the target audience. Positioning is the central concept in modern thinking about strategy. In their now celebrated book, *Positioning: The Battle for Your Mind*, advertising professionals Al Ries and Jack Trout draw analogies between military and business strategy. Their main idea is that success is determined not by the amount of force put behind the brand but by the way that force is used—the ability of a company to position itself to advantage in consumers' minds relative to the competition.[1]

If a company is market-driven, it will accept the premise that the most enduring form of competitive advantage is a perceived superiority in the eyes of its customers—the winning "position." This is not to be confused with the source of the advantage, which may well be an internal operation—the attitude of personnel in a service organization, for instance, or the handling of suppliers or the distribution chain.

Positioning is a useful word because it emphasizes that the key issue is how the offer is presented to customers, and how it is therefore perceived by them, rather than the ingredients of the offer. Branding is all about positioning.

The objective of strategy is a sustainable competitive advantage, which may come from any part of the organization's operations. The market is the judge of this advantage. Brand strategy is the process whereby the offer is positioned in the customer's mind to produce a perception of advantage.

The Process of Positioning

So what is positioning? It is really the other half of the branding issue: If a brand is essentially a customer perception, positioning is the process by which a company offers its brands to the consumer.

The message that is conveyed is far more than simply an advertisement, the most obvious form of marketing communication. It should be communicated by *all* the organization's activities, because any of them may be the salient attribute from which the customer takes the message and develops a perception. The Body Shop, for instance, has reached a strong global position without conventional media advertisements. It communicates its brand proposition of personal and environmental care through its products (natural ingredients only, never tested on animals); its packaging (simple, refillable, recyclable); its merchandising (detailed point-of-sale information involving the customer in conscious product choices rather than imitation of role models); its staff (young, informally dressed, committed to the brand values); its sourcing policies (using small local producers from around the world); its social action program (requiring each franchisee to run a local community project); and its public campaigns (generally on environmental issues).

The objective of the positioning process is to make the offer into a brand. If a brand is a simple, unified personality, then it follows that the variety of activities contributing to it must be guided by a similar target position. Each of the individual ways in which the consumer experiences the brand can then reinforce the basic position. The message can be adopted unaltered by the consumer as the brand image, and there is no dissonance between message and experience.

A model process is described by Philip Kotler, consisting of four stages that he calls the "Four P's of Strategic Marketing":

> The first step in the strategic marketing process is to research the market you are interested in. There's no way around it. I've got to know what the market's like, who's in it, what they need and want, and I call that *probing.* . . . Now after you probe the market you discover that the customers are not homogeneous, they're heterogeneous, but they do cluster into groups, into segments. Since they want different things it's not possible to satisfy them all with one offer. So we call that segmentation, albeit that my name for it is *partitioning.* . . . The third step is to realize that we don't have the resources to serve every customer need and group. So we target, which I call *prioritizing.* Finally, fourth, for each market we are going to make into a target, we *position* ourselves. We decide on the message we want to create about who we are for that target market.[2]

Kotler is punning on the traditional "four P's" known as the marketing mix: product, price, promotion, and place (better described as distribution). These are the set of activities that are commonly thought to constitute the tool kit with which a company can influence the perception of its customers. According to this scheme, a company makes a decisions about the type of product it offers, decides on the price that will best convey to the market the level of quality being offered, uses all promotion media to help customers understand and desire the product, and distributes it in a way that will make it easy to acquire. As long as it coordinates all the decisions so that a single clear message is given to the market, then the marketing can be said to be well done.

How is the organization to decide on the single clear message that is to guide its marketing mix decisions? Just as branding forces an organization to ask why its customers are buying, so positioning forces attention on how consumers will react to the marketing mix. The traditional four P's of the marketing mix are concerned with what the company does; positioning starts by considering what the market needs and wants. The marketing mix represents only the messenger, not the message.

Choosing a Brand Position

The brand position will, if successful, be something that consumers throughout the market understand and can express. Consumers around the world will tell you that Volvo builds the safest cars, or that Disney is the expert at entertaining children (of all ages).

Criteria for Selection

Many positions might be successful, but it is clear that certain criteria must be applied in selecting an appropriate one:

- The position must be *salient* to customers. It is absolutely no use positioning upon something that is not used by customers as an indicator of quality, such as positioning a hotel on the height of the building.
- The position must be based upon *real brand strengths*. If the message promises something that cannot be delivered, the consumer will be less likely to purchase the product regularly and may even be antagonized. It is easy for service companies to promise that they are faster, or friendlier, or more efficient. It is harder to build those positions into the operations.

- The position must reflect a *competitive advantage.* It is no use positioning on the same basis as a competitor. Without a perceived difference, there will be a risk that all products are seen as similar and the purchase gets made on price.
- The position must be *communicable* in a clear and motivating way to the market. If the position is too complex, or relies upon extensive use of the brand, consumers cannot be relied upon to put in the substantial effort required to discern the message.

A brand has therefore to be "designed" so that all elements of the marketing mix communicate the same salient, superior, and distinctive message. This design process will by definition involve nearly all the company's functions and operations.

The selection of position will probably involve a searching analysis of the company's own strengths and weaknesses. After this, aspects that do not contribute to the position can be designed out of the product or service. A brand cannot be strong on all counts, and it is better to attempt to excel on one attribute and perform adequately on the others, than to chase the impossible goal of excelling in every area.

Table 6.1 is an example of how the PIMS research into the results of marketing strategy rates market positions and shows clearly the need to understand the basis of the position. In this hypothetical example, Volvo has the weakest position, because it has a less distinct profile and is superior only on an attribute with low importance in the buying decision.

The Influence of Brand Personality

Tables like Table 6.1 are useful, but they do not necessarily reflect how customers see the market. While the customers will be able to rate brands against given attributes, they are still likely to use the shorthand of an overall brand personality, and this too must be understood. In his recent book *World Class Brands*,[3] Chris Macrae arrives at six stereotypes of brand personalities:

1. **The ritual.** Brands associated with particular occasions, to the extent that the brand is the whole experience. Examples include champagne (associated with any celebration); Pimm's (summer relaxation); or certain toys or foods associated with Christmas.

Table 6.1 **Purchase Decision by Customer for Heavy-Duty Trucks (hypothetical example)**

No differentiation

		Performance Rating			
ATTRIBUTE	WEIGHT	NAVISTAR	PACCAR	VOLVO	MACK
Durability	35	7	7	7	7
Fuel economy	25	8	8	8	8
Living features	20	6	6	6	6
Ride	20	9	9	9	9

Substantial Differentiation

ATTRIBUTE	WEIGHT	NAVISTAR	PACCAR	VOLVO	MACK
Durability	35	7	7	8	9
Fuel economy	30	9	8	7	7
Living features	20	6	9	7	6
Ride	15	5	7	8	6

Source: Robert D. Buzzell and Bradley T. Gale, *The PIMS Principles: Linking Strategy to Performance* (New York: Free Press, 1987), p. 122.

2. **The symbol.** Image brands where the symbol is the added value because of its associations. Examples include the Lacoste alligator or the Dunhill name, where the actual product category is almost unimportant.

3. **The heritage of good.** Usually the first brand to have established a specific set of benefits, which can then position itself as the pioneer of this sector. Examples include The Body Shop (environmentally conscious toiletries); Coca-Cola ("the real thing" in soft drinks); Kellogg's (still the experts in a "sunshine start" to the day).

4. **The aloof snob.** Brands that help a person give signals that he or she is different. Very common in "designer goods," examples include Chanel perfumes, Ferrari cars, or American Express Gold Cards.

5. **The belonging.** Brands that make the consumer feel part of a larger group with which they want to identify, such as Levi's jeans (the symbol of youth and informality) or Benetton clothes

(the "United Colors of Benetton," which endorses a "multi-racial global village").

6. **The legend**. Brands that have a real history and have become almost mythical, such as Levi's 501s (the first jeans ever made by the company in the nineteenth century); or Timberland shoes (made using the original Red Indian method of moccasin construction).

Such an exercise is subjective, but useful in understanding the focus of a brand position. Is it meant to make the customer feel good in using the brand, or in displaying it to friends? What is the balance between rational and emotional benefits? This may seem most applicable to emotional low-value markets like groceries, but in fact all buyers tend to pigeonhole alternative suppliers; industrial market research often shows positions like "fastest," "friendliest," "highest product quality," "most innovative," which are summary "company personalities."

Establishing a Focus

Within these overall generic positions, the brand must be analyzed to establish the exact nature of the position. For Coca-Cola, for instance, "the reason for our success . . . is the atmosphere of friendliness we create . . . customers actually want to identify with the product."[4] Clearly this appeal to the want for friendliness is suitable when the basic need is refreshment. Marlboro has a different set of values—"the brand for the strong, outdoor, independent man, the person who thinks for himself, lives his own life, does his own thing."[5] Importantly, this brand is positioned on the basis of its target customer (only a certain sort of man smokes Marlboro) rather than explicitly on the benefits of the product in use. The wants it meets are about self-image.

Kellogg's is a different sort of brand proposition; not a single product, but a family of products all endorsed with the brand name in a single product field. The focus is then very much on the quality of the physical product, with the Kellogg's name acting as a guarantee that it was indeed produced by the experts in this area. The appeal of Sony is somewhat similar: The name belongs to a supplier who is dedicated to a certain product field only, is constantly innovating within that field, and can be positioned as "the expert." This is obviously a strong position in product categories where loyalty to one brand is low, either because the range of products is wide (Sony) or the repertoire is large (Kellogg's).

IBM might by contrast be argued to be less product-quality oriented; the usual verdict is that IBM meets the need for security felt by the nonexpert computer user. To emphasize this, IBM marketing communications always stress that it is a service company. Position here is relative; IBM operates in a market where many suppliers have traditionally promoted product features rather than benefits (or "customer solutions" as IBM has long termed them).

Another service brand, McDonald's, shows how quickly a brand can grow when it is better at meeting a want that was previously not served (the brand was born as recently as 1955). The essence of McDonald's position is the predictability of its offer, and in particular its guaranteed standards on "quality, service, cleanliness, and value" (QSC&V, as the company calls it). While there are times when customers enjoy uncertainty when visiting a restaurant, there are many others—for example, when children are present—when unpredictability is the last thing required. The variety of possible positions is limited only by the variety of people's wants.

Brands as Market Leaders

A successful brand will eventually have the option of making its brand leadership part of the position. Many brands that are market leaders do indeed say or imply in their advertising that this is an endorsement of their superiority; and it works—plenty of consumers will buy the market leader because they assume it is better quality or because it is a lower-risk, more reliable option. Whether this assumption is right or not, it is such a powerful force that many marketing textbooks divide up their discussion of strategy into strategies for leaders and strategies for others.

A superior brand position can be built on anything of enduring value to customers. This may include images or simply that a brand is the biggest. The position should be consistently communicated by all elements of the marketing mix.

The case study of Michelob Dry reflects how the strength of an existing brand leader was used to defend a position in the U.S. beer market against a powerful new entrant.

Text continues on page 102, after the case study.

A New Face for an Established Brand—
The Dry Beer Threat

Anheuser-Busch/Michelob Dry

• • • • •

In March 1987, Asahi, the third largest Japanese brewing company, launched a new product in Japan known as "dry beer." The company had surveyed beer drinkers in 1985 and determined that there was a need for a drier-tasting product. Asahi Super Dry, characterized as tasting clean, crisp, slightly sweet, and with virtually no aftertaste, was loved by Japanese beer consumers.

Super Dry was Japan's biggest hit in domestic history. It grossed $680 million in its first nine months and increased the company's share by 2.5% to 12.9%. This phenomenal success led the other players in the industry quickly to introduce dry versions. In less than one year dry beer held 33% of the entire Japanese beer market. Table 6.2 represents the market share and number of cases sold in Japan by the four Japanese beer manufacturers in 1987. Also shown are the small number of cases imported to the United States.

Table 6.2 **Sales of Japanese Beer, 1987**

Imports to the United States

	Sapporo	Kirin	Asahi	Suntory	Total
Cases (thousand)	1,163	890	179	168	2,400
Change from 1986 (%)	+14	−1.5	+17	−11.5	+5.9
Market share (%)	48.4	37.1	7.5	7.0	100
In Japan					
Cases (thousand)	128,542	357,410	80,827	60,196	626,975
Change from 1986 (%)	+7	+3	+34	+12	+7.3
Market share (%)	20.5	57.0	12.9	9.6	100

Source: Japanese Ministry of the Treasury.

This was not so much another major Japanese innovation, but more a case of capitalizing on a 40-year-old American idea. In the 1950s dry beers were being produced in the United States under brand names such as Rheingold and Stag Pale Dry and by very small regional brewers. The beer giants like Anheuser-Busch and Miller did not take it up, and by the late 1960s dry beer had virtually disappeared. The Japanese were the first to make dry beer a national success, and by 1987 the U.S. brewing companies were starting to pay close attention.

Having a popular presence in Japan with its Budweiser brand, Anheuser-Busch was able to observe the dry beer phenomenon first-hand. The Japanese breweries were very open about their global intentions in early 1988. Business and trade magazines such as *Forbes* and *Beverage World* featured their very aggressive expansion strategy. The fact that all four major Japanese brewers had established a U.S. subsidiary for their nondry brews and nonalcoholic beverages made it obvious that the United States was their highest priority.

Anheuser-Busch Plans to Resist the Japanese Challenge

Seeing the dry beer success in Japan and fully aware of the Japanese brewers' aggressive U.S. strategy, Anheuser-Busch knew that dry beer would soon be introduced in the United States on a large scale. Among the major factors to consider were the following:

- Many Japanese products in other sectors were becoming preferred to U.S. products by U.S. consumers; why couldn't this occur in the beer industry?
- The Japanese had often improved upon U.S. innovation to make products that were more successful in the United States than those of U.S. companies.

Anheuser-Busch also faced several threats:

- Dry beer could be a fad. The Japanese constantly invent new tastes and this might not last more than a year.
- Sales could be stolen from existing Anheuser-Busch brands ("cannibalization" in marketing terminology).
- The dry concept could cause confusion since the term had been previously used in the alcohol business but not in regard to beer.

- A dry product offers no meaningful benefit.
- Dry beer fits into a small segment between premium and light beers.

In June 1988, Asahi and Kirin began full-scale exporting of their dry beers to the United States. Although they targeted Japanese restaurants, Anheuser-Busch anticipated that it would not be long before a national introduction was undertaken. Anheuser-Busch needed to test the dry beer concept quickly. If viable, it had to introduce a dry beer before the Japanese brewers made substantial inroads.

Anheuser-Busch started its analysis by sending a group brand executive to Japan for two weeks to talk with representatives from different brewers. Following this, the brewer conducted extensive qualitative and quantitative research. The studies revealed the following consumer responses:

- There was a readiness for a new, exciting beer.
- Consumers were very curious about dry beer—what it is, what it tastes like.
- Consumers were familiar with the "dry" concept for wine, champagne, or spirits but unsure how it related to beer.
- Beer drinkers wanted to know more about dry beer.

Anheuser-Busch believed the curiosity factor would make dry beer popular and encourage consumers to try it—a vital prerequisite for the successful introduction of a dry beer product.

Consumer testing also showed that consumers wanted "a beer providing refreshment but no aftertaste." The overwhelming response in favor of an up-market brand, Japan's proven success with dry beer, and Americans' general willingness to try new tastes led Anheuser-Busch to plan a national roll-out even before the results from test markets were collected. It was confident that the results of its consumer research indicated that the risks were worth taking.

Choosing Which Brand Would Go Dry

Although Anheuser-Busch had many brand names (Michelob, Budweiser, and Busch) in segments that could potentially have competed against each other, choosing the best brand to introduce first in a new category was not a difficult decision. The reasons for introducing Michelob Dry instead of other family brands were as follows:

- Since this was a new product category in the United States, the risks and investment were far greater than for a more routine product extension. A reliable brand name was needed to build sales through leveraging an already strong brand.
- The quality of dry beers in Japan seemed to fit the upscale image most characteristic of the Michelob name.
- Although both Michelob and Budweiser dry products could have been a hit, if the segment grew as projected then there could be room for both a Michelob Dry and Bud Dry. But if Bud Dry was introduced first and loyalty for the product was very strong due to the power of the Budweiser name, a Michelob Dry could have a difficult time attracting followers.
- Anheuser-Busch had a strong need to improve the sales of the Michelob line. In 1987 the family of Michelob, Michelob Light, and Michelob Classic Dark declined 3% in sales to 7.9 million barrels from its peak of 9.9 million barrels in 1981. By introducing Michelob Dry first, Anheuser-Busch sensed an opportunity for the new product to revitalize the whole family.

Anheuser-Busch had a definite target market in mind for Michelob Dry:

- Young educated adults with up-market tastes (many are attracted to the dry concept as they associate it with fine wine and champagne).
- Women (many like the no aftertaste feature).
- Light beer drinkers (Michelob Dry contained 133 calories, far less than Michelob's 155 calories and even 1 calorie less than Michelob Light).

With an apparently good fit between product and target market, the decision was made to launch Michelob Dry nationally after test marketing in September 1988.

Internal Brand Competition Brings Market Dominance

A year after its introduction, Michelob Dry had an 83% share of the dry beer segment. The only competition in 1988 and 1989 came from C. Heileman Beer, which had followed Anheuser-Busch's lead by introducing four regional dry beers.

Bud Dry was nationally introduced in April 1990. This gave Anheuser-Busch a year and a half to measure the performance and longevity of Michelob Dry. Strategically, it also gave ample time to position Michelob Dry firmly while conducting more thorough market research regarding Bud Dry's introduction. Even with regional distribution the previous year, Bud Dry managed to capture 14.3% of the dry beer market in the United States. Bud Dry's entry indicated that the dry beer market was to be taken seriously.

Bud Dry was quickly accepted. It took only one year for Michelob Dry and Bud Dry to switch market shares, with Bud Dry holding 75% and Michelob Dry 19%. This was a classic example of the internal competition so common to Anheuser-Busch's past success and a powerful signal of the Budweiser brand strength. So, by the end of 1990, Anheuser-Busch had a virtual monopoly of the dry beer segment, commanding a 94% share with its two brands.

By the end of 1990, Bud Dry was expected to have sold 4 million to 5 million barrels, with Michelob Dry selling some 1 million to 1.5 million. This is dramatic, considering that in 1988 the whole dry beer segment had sales of only 600,000 barrels.

CONCLUSION

In one industry sector at least, it appears that careful observation of impending foreign invasion and rapid response through brand leverage can help a domestic company win and maintain market dominance.

———

Text continued from page 97.

The Two Major Elements of Brand Strategy: The Offer and the Customer

Whatever position is chosen, the brand strategy will have to reflect the two partners in the brand marketing relationship: the offer and the customer.

When the positioning strategy is based upon the idea of uniqueness—Coca-Cola, Kellogg's, Sony, and McDonald's fall into this category—the brand is communicated to as many different types of customer as possible, and the actual customers self-select (they will identify with the brand). For this type of strategy, the key task is to determine exactly what it is that is being offered to the customer. The usual way of looking at this is the marketing mix. The brand may be differentiated on the basis of its advertising, its name, its price, the R&D that went into it, the speed with which it is delivered, the people who deliver it, the range of the product line, or anything else.

When, as with Lacoste or Marlboro, the positioning is on the type of person the brand is designed for, the key skill is the identification of the target customer. The assumption is that different customers will have different wants, and that these segments of the market can be addressed with distinct brands. The value of such a brand may be that it is intrinsically different, addressing the distinct want(s) of the segment, or that it is perceived as a specialist offering to a certain type of customer ("user imagery"). In either case, the brand position will contain or imply the message: "This is for you only if you are or if you want. . . ."

The relative emphasis of these two approaches is shifting in the 1990s and is the subject of some debate.

> *The two major elements of a brand strategy are the nature of the offer (the sum of the marketing mix) and the target segment(s) to which the offer is made. Either aspect can provide a competitive advantage.*

The Target Segment

Should a Brand Strategy Include Target Segments?

The 1990s have been described as the age of target marketing. Many markets are undoubtedly increasingly fragmented. However, a small but growing number of observers point out that, first, the globalization of markets is leading to more standardization and fewer real segments (see Chapter 11); second, while accepting that consumers are growing more varied in their tastes, it is argued that it is impossible to measure the differences between segments in any meaningful way. Consumers do not always sort themselves obligingly into distinct subgroups within a market. The research that reveals the importance of repertoires tends to fuel these doubts, as it demonstrates that all sorts of customers may include a given brand in their repertoire, even if they do buy in cycles of different frequencies, and that the number of loyal customers who buy little else is very small.

It would therefore seem unlikely that there are significant groups of consumers who are fundamentally different in ways reflected by their buying patterns.

This view, summed up by advertising researcher Stephen King, leads to the conclusion that market segments may not even exist:

> A development of market segmentation theory is product segmentation, which seems more promising. The only measurable factor that distinguishes the people who buy Brand A from those who do not (or those for whom Brand A makes up a high proportion of purchases from those for whom it makes up a low proportion) is their liking for Brand A. . . . The significant difference in implications between this theory and consumer segmentation theory is that the new brand must aim to have a unique blend of characteristics, not look for a unique group of consumers. . . . The basic principle is that the *brand sets its own pattern*. The brand, as it were, chooses its consumer, and not vice versa. The right group cannot be finally selected until the brand has been invented.[6]

According to this view, management had better just concentrate on producing something *different*. Provided there is some added value in the product, the offer will appeal to some segments and not to others. Indeed, the more added value in the product, the closer we can get to the customer and his or her wants.

To many nonmarketers familiar with the idea that the central principle of marketing is that everything begins with the consumer, this product-driven approach will seem heretical. It is nevertheless true that most of today's great brands did not originate from a carefully researched launch into a target part of the market; they were instead launched in a small way and emerged as the market developed.

In adding value and getting closer to some customers, it follows that a brand will be getting further away from the different wants of another group or segment in the same market. There is a trade-off that looks something like Figure 6.1.

This natural condition is being accelerated by several specific conditions of modern markets that may be summed up as market maturity:

- Now that society is a long way up the learning curve of technology and production, the genuine innovation, which changes the way a consumer need is met, is increasingly rare. The era

Figure 6.1 **The Trade-off Between Value Added and Breadth of Appeal**

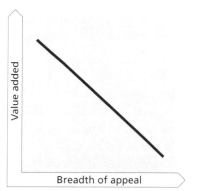

when consumers were buying into major new product categories, such as cars or televisions, is gone. Even when a real innovation comes along, it is now much more easily copied. This shifts the emphasis to "wants" or "extras," the basis of segments rather than overall market definition.

- Because of this, markets are not growing so quickly. To achieve growth, a company has to steal the customers of other brands. This increases the urgency of adding value, and the targeting of specific groups.

- The 1990s are seeing the emergence of the so-called "new consumers," with their emphasis on individualism, shunning the former mass-market trend of emulating role models in their consumption patterns and priding themselves on being different and independent-minded.

In such conditions, it becomes extremely unlikely that a single brand proposition will appeal to all parts of the market. Some sort of targeting will be necessary even to survive. So companies are deliberately accelerating the already strong trend toward fragmentation by helping subsegments to emerge.

The view that targeting is more vital than ever is well expressed by Kotler:

> The heart of modern strategic marketing can be described as STP marketing—namely, segmenting, targeting and positioning. This does not obviate the importance of LGD marketing—lunch, golf, and dinner—but

rather provides the broader framework for strategic success in the marketplace. . . . Today's companies are finding it increasingly unrewarding to practice mass marketing or product variety marketing. Mass markets are becoming "demassified." They are dissolving into hundreds of micromarkets.[7]

These two views of strategy are not incompatible if looked at in the right light. The distinction at heart is between segmentation (a characteristic of markets) and differentiation (a company action addressed to the market). In truth, both are necessary. Nobody denies that a great brand is both differentiated and ends up appealing to some consumers more than to others. In fact, market research is getting much better at understanding the one segmentation scheme everybody accepts—the difference between those who like the brand and those who do not (this is discussed in Chapter 4). It will become increasingly possible for marketers to build models of the market for specific product categories. With this more sophisticated information, it becomes possible for a brand team to gain a competitive edge purely by understanding the changing wants in the market better. To ignore this opportunity for getting closer to customers is to concede a potential advantage to competitors.

The other clinching factor in favor of more target marketing is that the megabrands are fragmenting their offerings: more line extensions in the form of different formulations, "diet" versions, and so on. This is powerful testimony that the forces leading to the fragmentation of mature markets are real.

If markets are changing, then marketing ought to change too. The product-driven approach to segmentation is in some ways a leftover of the days of growth markets when the balance of power was with the suppliers. It may still be the best approach when there is a chance of launching a major new innovation and consumers have to be educated to understand how the new product category meets their need. But companies today mainly operate in low-growth markets where competition is on the basis of meeting wants rather than needs. Growth is usually achieved by effecting a change in already well-established positions. This involves risk, the dilemma behind so many management decisions. If a new brand is developed without reference to the target consumer group, the chances of it being successful are obviously reduced. At the same time, the chances of it being a breakthrough that actually changes the market are increased, because its development has been outside the constraints of existing attitudes. A brand developed from a research base is more likely to gain acceptance but less likely to be a moldbreaker.

> *Although it is not easy to predict where a market will segment between users and nonusers of a brand, it is increasingly important to attempt to target brands to specific segments. In today's more fragmented markets a brand that is not targeted risks having no franchise at all.*

A good example of target marketing is demonstrated in the case study charting the launch of the Vector checking account by Midland Bank in the United Kingdom. In fact, this account has proved unsuccessful against its stated objectives, possibly because of pricing decisions. But the targeting of a new type of customer was exemplary in its approach.

Text continues on page 112, after the case study.

New Customers, New Brand Positions
The Midland Vector Account

• • • • •

In May 1987 Midland Bank launched a new style of checking account in the United Kingdom called Vector. It carried a fixed monthly charge of £10 but gave holders an automatic interest-free overdraft facility of £250 and paid interest on current balances.

From the launch date to the end of 1987 Midland spent £6 million on advertising the new account, 86% of that on television and the balance on press advertising. The target was to attract 250,000 account holders, with 60,000 of them coming from Midland's competitors.

A Segmented Approach

Vector was a brand very deliberately created and marketed to appeal to one of four segments that Midland had identified in its market base.

Its segmentation study was based on two axes, "Confidence" and "Authority." The first measured whether people were confident or diffident in their dealings with banks. While there are obvious relationships with financial standing, age, and class, confidence can also be "unlearned" and such relationships can be weak in individual cases. Authority is a more difficult concept. It measures a desire for structure and authority within a system. A high scorer would be someone who wants to know where they stand.

Using the two axes to create a matrix, Midland was able to arrive at extreme segment examples (see Figure 6.2 on page 109). These can be defined as follows:

- **New bankers:** They are low on confidence but have a high desire for authority. They respect banks and the position they view them as holding in society and expect them to maintain that position. They want bankers to act in a paternal way toward them.
- **Minimalists:** They have little confidence in dealing with banks and little respect for authority. They are poor users of the banking

Figure 6.2 **A Segmentation of the U.K. Personal Banking Market**

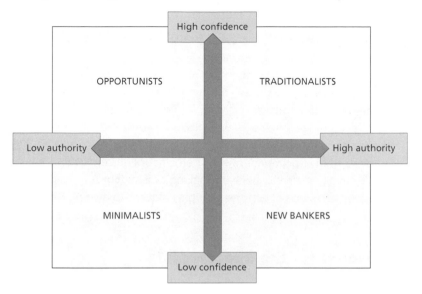

Source: Company data, 1986.

system and have no particular views of banks if and when they have to deal with them. Unlike the New Bankers, they are not interested in any ongoing relationship with banks.

- **Traditionalists:** High in confidence and respect for authority, they like structure and systems and also see themselves as highly placed within them. They want a relationship of mutual respect with banks. They see a bank as a professional adviser and confidant.
- **Opportunists:** High confidence and low respect for authority combine to produce a view of banks as simply another retail outlet for services that may or may not be useful at any given time. They regard banks as likely to be exploitative and as something to be exploited first. They view banking as a straightforward commercial operation, and they expect banks to be efficient, not friendly or disapproving.

These categories are not regarded as watertight. There will be a mix of characteristics and some shifting over time and circumstances between and within segments.

What was important from Midland's point of view was that each segment could also be described in terms of the likely "desired imagery" to which each would respond. For the purposes of this case study, the most important segment is the Opportunist, and the desired imagery of the other three will not be considered.

Opportunists were described as most likely to be happy with a banking system that they believe they can "beat" (though they also do not want the opposition to be too strong). A high-status credit card, but one without very strict requirements, was also a key attribute.

The Opportunists believe in offers being actively "sold" so that they can choose what to accept or reject. Their emotional satisfactions will be highest from a high-profile bank or banking system that sells its products aggressively. This kind of customer is highly influenced by advertising and imagery.

An Account for the Opportunists

It is thus not surprising that Midland targeted its first segmented brand, Vector, at the Opportunists. But there were other reasons.

It was argued that this was the segment most likely to try a new type of banking relationship. Research also showed that the Opportunist segment had the most complaints about how banks handle current accounts, especially small overdrafts and bank charges. They were also the group most likely to move their account from one bank to another, so an account specific to their requirements was the only one likely to inspire them to demonstrate any loyalty. Further, they were seen as attractive banking propositions because of their high financial activity and use of other services such as personal loans, credit cards, revolving credit accounts, and bank mortgages.

The profile of the segment was very positive:

- The highest social class of the four segments
- Predominantly male
- In the most financially active age group, 25 to 44
- Heavy users of financial products, especially credit products
- Likely to have paid bank charges
- Likely to have more than one account
- Likely to have transferred accounts from one bank to another

The rationale behind Vector was to meet the requirements of Opportunists to feel in charge. The account was specifically designed to meet

the needs and expectations of this group and to overcome their objec-
tions to existing accounts.

Vector has three main brand features to meet these requirements:

- The interest-free overdraft facility dispels perceptions of rigidity
  and small-mindedness.
- Interest on current balances establishes the account as nonex-
  ploitative and "fair."
- The fixed-charge fee overcomes one of the main dissatisfactions
  with bank charges—that they often appear arbitrary and are frequently debited from customers' accounts without their knowledge
  or prior consultation.

All combined to sell a powerful "image" of Vector as a distinct change in
the bank/customer relationship.

Selling the Message

The main features of the account had to be conveyed through advertising.
But it was also important to point out the emotional benefits: the basic
changes in bank/customer relationships.

Four possible advertisements were tested, using attitudinal segmentation to recruit people who were primary and secondary targets for
Vector. The final choice was the one that was shown to state most
powerfully the emotional as well as the practical benefits.

In the TV advertisement a young modern man confronts two traditional
banking figures and, in effect, dictates to them the special features of the
Vector account. This added modernity and style to the account, and, in
dealing so directly with the issue of bank/customer power relationships,
was highly motivating for the Opportunist segment. It also gave secondary messages that the bank was not authoritarian and was prepared to
listen to what customers want.

Researching the Impact

Both immediately after the launch and six months later, Midland carried
out research to assess the success of the Vector account.

This initially showed that awareness was high, though inertia was still
a problem in persuading people to change banks. The targeting had been
fairly accurate: 83% of Vector customers were in the ABC1 groups and
almost three-quarters in the target age group of 25 to 44; they were
much more likely to be men than women and most worked full time and

owned their own house. The vast majority of Vector account holders (89%) were previous Midland account holders. However, a 10% inroad is very respectable in the financial services sector.

Using attitudinal segmentation analysis, 57% of Vector users were defined as Opportunists. However, a surprising 25% emerged as Traditionalists. Subsequent research showed, indeed, that the authority axis is not as clear-cut as the confidence one. Traditionalists can exhibit Opportunistic values, and vice versa.

The biggest "pulling power" of the brand was the interest-free overdraft facility. Over 90% of Vector customers had been overdrawn, many on a regular basis. The fixed fee was the second attraction, seen as reducing "hassle." In any case, as overdraft users, most were used to paying bank charges.

Although ownership of a Vector account was not seen as conveying any particular status, the brand did possess a meaningful personality—though there were concerns that it had a "Yuppie" image. Overall, the account was seen as fairly or very good value for money.

CONCLUSION

Vector was developed as an innovative and differentiated product by using segmentation studies to anticipate the current as well as future needs of customers.

The brand was designed to contain the key practical benefit (a "free" overdraft) and the key emotional benefit (transfer of power from the bank to the customer) of the target segment. Advertising was used to communicate these benefits. The market communication therefore provided a synthesis of physical, aesthetic, rational, and emotional elements, which is one of the main attributes of a successful brand.

────────

Text continued from page 107.

Target Segments and the Market Life Cycle

It is a central task of brand management to understand the structure of the market. Only then is it possible to work on the first phase of a positioning strategy: Who is this brand for, and who is it not for? What is required is a map of consumer motivations, which are the only relevant way of differentiating between customer groups. (Other differences such as age groups are coincidental.)

Such a map of the market structure may prove an elusive goal. In many markets the same consumers have different wants on different occasions. In fashion, for instance, a consumer may want expensive imported designer label items for one occasion and cheap and cheerful items for another. Management therefore have to examine other possibilities for segments, such as situations, and not merely try to categorize consumers as individuals. (A detailed examination of segmentation methodologies is found in Chapter 5.)

This concept of market structure also needs qualifying by an awareness that markets are not all segmented, or constant in their structure. The usual dynamic of a market is to become more fragmented with time as customers become gradually more familiar with the product category, and therefore more discriminating in what they choose. This means that a brand's position will have to evolve as the market evolves.

The idea builds upon the well-known marketing theory of the product life cycle. This argues that a product goes through four distinct stages in its life (see Figure 6.3), with different characteristics and a different treatment required for each. This concept has some flaws. As far as brands are concerned, the notion of inevitable decline is contradicted by the evidence of longevity. The great brands are constantly fine-tuned to keep them updated, and they can certainly survive more than one generation.

The changing character of the market during its life cycle is in essence a change in the extent of segmentation. This translates into two considerations for brand strategy:

- The nature of the target, evolving from a broad mass-market approach to a need for target positioning.
- The nature of the differentiation, from a generic message about satisfaction of the basic need to positioning on specific differentiators.

Brand positions must be very carefully thought out in the introduction phase. It is a well-documented fact that most new product launches are disappointingly slow; in this, at least, the product life cycle is sound. The reason is that only a few experimentalists will take up a new product category. For most consumers, the perceived

Figure 6.3 **The Four Phases of the Product Life Cycle**

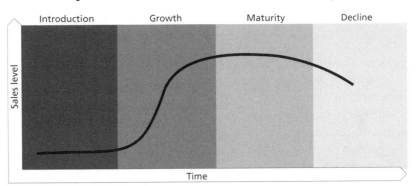

level of risk is a reason to delay the purchase until it has gained a critical mass of market acceptance.

For example, the consumer considering whether to buy a compact disc player for the first time is primarily pondering a choice of product categories—that is, whether to move into the new technology or to remain in the old technology. This consumer will not be familiar with the subtle differences between different CD player brands and will not respond to messages in that area. What is likely to influence a decision to buy is a message of a broad generic nature that focuses on the general functional benefits of the new technology.

This situation will change as the market matures. Just as recently happened with the microwave oven market, customers will become familiar with the technology and will then choose CD players on features, appearance, details of performance, and country or company of origin; in other words, all the variety of wants we see in mature markets.

But customer familiarity has to come first. It is interesting to note the problems encountered by the two companies attempting to introduce satellite TV into Britain. Initially, BSB and Sky positioned themselves competitively. All their promotion advocated their comparative benefits. This became the battle between their differently shaped receivers, one round and one square. What neither player did was explain to the potential consumer the benefits of satellite TV over the terrestrial channels. The result was a painfully slow adoption rate, large financial losses for both competitors, and the eventual merger of the two brands into one.

Most markets, of course, are well established and mature, but even in these markets there will be changes that require new brands or repositioning of existing brands. In this case it is a question not of the emergence of wants but shifts from one want to another. In the car market, the want for economy was very strong in the 1970s because of oil crisis–driven recessions. This faded during the relatively affluent 1980s, only to reemerge in the 1990s with worries about environmental issues in general and the Gulf War in particular. In the food market, many new wants have emerged in recent years with the growth in health consciousness. It is clear that even in markets that are static overall—that is, with no growth in sales—there are thermals of growth as wants change and segments reorder.

This emphasizes the importance of what leading Harvard strategy professor Michael Porter terms "the competitive scope" of a strategy. In mature markets—those with discriminating consumers, clear and distinct segments, and changing patterns of preference—close targeting of the offer is really essential. In less mature or growth markets, the key decision is when to fragment the offering to match the fragmentation of the market.

Options for Positioning Strategies

There are essentially three approaches to this aspect of positioning: mass-market, niche, and differentiated (see Figure 6.4).

Mass-Market Position

The essence of this position is that the company offers only one brand and hopes to pick up customers from all parts of the market. This is most effective in a young and unsegmented market, and the focus is on the need rather than the overlying wants. Alternatively, a company may take the view that, if its brand is unique, it simply needs to support its brand strongly enough for customers to be attracted in sufficient numbers. This may sound simplistic, but it is how most big brands came to be where they are today, and plenty of brand decisions are still taken on the assumption that the success of the brand has more to do with the uniqueness of the offer, and the level of the support, than the targeting of specific customer groups.

Niche Position

A niche position is achieved by offering only one brand and targeting it at only one segment. Obviously this assumes that at least one segment is distinct from the rest of the market. A niche player will usually have a perceived advantage over a mass company: Consumers offered two brands—one mass market and one "specialist"

Figure 6.4 **Three Approaches to Positioning**

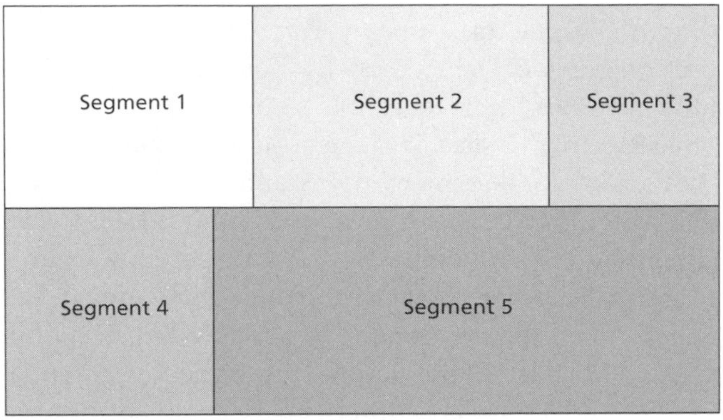

Segment 1	Segment 2	Segment 3
Segment 4	Segment 5	

Mass-market   Brand proposition A – Segments 1, 2, 3, 4, 5

Niche   Brand proposition A – Segment 5

Differentiated   Brand proposition A – 1
                                   B – 2
                                   C – 3
                                   D – 4

offering targeted specifically at their own type—will usually opt for the specialist offering. As a market matures, it is therefore important that a mass player is aware of the threat that will be posed by niche players as soon as segments begin to show.

While it is easy for niche players to pick off segments from major players, especially if the segments are small, there are also dangers in being a niche player. Segments, which are no more than clusters of customers sharing a want, are bound to change as the wants change. At worst, a segment may disappear, and the changing pattern of demand that gave the niche player its initial success is likely to be its undoing. To be a successful niche player, the ability to move and reposition the brand regularly is essential.

Differentiated Position

As a market matures and fragments, the obvious response is for a company to offer several distinct brands to attract the various segments. It can either launch new brands or introduce variants of the original brand (known as brand line extensions). A company with a portfolio of brands will be able to cover most of the market. Most of the large brand companies operate in this way: While each of Ford's vehicles is targeted at specific segments, the Ford portfolio in total covers most of the market.

Differentiation is clearly the least-risk approach. Because of the breadth of the portfolio, changing segmentation patterns will not be too dangerous. However, it is also the most expensive way of operating, because each brand will have to be supported with its own marketing mix.

The fact that most companies are inevitably operating in mature markets has several consequences for brand strategy:

1. **It means that a mass-market position is probably not a realistic option.** The market is very likely to be segmented and consumers discriminating, with well-established attitudes toward the product category and the brands offered.

2. **It means that achieving any sort of change in the market standing of a brand is going to be expensive.** Even if a company launches a unique brand having the potential to change the market's segmentation pattern, the cost of changing entrenched attitudes and buying behavior is likely to be prohibitively high. If a company is fortunate enough to own a well-established brand it is more attractive to try to launch a variant under the established brand's umbrella protection.

3. **It will probably mean that intangibles are the increasingly important battleground for brand differentiation.** Consumers tend to trade up in most markets and will eventually saturate the possibilities of physical or functional differentiation. When this happens, they tend to look to intangibles like image for their extra satisfactions and basis of choice. This may well explain the surge of interest in recent years in the whole topic of branding.

Most companies, then, are left with the options of a niche strategy or a differentiated position (which is arguably a collection of niche positions in one portfolio). In other words, they have to target their brands quite carefully, even if the target in some cases is a broad one. Understanding the target market occupies more time in marketing departments than ever before. Once the target has been clearly identified, attention will turn to the brand.

> *A key element of brand strategy is the competitive scope—how much of the market is the brand designed to cover? Brands will usually become more closely targeted as the market fragments over time.*

Alternative Brand Strategies

Brand strategy is essentially about two variables: the exact composition of the offer made to the market and the part(s) of the market to which the offer is made. The process of bridging these two areas is positioning. As a brand is at heart a position within the consumer's mind, the selection of the desired position is the brand strategy.

The importance of a brand strategy is shown in the case of Gatorade, the U.S. sports drink acquired by Quaker Oats. Gatorade had been too narrowly positioned, mainly on the basis of product features rather than benefits. Because of this slightly technical image, it had been associated with serious sports users, with no reach out to the mass market of sports enthusiasts or amateurs. Although the brand essence was well understood, no real effort had been made to study the target customers, and the brand franchise remained underdeveloped.

Text continues on page 126, after the case study.

Figure 6.5 **Brand Positioning: The Bridge Between the Marketing Mix and Consumer Perception**

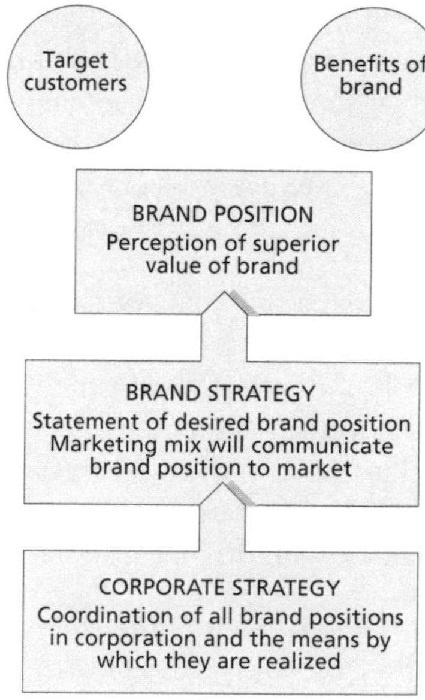

Getting More Performance from the Energy Drink
Gatorade Sports Drink

· · · · ·

In 1983 Quaker Oats purchased Gatorade, the leading brand in the U.S. sports drink segment. Developed in the 1960s by University of Florida sports researchers, this "isotonic" drink had been proved to prevent dehydration caused by physical exertion. Endorsed by professional athletes and a favorite of the athletically minded for 15 years, Gatorade had annual sales of $80 million.

Quaker Oats saw Gatorade as a product that fitted its criteria for brand strength as a market leader. The trend toward increased physical fitness offered great potential and, since Quaker's Grocery Products Division was relatively small, Gatorade would also serve to build the division.

Broadening the Gatorade Brand

There were several shortcomings connected with the Gatorade brand that Quaker Oats sought to improve:

- **Regionality:** Over 70% of sales were concentrated in the Southeast and Southwest. The product had been developed and marketed in the South, and it was assisted by its warmer climate.
- **Seasonality:** As a sports drink, sales peaked in the warmer months between April and September.
- **Limited user base:** Most consumers were male athletes aged 15 to 49 and the majority of promotions took place at male-dominated sporting events such as motor racing and football.

Table 6.3 (see page 121) illustrates Gatorade's positioning prior to 1984 as viewed by the marketing research department at Quaker Oats. It also illustrates the format used by Quaker Oats management for defining the position of their brands. In essence, the department saw a lack of focus on key positioning elements. In particular, there were few messages on the use of the product.

Quaker Oats plans to capitalize aggressively on Gatorade's untapped potential were as follows:

- Geographical expansion to stimulate growth supported by the product's first national TV advertising.
- Marketing to women and children rather than just men.
- Moving the product closer to general thirst environments, rather than just sports occasions.
- Researching the use of aseptic packaging, which could expand the user base.

To address some of these issues, Quaker Oats hired Rabin Research Company to study the market potential of Gatorade in the northern United States. The study involved 607 mall intercept interviews in 17 markets. It showed that users in the North and South were quite similar in how they related to and used Gatorade. Both user groups understood and were committed to the product in terms of actual usage, tactile drinking experience, thirst-quenching/body benefits, and sports orientation. There were, though, signs that users in the North related to the thrist-quenching benefits of Gatorade, while users in the South related more to the replenishing effects. Overall, there appeared to be no need for separate North and South advertising campaigns based on user orientation.

The conclusions of the research study were as follows:

- There are no major resistances toward Gatorade. Consumers know Gatorade and do not express dramatic resistance or negatives that could impede acceptance.
- Achieving additional acceptance among users and trial among non-users will not be easy. Consumers understand the claimed function of Gatorade but they have not totally accepted it.
- In some ways users in the North are very similar to users in the South, but two areas need to be strengthened. The user image needs to be broadened and users need to be made more comfortable with the fact that they use and enjoy Gatorade.
- Nontriers have not internalized the Gatorade experience at all. They are familiar with what Gatorade is supposed to do but really have no idea what the product is, how it will taste, and what it can do.

Table 6.3 **Historical Gatorade "Positioning"**

Target market	
Users:	Competitive athletes
	Adult men
	Teens
	Stuntmen
Occasions:	Everyday, just thirsty
	Work around the house
	Dancing
	Card playing
	Sports
	Beach
	Illness
Frame of Reference	
	All beverages
Point of Difference	
	12 times faster than water
	Quenches
	Replaces
	Cools
	Scientifically formulated

- Nontriers recognize Gatorade's sports linkage and are willing to accept it. The focus needs to be on letting consumers feel the benefit and respect the user imagery. These elements also need to be reinforced among users.

In terms of marketing applications, this translated into the following:

- Gatorade usage and purchase can be extended.
- User imagery must be sharpened so that enjoying Gatorade and feeling the Gatorade experience are seen as being for everyone.
- With nontriers, the product and its taste/consumption and quenching (mouth and body) benefits have to be felt.
- The product needs to be positioned as being a unique and rewarding experience compared with other beverages.
- The sports linkage should not be dropped. However, the focus of the positioning and creative support should be that the tactile and body benefits of Gatorade are for everyone.

Repositioning Gatorade

As the attitudinal research conducted by Rabin indicated that the target could be expanded geographically, Quaker Oats quickly set up the distribution and advertising to support this move.

Management saw a well-focused positioning of the brand as the key to building the franchise. They formulated a new positioning strategy for 1984:

> To Physical Activity Enthusiasts who work up a thirst through hot and sweaty activities, Gatorade is a beverage which quenches thirst and replaces lost fluids and minerals.

The national advertising created in 1984 revolved around this positioning with the slogan "Gatorade is the thirst aid . . . for that deep-down body thirst." The new position is summed up in Table 6.4.

To track brand awareness based on the new campaign, the marketing research department conducted four surveys in 1984, from one week prior to advertising to 24 weeks after. Included was a comparison of attitudes among different consumer segments: Sunbelt versus non-Sunbelt

Table 6.4 **Gatorade Positioning—Refinements**

Target market

Users:	Accomplished, but not professional athletes
	Not too competitive
	Camaraderie, but not social
	Aspirational
Occasions:	Sports, not physical work
	Not too intense, sweaty
	Proper motivations behind sports activity
	Fun but not frivolous

Point of difference

Maintained point of difference vs. other beverages to communicate key benefits:
- Thirst-quenching and replenishment (1984, 1985)
- "Thirst in throat" (1986)
- "Supplies energy to working muscles" (1987)
- "Nothing works better" (1989)
- "Accept no substitutes" (1990)

Table 6.5 **Attitudes Toward Gatorade**

% agree/disagree strongly or somewhat

	WAVE I (MAY)	WAVE IV (NOVEMBER)	POINT CHANGE
Perceived users			
Not for women (disagree)	84	89	+5
Not for kids (disagree)	74	76	+2
Only for super jocks (disagree)	86	88	+2
Useful to everyone (agree)	80	79	+2
Usage occasions			
I don't get thirsty enough (disagree)	60	62	+2
Would taste good after exercise (agree)	76	76	—
Product			
Bothers me that I don't know what it is (disagree)	41	49	+8
A gimmick (disagree)	57	54	+3
Good for you (disagree)	58	59	+1
Unique (agree)	61	62	+1
Would quench thirst (agree)	68	69	+1
Replenishes (agree)	68	66	−2

and males versus females. This seemed to address the product's narrow focus on southern regions and male users.

Overall, although the 1984 advertising was unable to increase the already high levels (93%) of Gatorade awareness among consumers, the campaign was recalled by a significant proportion. More importantly, positive attitude shifts toward the product and perceived users occurred between the initial and final survey waves. Table 6.5 illustrates some of the changes.

The greatest positive change was that females emerged as perceived users of Gatorade sports drink. To a somewhat lesser degree, Gatorade was more likely to be thought to be suitable for kids and less likely to be perceived as for "pros or super jocks" only. These attitude changes toward a broader perceived user base were consistent across the user segments interviewed.

Large changes in attitudes were evident in statements related to negative, or limited, information about the Gatorade product. In the final survey wave, many more respondents (49% versus 41% in Wave I) disagreed that it "bothered them" that they didn't know exactly what was in Gatorade. This positive attitudinal change was consistently strong across all segments (particularly the non-Sunbelt). In addition, fewer respondents felt Gatorade "was a gimmick."

However, there was a lack of increase in the percentage of respondents agreeing that Gatorade would "replenish fluids and minerals lost." This was consistent across all segments, with a 5% decline in the Sunbelt.

Attitudes regarding perceived occasions for Gatorade sports drink use showed little or no change. However, a high proportion of respondents (76%) agreed that the product would taste good following exercise; and two-thirds disagreed with the statement that they "didn't get thirsty enough to drink something like Gatorade."

With effective advertising, increased distribution, and better positioning, Gatorade averaged growth of more than 20% annually from 1983 to 1987, and the brand was able to achieve its secondary aim of helping the Grocery Products Division develop into a powerful unit. Table 6.6 shows the product's volume increases, percentage of sales by region, and percentage of households buying in each region from 1982 to 1986. Clearly, the regionality problem mentioned earlier had been eliminated, as the percentage of sales in the Sunbelt decreased from 72% to 54% between 1983 and 1986.

Growth Attracts Competition

During Gatorade's rapid growth from 1983 to 1987, the brand maintained over 90% market share in the sports drink segment despite significant competitive entry. Gatorade's marketing strength was achieved by continuously adding new flavors and sizes, updating packaging and refining advertising.

By the end of 1987 Gatorade's annual sales exceeded $200 million. As industry analysts projected the sports drink segment to grow to $1 billion in the 1990s, more competitors appeared.

In late May 1988, General Foods introduced Kool-Aid Sports Koolers, aseptically packaged to target younger athletes. Although General Foods failed to steal market share, Gatorade's management recognized the importance of targeting young athletes. By the autumn of 1989, they had introduced Gatorbox aseptic packages, marketed through vending machines. They also introduced 8.5-ounce (250-milliliter) aseptic cartons to entice mothers to buy Gatorade for young, active children.

Table 6.6 **Gatorade Historic Measures**

	FY83*	FY84	FY85	FY86
Volume growth vs. prior year (shipments)	−11.0	+24.8	+22.4	+16.8
% of sales by region				
Sunbelt	72	64	57	54
Non-Sunbelt	28	36	43	46
% households buying	FY83*	FY84	FY85	
Sunbelt	17	21	22	
Non-Sunbelt	5	9	12	

*FY83 covers July 1982 through June 1983.

Despite the 1988 competition, Gatorade sales grew 30% to $285 million, retaining over 90% of the sports drink segment. In order to prevent Gatorade sports drink from becoming a mature brand vulnerable to new entrants, management had to give Gatorade more support through marketing efforts. In 1989 they spent a sports drink industry record $100 million on marketing. This consisted mostly of sports tie-ins and promotions, with $30 million devoted to advertising.

Although Kool-Aid Sports Koolers was another victim of Gatorade's dominance, several potentially challenging sports drink introductions took place in 1989. These were targeted to new segments (women), improved tastes, and new distribution.

In September 1989, competition stiffened as Pepsi began test marketing Mountain Dew Sport to leverage the Mountain Dew franchise success in the sports drink category at the same time trying to steal share based on flavor. In March 1990, Coca-Cola introduced Powerade, a sports drink sold at convenience stores to preempt this untapped segment. The fact that it had recently made an isotonic product extremely successful in Japan was a concern.

Reacting to increased competition, Gatorade increased marketing expenditures from $100 million to $140 million. This supported two new Gatorade family introductions:

Gatorade Light: To fight the lower-calorie, lower-sodium entrants and to target more women.

Freestyle: A nonisotonic with improved taste to combat Pepsi and Coke on their home turf.

Quaker also used public relations to dismiss the competition, using the following national campaigns:

Powerade: "A me-too product with no consumer franchise"
Mountain Dew Sport: "Not an optimal sports beverage"

The sports drink segment had become a vicious battleground with the potential of developing into a new cola war. It became worse when, in October 1990, number three soft-drink marketer, Dr. Pepper/7-Up, introduced Nautilus as a "world-class thirst quencher."

CONCLUSION

Although the sports drink segment has become extremely competitive, in late 1990 Gatorade still maintained over 90% market share. From 1987 to 1990, with the proliferation of new products, flavors, sizes, and packaging improvements, Gatorade sales consistently increased by 25% to 30% annually, further strengthening the once small Quaker Oats Grocery Products Division, which grew from $26 million (1983) to $765 million (1990), largely due to the acquisition and management of Gatorade.

From acquisition of the brand in 1983, strong brand management and research had helped increase the Gatorade franchise by 449%. With this spectacular growth came gradual refinements that improved the product's positioning in regard to users, occasions, and points of difference.

Text continued from page 118

Generic Strategy Theories

Given the essential simplicity of brand strategy, it is possible to draw up simple alternatives by looking at the extremes of the two variables. This has given rise to the gamut of so-called "generic" strategies in various textbooks. Perhaps the most famous is that of Harvard's Michael Porter, who arrives at four generic strategies according to the position taken on two decisions: Is the competitive advantage to be low cost or some form of differentiation? Is the offer aimed at a broad or narrow target area in the market? (See Figure 6.6 on page 127.)

Figure 6.6 **Generic Brand Strategies**

COMPETITIVE ADVANTAGE

	Low cost	Differentiation
Broad	1. Cost leadership	2. Differentiation
TARGET Narrow	3(A). Cost focus	3(B). Differentiation focus

Source: Michael Porter, *Competitive Advantage* (New York: Free Press, 1985), p. 12.

This is helpful in initial thinking, even if somewhat simplistic. Porter, for instance, leaves it to management to decide what "differentiation" might mean, and this is the difficult bit. It is also what branding is all about. All the same, in so far as his model encourages managers to make decisions on the two key variables, it can only be good. Porter's key message is that a company or brand must have a distinct position; if it does not make choices, it will be "stuck in the middle" or "in the crisis zone." This at least is generally true: The most common reason for brand failure is that management did not define or understand the need to develop a clear competitive advantage.

With a brand, however, there is the potential to make the offer at the multiproduct level through brand extensions. Both variables then become more complex. Another grid, this one from Peter Doyle of Warwick University,[8] may be helpful here (Figure 6.7 on page 128). Doyle's grid addresses the question of the scope of the brand in relation to the target segment(s), and so produces generic brand extension strategies.

Figure 6.7 **Brand Positioning Grid**

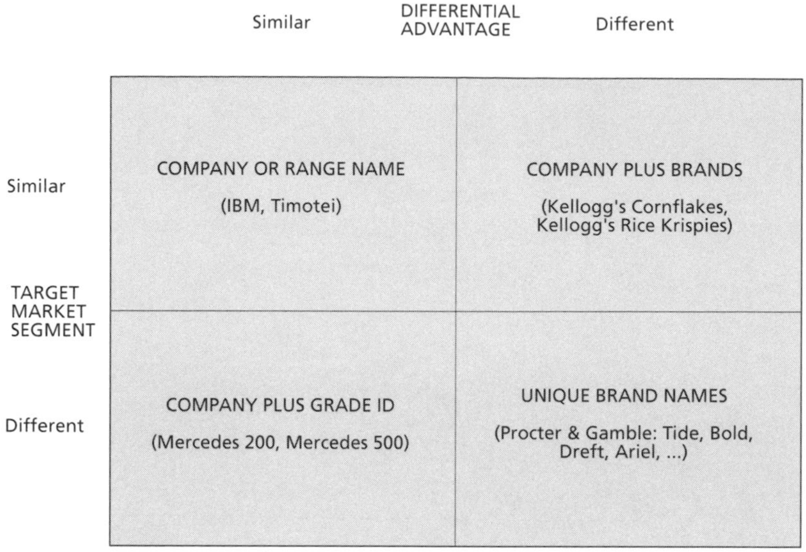

Similar   DIFFERENTIAL ADVANTAGE   Different

	Similar	Different
Similar	COMPANY OR RANGE NAME (IBM, Timotei)	COMPANY PLUS BRANDS (Kellogg's Cornflakes, Kellogg's Rice Krispies)
Different	COMPANY PLUS GRADE ID (Mercedes 200, Mercedes 500)	UNIQUE BRAND NAMES (Procter & Gamble: Tide, Bold, Dreft, Ariel, ...)

TARGET MARKET SEGMENT

Source: Peter Doyle, "Building Brands: The Strategic Options," *Journal of Consumer Marketing 7*, no. 2, and *Journal of Marketing Management 5*, no. 1 (Spring 1990).

While the concept of generic strategies is helpful, it is not a way of formulating brand strategies. It is more useful in deciding the general focus of the brand strategy, such as finding new segments to maximize the potential of a brand personality, or extending the line as a defensive move.

> *A brand strategy is a specific statement of the brand's sustainable competitive advantage, usually consisting of a description of the target customers and the benefits they get from the brand. The strategy should specify why the customers will prefer this brand. It is* **not**:
>
> *A sum of the marketing mix plans*
> *A statement of an objective (e.g., gain 5% more market share)*
> *A general focus (e.g., extend product range to meet emerging segments)*

SUMMARY

The purpose of branding is to achieve a market position that will represent a sustainable competitive advantage. The brand position is how the brand is perceived by consumers. It is not to be confused with the corporate activities that, along with other forces like competitor activity, result in that perception. The company can influence the market position of the brand using these activities (usually known as the marketing mix), but a strategy must begin with an in-depth understanding of the whole market.

There are two central elements to a brand position: the type of benefits offered by the brand and the type of consumer who will value them. The 1990s are regarded as the decade of target marketing. As markets fragment, brands must be targeted at smaller groups or niches. The concept of the market life cycle encourages the belief that more segments will emerge in maturity. The scope of the target for a brand is therefore becoming more important than ever.

CHECKLIST

Positioning is at the heart of strategy in a brand company. It is vital to understand

- The current and potential positions in the market.
- The corporate capabilities that will produce the desired position.

The eventual position chosen for a brand must be

- Salient to consumers and offering real added value to them.
- Built upon real brand strengths which reflect corporate capabilities.
- Differentiated from competitor brand positions.
- Capable of being clearly communicated to the market.

A positioning statement should as a minimum have a clear statement of

- The benefits offered by the brand.
- A description of the target consumer segment(s) within the market.
- A description of the desired consumer perception of the brand.

REFERENCES

1. Al Ries and Jack Trout, *Positioning: The Battle for Your Mind* (New York: Warner Books, 1982).

2. Philip Kotler, "Kotler on. . .," *Management Decision* 29, no. 2 (1991), p. 45.

3. Chris Macrae, *World Class Brands* (Reading, Mass.: Addison Wesley, 1991), pp. 87–107.

4. Interbrand, *Brands: An International Review* (Mercury Business Books, 1990), p. 30.

5. Interbrand, *Brands*, p. 37.

6. Stephen King, *Developing New Brands* (London: Pitman, 1973), pp. 94–95.

7. Philip Kotler, *Marketing Management*, 7th ed. (Englewood Cliffs, N.J.: Prentice Hall, 1991).

8. Peter Doyle, "Building Brands: The Strategic Options," *Journal of Consumer Marketing* 7, no. 2 (1990), and *Journal of Marketing Management* 5, no. 1 (1990).

The Scope of a Brand—
Brand Stretching

. . . .

The Level of a Brand—Corporate or Product Brand?

The first issue to consider is the level at which the branding should be put in place. This is often posed as, "What is a brand—a company, a range of products, or an individual product line?" But branding can occur at any of these levels, so this is the wrong question. The decisions can be made only when the desired position, in terms of target and brand essence, has been determined.

Many companies now want all their products labeled with their corporate brand. It is noticeable that more companies are trying to "stretch" their brands by launching more variants under a single brand name or identity, thus creating families of brands. Others continue in the tradition of branding at the product level. Most consumers have no idea which detergents are produced by Unilever and which by Procter & Gamble.

The most noticeable explosion of corporate brands is in the service sector. Brands like McDonald's and Marriott have led the way, and the financial services sector and retailers are also now working hard to build up the kind of brand strength associated with long-standing FMCG goods. It is also standard practice in industrial or business-to-business markets for any branding to take place at the corporate rather than the product level. Perhaps the most contentious issue is the rise of "own-label" goods: Companies that were previously only distributors of other people's brands (most notably retailers) have developed their own brands and compete with their suppliers for the consumer's attention.

Corporate branding is not limited to the service industries. It is increasingly common to see a corporate brand endorsing a product brand. This may happen, for example, at the end of a TV advertisement when the corporate logo suddenly appears in the corner, or on the back of a package where the corporate brand is displayed to identify the company that owns the brand.

These are strategic issues for any branding company, but often the decisions seem to be taken without reference to branding principles. Insofar as these companies are trying to get closer to their customers and sharpen their position in the market by adopting branding practice, one can only applaud their management. But questions need to be asked about the possible confusion of objectives. A company that inserts its corporate logo onto a set of perfectly strong but distinct brands within its portfolio risks confusing the consumer.

Objectives in Building a Corporate Brand

There may be several valid objectives to trying to build a corporate brand. Some or all of these issues face most companies, and management needs to take action. Combined with a spreading awareness of the importance of branding and with the growing stature of the graphic design industry, they have led to an explosion of corporate branding.

- **Corporate identity:** There is currently a fashion for corporate identity, fueled by changing ideas of the way a company should be perceived. Since the "excellence revolution" of the 1980s, management often wants to build an organization with a mission, which will inspire its people with affection and commitment. The company, in other words, becomes a brand to the people who work for it.
- **Different corporate audiences:** Modern corporations have a much more acute sense of the wide number of audiences with which to communicate. This includes not just suppliers and customers but also the community, the financial sector, regulatory authorities, shareholders, and others. As the number of

publics increases, so does the need for a more clearly defined and closely controlled message—in other words, a corporate brand.

- **Defending a company against acquisition:** Companies are now more aware of the danger of acquisition. In particular, corporate raiders are bound to be interested when they perceive part of a company (such as a brand or group of brands) to be thriving without much apparent help from its corporate parent, and which may well benefit from being "unbundled." Parent corporations are therefore keen to demonstrate that the corporate management adds real value. Again, they turn to corporate branding to position themselves in this way.

These are worthy objectives, but it is immediately noticeable that they are all company-oriented, rather than consumer-driven. While few would argue against the value of a corporation having a consistent visual identity, branding decisions must address preference, not just identification. While the financial community may need to be reminded that a large corporation is the owner of a certain range of apparently unrelated brands, it will only confuse the consumer to have two different messages—product and corporate—to take in. The whole purpose of branding is to give the customer something clear and compelling with which to identify, and if this is diluted then the power of the whole brand is diluted too.

Criteria for Choosing Corporate Branding

The following criteria are therefore important when considering the level of branding:

1. *Is the corporation a salient attribute?*
The growth of retailers' own labels has come about because the shop in which the consumer buys the products is a salient attribute; that is to say, the shop is more likely to be at the center of the experience of shopping than the products that are purchased. For the same reason, the hospitality industry tends to brand at the corporate level: The experience of going into McDonald's is a productive focus for consumer perception. In industrial markets, the focus of customer perception is not so much the individual products as the *range* of products offered and the service capability to provide backup, both of which argue for corporate branding.

All brand communication should be directed to reinforce what the consumer might perceive anyway. If the corporation providing the product or service is unlikely to be of interest to the consumer, then a corporate brand is more likely to do harm than good. *A corporate brand is applicable only where the company, rather than the specific product or service, is a salient attribute.*

2. *Does the corporation have values?*
At the heart of all brands are values that motivate the customer. Many corporations possess several individual brands at the product or product group level that have distinct identities. The corporation will therefore have to dilute its own character to little more than a label, without values, in order to be applicable to all its subbrands. Once it is this weak, it is as likely to cause harm as good.

If a corporation is a salient attribute, then we must analyze it like any other brand, including the emotional values attached to it. The message given out by many corporations—that their name is an endorsement of quality—is not enough. The corporate brand must convey exactly what is meant by quality (technological excellence, efficiency, friendliness) and not be afraid to nail its colors to the mast. *A corporate brand must be more than just a label; it must convey values that motivate the customer.*

3. *Does the corporate brand have a brand property that is evident in use?*
The brand property is the unique identity of the brand that is a rein-forcement (usually visual) to the customer of what is being bought. Most corporations do now have a corporate identity that can be used as a brand property, but it is important that it will be evident to the customer at the point of purchase or use. A corporate logo on the back of a package, for instance, is unlikely to get noticed. The atrium concept of Marriott hotels, by contrast, is not only distinctive but something that the customer is bound to encounter and experi-ence. *A corporate brand must be easily identified and evident and relevant at purchase or during use.*

There is little doubt that, if these mainstream branding criteria were applied, we would encounter far fewer corporate brands than at present. Unless a corporation is dedicated to providing just one thing to just one type of customer, a corporate brand is unlikely to be successful. This, of course, is not true of most companies.

Extending Brand Families as Markets Evolve

The corporate brand is clearly more suited to service markets, where customers focus more on the overall package and its provider. This does not mean that the brand does not have to evolve continually, as the case study on Pizza Hut illustrates. The pizza market demonstrates typical life cycle issues, as segments become clear while the market is still in its growth phase. It would have been all too easy for Pizza Hut to relax and refrain from developing its brand while the market was still growing, but it responded quickly to the early signs of segmentation. The Pizza Hut brand was easily stretched to include a wider variety of product variants and a variety of distribution systems; the umbrella brand clearly identifies pizza only as the brand essence. If Pizza Hut had not responded so quickly, the whole company, being so indelibly associated with the one offering, would have sunk. Pizza Hut is thus clearly marked as a service brand, despite the fact that it actually sells tangible products, and it is best regarded as a retailer rather than a producer. It is interesting to speculate how the brand would evolve if the American public had a love affair with another type of food.

A service package such as Pizza Hut makes brand stretching easy in growth markets. This is why retailers have been able to develop their own brands. Interestingly, retailers' "own-label" brands have to date simply reflected their corporation's strength. To grow in the future, a much clearer definition of the brand essence is called for. Is the dealer's own brand a low-price generic substitute, or does it have some other values added in? Is the corporation a retailer, or a provider of brands in certain product categories? These questions have often been ignored by retailers as their sales profit from the previously underutilized resource of their own corporate brand. Once a retailer has more than a few of its own brands, however, the game will slowly start to shift, changing the way that the whole corporation is seen. The company will no longer be seen as a retailer that provides variety and choice but as a retailer-cum-brand manufacturer. The normal rules of brand management will then apply, and the management challenge will be to decide whether the product lines or the store image drive the brand.

Text continues on page 140, after the case study.

Pizza Hut Recharges Its Brand

PepsiCo/Pizza Hut

· · · · ·

Founded in the late 1950s, Pizza Hut—part of the PepsiCo group—was always the U.S. market leader in the pizza sector. By 1985 its eat-in restaurant concept, in one of the fastest-growing segments of the food industry, had taken it to over 4,000 outlets in the United States. The number of units had grown steadily and so had unit sales. Revenue grew from $1.3 billion in 1982 to $2 billion in 1985.

Pizza Hut was a generalist operation. It served all types of pizza to all types of people. By the mid-1980s, however, a number of niche-based competitors were emerging, determined to take advantage of this growth business by specializing in areas not covered by Pizza Hut. In line with life-cycle models, the market was starting to segment. Niche players were stealing small areas of Pizza Hut's mass-market proposition.

The main threat to Pizza Hut's market dominance came from Domino's, Little Caesar's, and Godfather's. Domino's aggressive expansion into the home delivery market had allowed it to lead this growing off-premise segment. Little Caesar's offered a two-for-one discount strategy that challenged Pizza Hut's own moderate pricing policy.

The rapid expansion of these pizza chains, based on specific components of the marketing mix (Domino's—more convenient distribution; Little Caesar's—lower price), led Pizza Hut to begin rethinking its eat-in restaurant strategy.

In 1985 a new president, Steve Reinemund, joined Pizza Hut to start change moving. He also produced a new mission statement:

> To consistently demonstrate to America that Pizza Hut is the best choice for every pizza occasion.

Slicing Up the Pizza Market

There were good reasons why competitors like Domino's were making healthy profits and threatening the market leader and why Pizza Hut needed to make major changes. Significant developments were taking place in the pizza market.

For example, the industry research firm CREST estimated in 1985 that the delivery and carryout segments of the pizza market offered growth potential of 25% and 18% respectively, compared with only 4% in the eat-in restaurant business, where Pizza Hut was concentrated. CREST also looked at research into more fundamental factors affecting the restaurant/eating industry in general and the pizza business in particular.

Trend research showed that three major lifestyle changes were affecting the sector:

- Increasing demand for convenience
- Decreasing discretionary time
- A love affair with pizza

In addition, CREST identified a number of external influences that were having an impact on the restaurant industry in the mid-1980s:

- Growth of female labor
- Rising gross national product
- Rising real disposable incomes
- Rising consumer confidence
- Rising price of food eaten at home relative to that eaten in a restaurant
- Advertising activity
- Coupon offers

Some of these factors had a direct effect on the increasing demand for convenience. One of the most significant was the number of women entering the work force. This had risen considerably during the first half of the 1980s. The effect was to raise the disposable income of many family groups. At the same time, discretionary time decreased, which in itself provoked an increased demand for convenience. All this led to a growth in restaurant traffic.

The effects during this period of rising gross national product, disposable incomes, and consumer confidence and an acceptable imbalance between the cost of eating out and eating at home were obvious.

More significantly, advertising expenditure in the sector shot up in the 1980s as competitors fought for market share and generally increased consumer awareness. Similarly, coupon offers were on the increase. By 1985, coupon redemptions affected 2.2 billion restaurant meal occasions, according to CREST.

The third lifestyle change—a love affair with pizza—was tracked by *Nation's Restaurant News*, a trade journal. Its studies, which provided an accurate measure of the total number of meal occasions and number of outlets, confirmed that pizza was America's favorite food, even more popular than the hamburger.

Pizza Hut's Response

Pizza Hut was determined to avoid losing its dominance of the pizza industry to rapidly expanding competitors. It developed a strategy to incorporate these consumer trends and hold off the competition.

The company had to conduct extensive consumer research to ensure that it understood the reasons behind the new market structure. The main variables were not the consumer types, but the occasion and the type of pizza required.

Product Segmentation

Given that "pizza-eating" is a segment of the leisure market, the type of pizza becomes the important variable. The three most salient attributes of pizza were crust, sauce, and cheese, and a table of "ideal pizzas" was drawn up with a measure of how many of the total pizza-eating occasions they were suitable for (see Table 7.1). With these insights, Pizza Hut was able to widen its product range to suit its new variety of distribution outlets.

Traditionally, Pizza Hut offered a thick-crust pan pizza (the "Pan Pizza") and a thin-crust pizza (the "Thin 'n' Crispy"). In-depth statistical research of consumer attitudes and preferences revealed that there was an enormous market for an in-between, middle-thickness crust product. In fact, an extra $7 billion in sales could be generated. This competitive analysis followed by product development led to the "Hand-Tossed Traditional Pizza" product offering.

Market Segmentation

Pizza Hut's goal in distribution was to "get its pizza to consumers wherever they want it: at home, in the malls, in the airports, in cafeterias—wherever they are." Achieving this strategy meant developing several types of new outlets, described below. The comments relate to the results obtained by 1991.

Table 7.1 **Ideal Pizzas**

New York Foldable (14%)	Crust:	Thin, foldable, mild
	Sauce:	Mild
	Cheese:	Little mozzarella
Traditional (23%)	Crust:	Thin, foldable, doughy, dark, flaky
	Sauce:	Average
	Cheese:	Variety of white cheeses
Italian Crispy (23%)	Crust:	Thin, crispy, Italian flavored
	Sauce:	Mild, sparse
	Cheese:	Ample mozzarella
Pizza Bread (20%)	Crust:	Thick, light, bready, mild
	Sauce:	Mild
	Cheese:	Variety of white cheeses
Thick 'n Gusto (20%)	Crust:	Thick, flaky, Italian flavored
	Sauce:	Ample, spicy
	Cheese:	Variety of yellow cheeses

Delivery: Outlets capable of home delivery grew to 3,000 in four years. This included 2,000 Delco units—small delivery and carryout systems—and 1,000 traditional eat-in restaurants capable of handling delivery.

Kiosks: By 1991 several hundred of these indoor units were in operation. Major targets were colleges, ballparks, and the $4 billion schools sector.

Express: Set up in malls and in-line locations, these units offer fast service of a limited menu.

Modular: These are quick-construct units used to target smaller markets and to react to population shifts.

Pizza-Mat: These are drive-through express units designed on the Fotomat principle.

Success

Successful growth in the delivery segment and innovation through express and kiosk units led to Pizza Hut being named Company of the Year 1988 by *Restaurant Business*.

Before its "Pizza Distribution Company" strategic response, the company had depended on eat-in restaurants for virtually all of its business. By 1989 it already held 13% of the delivery segment, once totally controlled by Domino's. Between 1989 and 1990, Pizza Hut's share of deliveries rose further, to 18%. In terms of contribution to turnover, the delivery sector rose from just under 10% in 1988 to just over 20% in 1990. Over the same period, the contribution to turnover of eat-in restaurants fell from 58% to 49%.

Conclusion

Pizza Hut's extensive market research and close adherence to a corporate mission allowed it to meet successfully the changing needs of American consumers and to maintain its market leadership.

Pizza Hut's rapid gain of market share in a new market segment is a classic example of how an aggressive strategy supported by strong research can bring about success.

Pizza Hut did not participate in the preparation of this case study, and does not warrant the accuracy of the representations contained herein.

Text continued from page 135.

The argument that corporate branding is overused rests on the assumption that as markets grow more fragmented, and targeting more important, brands will have to be more distinct within the same portfolio. There is another way of looking at the issue: That attention will shift away from individual product lines as more industries become dominated by service attributes. As the intangibles become more important, and the concept of total value packages more prevalent, the corporate brand could become more important in reassuring customers that they are getting more than a superficial dressing up of a mediocre offer. Marketer Stephen King, writing in 1991, comments:

> The company brand will become the main discriminator. That is, consumers' choice of what they buy will depend less upon an evaluation of the functional benefits to them of a product or service, rather more on their assessment of the people in the company behind it, their skills, attitudes, behavior, design, style, language, greenism, altruism, modes of communication, speed of response, and so on—the whole company

culture, in fact. In essence, brand building in the 1990s will . . . be a lot closer to the marketing of services than to the brand-building of the classic brands.[1]

Consumers will, of course, always judge products by their experience of them in use, and many markets remain product-based, even if the service "add-ons" are increasing. King is also assuming that these new corporate service brands will be the output of a level of quality of brand management that we have traditionally seen on the classic FMCG brands. Too many corporate brands currently in existence are not like this.

Where a corporate brand is effective, the benefits are substantial, perhaps the principal one being the "umbrella brand" effect. This creates another level of shorthand for the consumer, and whenever the corporation launches a new product or service, it is not starting from scratch in building up awareness of the brand identity. The investment required in the new line is accordingly reduced. Companies are quick to see this benefit, and it is another motivation for the proliferation of corporate brands. However, companies are slower to see the increased risk of putting all their investment behind one brand—if anything goes wrong, everything suffers by association.

It is possible to settle on a halfway house between corporate and individual brand—the family of brands. The same umbrella effect works, but it applies to a group of products or services and not to the whole corporation.

The Extent of a Brand: Brand Stretching

Companies are increasingly extending the line of variants available under a given brand, resulting in a family of related offerings. A study of FMCG products introduced into American supermarkets over a period of ten years showed that of those that were successful (defined as reaching $15 million in sales), fully two-thirds were line extensions rather than new brands.[2]

The reason for this is essentially economic. All companies need growth, but more and more of them operate in markets characterized by the symptoms of maturity (notably, discerning customers with well-defined attitudes). As consumers become more knowledgeable and opinionated, it becomes ever more expensive to launch something new and reshape consumer perception of the product category.

At the same time, technological and information advances make it harder to gain, let alone sustain, a "hard" physical advantage in terms of product or service operations.

While the line extension may be undertaken for the company's own need for growth, it will work in the market over the long term only if it meets a want that was previously unfulfilled by the brand. Too often, a company will launch a line extension without a prompt from the market that there are real opportunities for new positions.

Benefits and Dangers of Line Extension

Where a line extension is successful, there are three principal benefits:

1. It increases the probability that consumers will accept other messages about new brands or new positioning when a familiar element is involved. (It is known that new messages are harder to get through to the recipient than familiar ones.)
2. The new offering will refresh the existing brand or group of brand variants. It will enhance the total offering under the umbrella brand, improving the total offer to the consumer.
3. It will improve the cost-effectiveness of resources spent on supporting the brand family, as the synergy should mean benefits for all lines, achieving an economy of scale in marketing support expenditure.

The case study on Schering-Plough's extension of the Coppertone sunscreen brand to its new Water Babies line is a perfect example of a successful brand stretch. The extension was launched not because the company was searching hard for sources of growth but because there were fundamental shifts in the consumer perception of tanning that led to the emergence of new segments. Coppertone wanted to take advantage of these new opportunities. As it turned out, the company not only launched a successful extension but in the process managed to alter the positioning of the core brand away from tanning toward sun protection. The extension enriched the core brand and was so successful in its own right that it is on the way to standing alone as a new brand.

The biggest single danger with a brand extension program is that of diluting the original personality of the brand. If this is allowed to happen, consumers will become confused and the bond between them and the original brand will be lost. Consistency is the prime criterion—as long as any extension offers the market satisfactions that are similar to those offered by the original brand, the extension can be considered. If it does not, then even if the new brand does well (unlikely) it may only be at the expense of the original core brand.

There is a spectrum of effects, from the most successful extension to the most disastrous:

- **Enrichment.** Both the core brand and the extension benefit from association with each other.
- **Extension.** The extension benefits from being associated with the original core brand and grows more quickly than it would on its own.
- **Neutral.** The extension gains nothing from its association with the core brand. This is rare, as an extension draws attention to its parentage and some reaction is almost inevitable.
- **Conflict.** The extension is at odds with the position or values of the core brand, and it fails because consumers are confused.
- **Brand damage.** The extension not only fails but damages the position of the core brand; because the extension is at odds with the core brand, it changes the consumer perception of the worth or values of the parent brand.

Text continues on page 152, after the case study.

A New Baby for Water Babies

Coppertone and Water Babies Sunscreens

$\bullet \quad \bullet \quad \bullet \quad \bullet \quad \bullet$

For many years Schering-Plough had enjoyed the lead in the United States in sun care products with its Coppertone line. In the late 1970s the company was serving three fairly evenly distributed consumer groups identified from attitudinal research: "Sun Worshippers" (35%), "Sun Concerned" (32%), and "Pragmatists" (31%). To meet the different needs of each segment, Schering-Plough had developed a variety of product lines, the main ones being Tropical Blend Shade, Coppertone, and Solarcaine.

Changing Usage and Competition

In the early 1980s numerous reports surfaced about the harmful effects of the sun. Consumers grew much more cautious of overexposure to the sun. This growing concern created the necessity for products that offered sun protection factors (SPFs). While Schering-Plough quickly responded to this need, other competitors were aggressive as well.

In August 1983 Schering-Plough decided to conduct extensive research. The research team chose a national sample of 1,153 women who were users of suntan or sunscreen products. This study clearly showed changes in the attitudinal groupings identified in the 1977 study. While Sun Worshippers and Sun Concerned remained major groups at 31% and 42% respectively, Pragmatists were reclassified into Cautious Tanners (20%) and Sun Actives (7%).

The fragmentation of the Pragmatists, closely linked to the Coppertone brand, into these major new groups made Schering-Plough aware of the urgency of new product development. Below is a description of the four groups in terms of age and psychographic profile:

1. **Sun Worshippers.** This group tends to be younger, aged 14 to 25. They have medium to dark skin, are frequent users of suntan products, and heavy users of suntan oils. In deciding upon a brand,

they are much more influenced by advertising than cost. Their main goal is to obtain a deep, dark, long-lasting tan as quickly as possible. Individuals feel that a tan makes them look attractive and healthy and means they care about themselves. Tanning is clearly more important to them than sun protection.

2. **Sun Concerned.** These users are older, aged 26 to 49, married, with children living at home, and employed. They have fair or sensitive skin, use lotion but are not heavy users, and consider getting a tan a chore. Their main goal is to obtain a light, gradual golden tan but with maximum protection from sunburn. They desire ingredients like PABA that prevent the aging, wrinkling, and peeling caused by sun exposure.

3. **Cautious Tanners.** These users are classified as 19- to 25-year-old single students. Their skin is medium to dark and is often oily. They most often use suntan oil and are heavy users. Their most important purchasing criterion is a brand's image, which has to be familiar, contemporary, and sophisticated. The ingredients of the product are seen to be important in preventing aging, wrinkling, and peeling. Ingredients sought are aloe, PABA, and a moisturizer. This group must work hard for a tan but feel it is worth the effort since it makes them look healthier and attractive and shows they care about themselves. They want a tan but do not want to burn. Thus, protection from burning is equally important. Although they prefer to tan quickly, a gradual, golden, light tan is acceptable.

4. **Sun Active.** This is the smallest group (7%) and is younger (14 to 18). They are single students and most often live in the South. This group consists of two skin types: dark skin and sensitive or fair skin. They do not use one particular form of a product but prefer a brand that is familiar through image advertising. Their preference is for contemporary brands that are sophisticated, modern, and associated with the tropics. They have little concern for the effects of the sun such as skin cancer, aging, peeling, and wrinkling. They like to tan naturally from sports and outdoor activities.

Figure 7.1 (see page 146) reveals differences in the importance of getting a suntan from 1977 to 1983.

The 1983 reclassification of sun care industry psychographic groupings provided Schering-Plough with important considerations for new products.

Figure 7.1 **Importance of Getting a Suntan: Comparison 1977 to 1983**

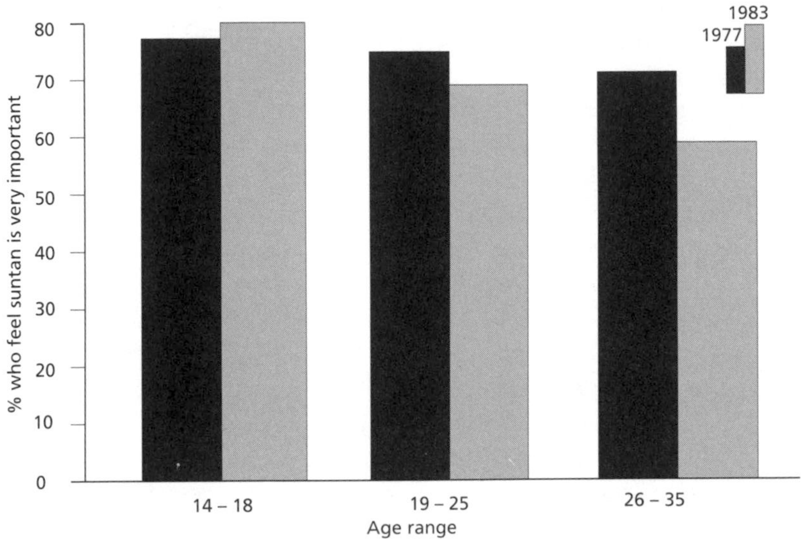

Source: Company data.

Product Line Extension Possibilities

The following 11 product ideas were revealed from the 1983 study:

1. A quick-tanning product that does not turn skin orange. This continues to be a high-volume opportunity.
2. A competitor to baby oil. Baby oil continues to get a large share of users. Its 34% past season usage is not far below that of Coppertone sunblock (40%).
3. A spot bronzer line extender. This would touch up strap marks and other small areas.
4. A suntan product for teens with natural ingredients. Teens show the strongest interest in this, but interest also spills over into older age groups.
5. A suntan/sunscreen with special moisturizer to prevent aging/ wrinkling and peeling. This would appeal to the Sun Concerned (42% of the user base).
6. A sunscreen product especially designed for children. Women's attitudes toward such a product have changed since 1977. The

product should be waterproof and provide good protection from burning.

7. A hypoallergenic product for the face to overcome the problem cited by 65% of the respondents that suntan products cause their faces to break out.

8. A greaseless product for the face to answer the problem that "suntan products are too greasy on my face."

9. A product that contains aloe. Interest in this ingredient has significantly increased since 1977 (59% in 1983).

10. A product that contains PABA to satisfy consumer interest in it (51% in 1983).

11. A cream or creamy lotion as a line extender. There appears to be a small group of consumers who like this form.

More Research and Information

A major concern was that many consumers associated Coppertone with tanning at a time when sun blocking was more essential. Clearly, Schering-Plough had to reposition Coppertone sunblock in the minds of the consumer as a protective product. It also needed to spot future consumer trends before its major competitors did.

More research and information were added to the debate from many sources: the American Academy of Dermatologists; the Skin Cancer Foundation; ongoing focus groups; Simmons and Nielsen market research information; mail intercept studies; Sunbelt perception studies—directly analyzing consumers in the warmest areas of the United States. These indicated that consumers wanted the additional skin benefits of vitamin E and aloe. In 1986 the Coppertone and Tropical Blend lines were reformulated to contain these important ingredients and repackaged to let consumers know of this improvement.

The studies had also reinforced just how fragmented the sun care product category was. Many of the subsegments that were identified did not have a product entry as yet (i.e., higher SPFs, products with new skin care ingredients, oils, additional waterproofing, pretan accelerators, sprays, children's products, sunless tanning formulas, and even pills). Schering's product management and market research needed to perform extensive testing of all these concepts to find the most viable new product entry. To develop this new product, the company used the services of new products and brand leveraging consultants.

New Products and Brand Leveraging

The consulting firm evaluated the conceptual attractiveness of many of the subsegments identified by Schering-Plough and several others. It tested 20 to 30 different concepts and product ideas, using 25 to 35 different techniques on focus groups and with mail intercepts.

The main new product or restaging programs behind the consumer studies were as follows:

- **Concept research directed toward consumers.** This used positionings of competing products, substituting the client's brand name for theirs in advertising, etc.
- **Brand heritage research.** This procedure involved looking at the original theme of the brand from 30 to 40 years ago. A close look at a brand's earliest advertising tells how the product originally made an impact on the mind of the consumer.
- **Research into creating a new product category or market for the client.** This research is based on the premise that a quality product can change the entire product category and that a great new product can actually start a totally new category.

The combination of these three methods served to separate the effective from the ineffective product concepts.

Three dominant concepts were tested: ease of application, sunproofing, and waterproofing. Of these, the one that carried the strongest appeal was waterproofing. From the focus groups, a very important buying group—mothers with children—was evident. The national segmentation study had pointed to a sunscreen product for children as a possible line extension. Figure 7.2 (see page 149) compares female buyers from the 1977 and 1983 studies. All groups from age 14 to 35 showed significantly less agreement that the same suntan product can be used on children. Health reports showing that skin cancer was developed at early ages also reinforced the need for a special product for children.

Market research at Schering then tested the waterproofing concept board using more quantitative methods. A group of 150 target users, mothers with children who had recently purchased sun care products, was surveyed. The users were mainly tested for intent to purchase and uniqueness of the concept of Water Babies SPF 15 sunblock versus an average sun care product. The results showed that mothers had a strong likelihood of purchasing the product that waterproofed children from the effects of

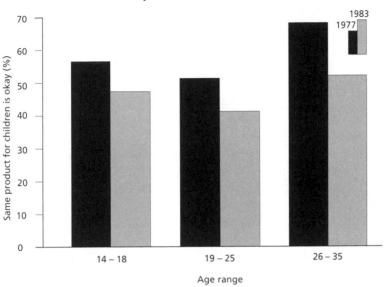

Figure 7.2 **Should the Same Suntan Products Be Used on Children?—Comparison of Data from 1977 to 1983**

Source: Company data.

the sun, with over 60% stating "Definitely Buy" and 42% "Probably Buy" with favorable reactions to descriptions of the concept (see Figures 7.3 and 7.4 on page 150).

The consumer profile studies indicated that children spend a lot of time outdoors and are exposed to more sun than adults. As the children's segment in other product categories was growing the fastest, introducing a sun care product for children seemed very sensible. Furthermore, Schering-Plough listened to skin care "thought leaders," such as pediatricians, who endorsed a need for a children's product to care for their tender skin.

Research and information showed that there was great potential for a sun care product for children. However, Schering-Plough was faced with two choices:

- Leverage the Coppertone brand name to introduce a skin care product for children.
- Introduce a new line of sun care products (as was done with the Tropical Blend, Shade, and Solarcaine brands).

Figure 7.3 **"My Kind of Product": Water Babies Concept Test, 1987**

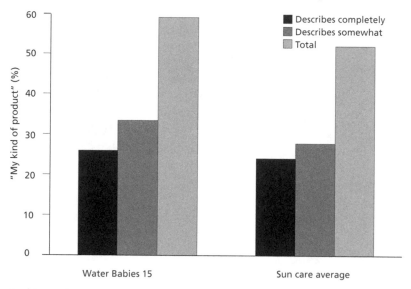

Source: Company data.

Figure 7.4 **"High-Quality Product ": Water Babies Concept Test, 1987**

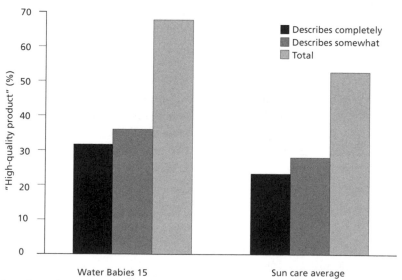

Source: Company data.

Since Coppertone was more known for tanning than blocking, how could it market the name to mothers who were very sensitive to their children's tender skin? Yet, in such a competitive market, how could it introduce a new line without leveraging the Coppertone marketing strength?

Using brand heritage research, brand leverage consultants took a historical look at Schering-Plough's advertising. What they found was a scene portraying a little girl with a dog pulling at her bathing suit. As this was a children's product, this theme seemed to fit the new market. The original slogan—"Tan don't burn"—was very suitable for the mother's main concern of protecting her child. It also seemed to match the message that Coppertone sunblock needed to convey in the ever-increasing SPF market. An alternative slogan studied was Schering-Plough's old advertising of an Indian saying "Don't be a pale face." Testing showed that "Tan don't burn" with the picture of the girl and dog was most effective.

With the logo decided, two questions remained: What should the product be called? Should it use the Coppertone name?

A name for the old logo seemed to come very easily and was unanimously approved. Research had indicated that mothers considered waterproofing to be the most important feature for a children's sun block. Thus the consultants knew that the word "water" had to be contained within the product name. The most popular name from focus group, mall intercept, and other quantitative research was Water Babies; short, easy to remember, and with literary associations. The word "babies" was found to be suitable for the whole young children's segment (infants to 10-year-olds) that Schering-Plough was targeting.

It was decided that the name "Water Babies" would be shown on the package in large bold letters. The Coppertone name was featured below for credibility and leverage but its size was considerably smaller. The package color that was found to be most appealing to mothers was pink and blue.

Product Introduction and Results

In 1987 Coppertone Water Babies sunblock was nationally launched. It was formulated so that it did not sting young children's tender skin. Water Babies was the first hypoallergenic, high-protection waterproof lotion for children. Introduced with an SPF of 15, Water Babies has been proved to be effective in water for as long as 80 minutes.

The product has clearly been a success, due to its effective positioning. In 1991, the product maintained 50% of the children's segment and its dollar volume was three times greater than the competition.

Water Babies sunscreen is also the product recommended by most pediatricians. This endorsement, market share success, and a name that has become synonymous with good sun care has allowed Water Babies to stand on its own. Water Babies is now manufactured with an SPF of 45 and has added to its line Sunblock Cream, Sunburn Relief Mist, Swimmer's Ear Prevention Formula, and Little Licks Sunblock Lip Balm. The Coppertone name on the Water Babies product has been further and further reduced.

Although the Coppertone name was used with Water Babies sunscreen for leveraging purposes, the relationship between the two lines is now more synergistic. Since Water Babies stands for sun care it has helped Schering-Plough adjust to consumer trends for higher SPFs and maintain its dominant market share in the industry.

―――――――――

Text continued from page 143.

Criteria in Line Extension Decisions

The variety of ways in which two or more subbrands can be complementary may involve any of the following:

- The key ingredient of the product
- The delivery system of a service
- General associations of technological expertise
- A shared benefit
- A similar user imagery

What is vital is that extensions are undertaken only where the similarity is more than superficial. Only that way can the extension in its turn grow and develop into a long-term success.

To be able to manage this process effectively, the starting point must be an in-depth understanding of the original brand proposition. Using the type of analytical approaches discussed in Chapter 1, the essence, values, and properties of the brand can be identified and used as criteria in line extension decisions:

1. *Is the brand essence still applicable?*
If the proposed extension draws upon different fundamental values, then the consumer is unlikely to be able to cope with the two brands under the single identity. It would be impossible for Philip Morris, for instance, to use the Marlboro brand name to launch a pipe tobacco. The Marlboro essence of rugged independence is unsuited to the more mellow and contemplative values characteristic of pipe tobacco as a category.

2. *Is the brand property transferable?*
The brand property is one of its great strengths, and certainly necessary in any extension so that the consumer can instantly recognize the brand offer and its associated values. More often than not the property is a visual one, such as package color or design, and in such cases the judgment need not be too difficult. However, the brand property may be more subtle. Take, for example, the fruit drink Ribena. It is well established in the U.K. as a black currant drink with values such as a strong and attractive flavor and high nutritional value, especially in vitamin C and is seen as very suitable for children. While the launch of a strawberry version of the drink (undertaken in 1989 without much success) clearly made use of the values of the brand, it is arguable that Ribena is so indelibly associated with black currants, in its use of a purple color pack and animated black currant characters in its advertising, that this constitutes the brand property. In this case, a more logical extension would have been into other tasty and nutritious black currant products rather than fruit drinks in general.

3. *Can the variants be promoted and distributed together?*
This question is an acid test of the suitability of a line extension decision, putting management in the consumer's position. The whole purpose of extension is to achieve synergy between the individual lines; the consumer needs to associate one line with the other whenever receiving a stimulus for either. If the two lines would be incongruous if they were promoted or sold together, this suggests that there is something wrong with the idea of the line extension in the first place.

As with corporate branding, proper use of these criteria would lead to more conservative decisions than we often see. If a brand is overused or indiscriminately applied to another offer, then the entire value of the brand is being risked—it is not just the new variant whose future is at stake. Line extensions such as Mars ice-cream or Cherry Coke are among the biggest decisions these corporations have ever made.

Edward Tauber, a recognized expert in the area of what he refers to as "leverage" of a brand, writes enthusiastically of the benefits of stretching brands as far as they will go.[3] He cites such examples as Hershey moving into chocolate milk, since the essence of Hershey is chocolate, and Bic moving from pens to lighters and razors, where he claims that the brand integrity is intact because the brand essence is all about the skills of manufacturing cheap and disposable plastic items. It is certainly true that a move into a relatively new market segment minimizes the risk of cannibalization of existing brands, and at the same time holds up the prospect of more significant gains in volume, but business history is littered with more failures than successes in the area of what he calls "brand franchise extension." The major risk, of course, is not of failure in the new area but of repositioning the existing brand by accident. One might argue that if the premise is that new brands are harder than ever to build, then the more appropriate response is to be ever more conservative in guarding the position of existing brands.

When Is Line Extension Suitable?

The following guidelines will apply in most cases:

1. **When the proposed extension is in a closely allied product area.** If the core values of the whole category (the need) are the same or similar, this is likely to mean that the brand property is still applicable in purchase or use.

2. **When repertoires are important.** When some switching between brands is inevitable, it is appropriate to try to ensure that there are several brands positioned as alternatives. This will also offer flexibility in reshaping the portfolio, useful because the desire for novelty tends to be strong in these areas. Flexibility may be necessary for simple factual reasons; a skin-care range needs to offer alternatives for different summer and winter conditions. Kellogg's umbrella branding strategy in the breakfast cereal market works well because there is a large repertoire for most people in this category. In areas such as cigarettes,

where consumers tend to be more loyal to single brands, line extensions are less successful.

3. **When variety is one of the clearly defined consumer wants in the market.** When the consumer actually wants to feel that there is a choice at the point of purchase or consumption (in buying wine, for instance), it is inappropriate to brand a single variety. The process of choosing is actually part of the satisfaction. Only an umbrella brand will succeed for holidays, books, music, or clothes. Perhaps this is why these are areas where branding has been late in developing. In other categories, most extensions are developed from a strong, simple, single brand that grew up alone and then spawned extensions at a later stage. But here the branding has to be a family of variants right from the start, which obviously makes the management task even more difficult.

Once these criteria are met, the management challenge is to develop the portfolio as well as maximizing the potential of its individual brands. The main problem is to prevent the brands from stealing sales from each other rather than from competitor brands.

Cross-Branding

Line extensions should not be confused with what might be termed cross-branding—a process that occurs when a company transfers a brand personality out of one market and uses it in another market altogether. In this case the brand is being used as an endorsement. Consider a cashmere sweater carrying the BMW logo. The sweater obviously needs to be high quality so as not to detract from the BMW name, but even so the consumer would never assume that BMW is seriously considering entering the clothing market. It is perceived all along as an accessory, not part of the core business of BMW as a firm nor an important element of the BMW brand.

Contrast this with a sweater with the Dunhill name. Dunhill, originally a tobacco goods firm, began cross-branding in just the same way as the BMW example, but at some point crossed the line into the luxury goods market. A Dunhill cashmere sweater is salient to the Dunhill brand because Dunhill deliberately positions its general luxury goods brand across many categories of product. The price it pays for this, of course, is that it is no longer perceived as a dedicated manufacturer of tobacco goods, and it has lost much of its presence in that market. In the unlikely event that the firm would try to rebuild Dunhill as a major cigarette brand, it would face an uphill task.

SUMMARY

There is a noticeable trend toward stretching brands further, evident as the development of corporate or "umbrella" brands, and the launching of more subbrands or line extensions. Corporate brands are often developed for an organization's own reasons, instead of on sound branding principles. The risk is that consumers will become confused by parent and subsidiary brands, and some of the core brand's market presence will then be in danger. Only when certain criteria are met can a corporate brand be said to add real value to the proposition. The most obvious examples are in the service sector or in technology-driven markets. Line extensions are usually employed to launch new entrants into established markets or segments, and when successful they offer major savings in the time and resources required to build a new brand from scratch. Again, however, strict branding criteria must be used to prevent the core or parent brand from being diluted by extension into more than one proposition. This will be possible only if the brand essence is properly understood.

CHECKLIST

A corporate brand is likely to be successful only under the following circumstances:

- The corporation is a salient attribute.
- The corporation has an identity with associated clear values.
- The corporation has a brand property that is evident in the use or consumption of its products.

A line extension is likely to be successful only under the following circumstances:

- The brand essence is still applicable.
- The brand property is transferable.

- The brand variants could be promoted and distributed together.
- The repertoires are a hallmark of consumer behavior in the category.

REFERENCES

1. Stephen King, "Brand Building in the 1990s," *Journal of Marketing Management* 7, no. 1, 1990.

2. Edward Tauber, "Brand Leverage: Strategy for Growth in a Cost-Controlled World," *Journal of Advertising Research* 28, no. 4 (August/September 1988), pp. 26–30.

3. Tauber, "Brand Leverage," pp. 26–30.

The Role of Promotion

• • • • • • • • • • • • •

"I know that half of my advertising budget is wasted. The trouble is, I don't know which half." Lord Leverhulme's famous *cri de coeur* still echoes throughout marketing textbooks, just as the questions behind it echo throughout boardrooms at budgeting time.

As it becomes harder to find any other differentiator than "image," "reputation," or "personality," promotion becomes ever more important. The added values of a brand start and end with consumer *perception*. As it is communication that feeds perception, promotion is necessarily at the heart of branding. Like branding as a whole, therefore, promotion must be a general management concern, not a marketing department property.

Branding and advertising used to be almost synonymous. In FMCG markets there was an unspoken assumption:

Product + Advertising = Brand

The "advertising idea," in other words, was the brand property. To some extent, this is still true: Promotion, and advertising in particular, is still the critical activity in the life of most brand managers. Advertising is a powerful medium for building the personality that in many cases *is* the brand. And promotion is still where most of a brand's budget is spent. The world's great brand companies place the highest importance on their promotion campaigns. But to many onlookers the amounts of expenditure involved are incomprehensible. What decision processes result in Pepsi paying millions to pop stars like Michael Jackson or Madonna to appear in their advertisements? How can brands that retail for small amounts of pocket money make a profit if they have advertising budgets of tens of millions?

In fact, despite the huge budgets that still make the headlines, advertising is undergoing something of a crisis of confidence in the 1990s, and there are distinct signs that we are at the end of an era. This is partly owing to the rise in the power and sophistication of other forms of promotion, such as direct marketing. We also now know a little more about how advertising works, in particular its limitations, which has led to its more discriminating use. The other major factor is the increasing need for all expenditure to be accounted for. Managers, used to appraising returns from tangible investments in direct quantified terms, expect understandably to be able to judge promotional expenditure in a similar fashion. Is advertising contributing to sales, and if so how? If not, what is it contributing?

The management of promotion, then, is likely to become both more complex and more important. The fact that there is a creative element to promotion should not be an excuse to regard the whole thing as a mysterious art form and to abandon the usual decision processes in favor of intuition and emotion. This chapter examines the increasingly critical debate on the role of advertising. It also looks at the key decisions in promotion management, on the assumption that this will continue to be a vital part of building and maintaining brands.

Advertising in Crisis: The End of an Era?

Other methods of promotion, such as direct mail, sales promotions, or face-to-face selling, are all more productive of short-term observable responses. So why has advertising always dominated promotional budgets in consumer markets? Originally, there were several good reasons: Only advertising could economically reach the vast numbers of consumers involved; only advertising agencies had people with real marketing and branding expertise; and the alternative promotional methods seemed poorly conceived and researched when compared with the professional way that advertising was managed.

However, the world of branding is no longer as dominated by advertising agencies as it used to be. There are several reasons for this:

1. Branding has now been extended to industries where advertising is not the obvious means of communication with customers. In industrial markets, for instance, the relatively small

number of customers and the complexity of the products argues for a face-to-face salesperson; in service industries like hotels, customers meet the providers of the service as they are buying it.

2. Other industries are catching up with advertising and are able to use technology to offer highly targeted contacts with markets through means such as direct mail, telemarketing, and event marketing.

3. We now have a wider view of how brand franchises develop than the traditional wisdom of weight of advertising exposure. Other areas, such as product design, packaging, supporting literature, and trade promotions all come into the center of brand management in order to reinforce the unified brand proposition.

4. The fragmentation of the media, a common phenomenon in most of the developed world, is robbing advertising of one of its great strengths—the power to reach vast audiences with one exposure—and is making advertising more expensive at the same time.

This adds up to tougher years ahead for the advertising industry. Some major clients now put far less of their promotional budget through their agencies and more into "below-the-line" activities (so called because they are paid for on a fee basis, a departure from the commission system by which advertising agencies were traditionally rewarded). The most acute pressure is perhaps that of technology. With the huge customer data bases, which are now commonplace, companies can often target their activities at the level of the individual consumer. In some cases—for example, in promotional magazine publishing or industrial markets—flexible production systems mean that the number of personalized touches that can be introduced lead to the product, as well as the promotion, being customized to the level of the individual customer.

Some commentators take the view that this spells the end of the road for the large advertising agencies. Marketing consultant Regis McKenna, a champion of this school of thought, calls it "knowledge-based marketing":

We are witnessing the obsolescence of advertising. In the old model of marketing, it made sense as part of the whole formula: you sell mass-produced goods to a mass market through mass-media. Marketing's job was to deliver a message to the consumer in a one-way communication: "Buy this!" . . . In today's market, advertising simply misses the fundamental point of marketing—adaptability, flexibility, and responsiveness. The new marketing requires a feedback loop; it is the element that is missing from the monologue of advertising but that is built into the dialogue of marketing. . . . It is accomplished through experience-based marketing, where companies create opportunities for customers and potential customers to sample their products and then provide feedback. . . . Sensitivity comes from having a variety of modes and channels through which companies can read the environment, from user groups that offer live feedback to sophisticated consumer scanners that provide data on customer choice in real time.[1]

By 1989, expenditure on all other forms of "marketing services" totalled $380 billion compared with $240 billion for advertising, according to the WPP Group, owners of J. Walter Thompson.[2] Statistics regularly demonstrate that advertising expenditure is either stagnant or declining in various countries. While this trend has accelerated in recent years, a study by John Philip Jones of Syracuse University concluded: "Since the 1920s, there has been a subtle, almost undetectable, but nevertheless real downward pressure on advertising appropriations. This has applied particularly to FMCG. . . . There is no reason to suppose that these causes of downward pressure will become less important in the future."[3]

Promotional expenditure is increasingly being moved into sponsorship of events or TV programs, sales promotions, activities directed at distributors such as retailers, and public relations activities of various sorts. New types of company are springing up, such as the "product placement" agencies that specialize in getting their brands used and visible in TV shows, movies, and the like. The proliferation of forms of market communication apparently knows no bounds. This will further shift the balance of power to the brand marketers, who can bring prices down by playing the media off against one another.

There are good marketing reasons as well as economic reasons for companies to follow this trend. The most persuasive is the increasing advertising literacy of many consumers. As consumers become more critical recipients of advertising, brand companies have to turn to more indirect and subtle media in order to get their message across. The sum of all these factors is that the promotions industry will change for good.

To date, the advertising agencies have been in a league of their own, with PR, promotions, or design agencies languishing behind in a motley second division. In the future, all will have to compete on more or less equal terms. Some advertising agencies have been responding by widening their activities into other marketing services, most notably the British-based WPP Group and Saatchi & Saatchi, the latter even going so far as to include management consultancy in its portfolio (unsuccessfully). The industry seems likely to polarize between large multiservice agencies, which can see that the answer to a marketing problem is not automatically an advertising one, and small specialist agencies with outstanding strength in one field. The balance of power will lie firmly with the client.

On the "client" side of the industry, the brand companies will have to get better at managing promotions. With greater choice of media, it will be more important to understand the exact role of each and every promotion in building a single brand personality, so that all activities are complementary. Failure to coordinate all the different promotions could potentially be a brand-killer. It will certainly be impossible without a clear understanding of the brand and its strategy (see Chapter 7), and the role of promotion in implementing that strategy (the subject of the rest of this chapter).

Advertising seems unlikely to dominate the world of branding as it has in the past. The development of more sophisticated and better-managed alternatives will lead to a more varied promotions mix for most brands, placing new demands on brand management.

Why Promote at All?

It is important to start at the beginning. In line with the widespread and clearly sensible modern practice of zero-base budgeting (whereby budgets are not simply adjusted versions of the previous year's figures but start by questioning the purpose of every single expenditure item), many companies might ask why they should spend anything on promotion. The elder statesman of marketing academics, Ted Levitt, once commented that "marketing exists to make selling redundant." Is heavy promotional support a sign that the marketing was poor in the first place?

The Effect on Sales

There is only one real reason for promoting a brand—to increase sales, in either the short or the long run. There are therefore two key questions in deciding whether to promote:

1. What would be the level of sales without promotion?
2. Will the value of the extra sales be more than the cost of the promotion?

These are difficult questions, which is why the modern manager still feels at times as puzzled as Lord Leverhulme. If the brand has never been on sale without promotion, then the first question is impossible to answer. However, it is important to remember that there will be an underlying level of sales for a brand, and promotional experiments can be carried out in a specific area and the results tested against a control prediction. This may give clues to help address the second question; this will often then come down to an assessment of the costs and benefits of different forms of promotion, such as advertising, public relations, publicity, face-to-face selling, direct marketing, exhibitions, sponsorship, and telemarketing. In either case, a management team must have information on underlying sales trends that they can use as baselines for comparison.

What is known about consumer behavior provides ample justification for promotional activity. Most importantly, available evidence shows that there is a causal relationship between promotional support and sales, and conversely that if left unpromoted a brand's strength in the market will decay.

The Dynamic Difference Model

Probably the best-known and most reliable work on this is the "dynamic difference" model, originally developed in FMCG giant Unilever by Michael Moroney and now widely used. This consists of plotting levels of promotional expenditure (measured as a share of the total advertising in the market, or "share of voice") against a brand's market share over a number of years. Shifts in promotional support tend to result in shifts in market share over the long term (approximately five years' data are generally needed). In subsequent tests by Nielsen, this was found in 70% of cases.

More recent research projects also confirm that brands that consistently advertise will do better. A project conducted jointly by the

Table 8.1 **Relative Advertising Expenditures and Perceived Quality Percentile, _x_ Return on Investment (%), and _x_ Average Share of Market (%)**

A/S vs. direct competitor	Perceived quality percentile	Average ROI (%)	Average share of market (%)
Much less	44	17	14
Less	50	22	20
Equal	56	22	25
More	60	25	26
Much more	69	32	32

Source: Center for Research & Development/Strategic Planning Institute.

Californian Center for Research & Development and the Strategic Planning Institute (which runs the well-known PIMS data base) compared companies with different proportions of their sales devoted to advertising (the A/S ratio). It was found that companies investing more in advertising enjoyed a superior quality image, higher market share, and better profitability (see Table 8.1 above).[4] Further findings from this important study confirm that increases in advertising budgets often lead to increases in sales, and that the effects of the advertising are lasting, altering the perception of quality and building superior brands.

In FMCG markets at least, it can therefore be said with some confidence that advertising does work in most cases. Importantly, though, the dynamic difference model is based upon sheer weight or pressure of advertising, rather than the creative content, and so it is not possible to deduce how it works.

Many management teams remain skeptical about the value of the substantial investment needed for major advertising campaigns. They are turning to other forms of promotion, such as sales promotions (special offers, discounts, competitions, etc.) and direct mail or telephone promotion, where there is more direct evidence of an effect on buying patterns with better records of the consumers exposed to the promotion and their response. In many such cases promotion is effective, in the sense that it elicits a response. What is not so well understood is the long-term effect of such responses; research is only just beginning into the extent to which brand switching induced by short-term sales promotions is consolidated into the consumer's repertoire over the long term.

High-Tech Tests into Promotional Effects

New technology is helping marketers run ever more sophisticated tests on the effectiveness of promotions. Perhaps the most exciting are the BehaviorScan tests first run in the United States by researchers at IRI. These tests focus on a geographically isolated community where all consumers operate in the same context of distribution, price, and promotional activity. Through the use of electronic ID cards at the store checkouts, all the purchases of certain households are recorded. Then some households are exposed to TV advertisements while others are not—hence the name of "split-cable" tests— and the effects on purchasing patterns observed. These tests have not been running for long enough to draw firm conclusions, and as they are expensive they will not be widespread. Early results, however, are believed to show distinct effects on buying behavior where there is some "news" in the promotion, such as a new brand launch, a repositioning or a major sales promotion. Findings on the effects of normal advertising are not yet clear, which must indicate that no dramatic immediate effects are observable.

The Need to Be Heard

Absolute effects apart, there is one other good reason why promotion is necessary. "Noise" is the marketing jargon term for the total quantity of promotional messages to which almost every consumer is exposed. In most markets, the amount of noise has increased substantially in the last ten years. Common sense tells us that consumers have long been well past the point of taking in all the messages to which they are exposed. In simple terms this means that a brand has to be promoted simply because its rivals are. An unpromoted brand might not even be noticed by consumers, and distributors or retailers might not be willing to carry it. This has two implications for marketers:

1. Greater efforts will have to be made to grab even a tiny part of the consumer's attention—making it more imperative than ever to promote.
2. Whatever promotion is undertaken will have to be better targeted in terms of message, tone, and timing; amid such "noise," mere weight of exposure is not enough.

It all adds to a fiercer battle than ever for "share of mind."

> *New measures of response to promotion show that it is effective
> in general, even though advertising returns are unlikely ever to be
> measured very precisely.*

How Does It Work?

Assessing Advertising Expenditure in Terms of Sales

As long-run perceptions of products, brands tend to have relatively
stable sales patterns. Even if promotion can produce short-term
variations in sales figures, a brand will usually revert to its long-run
sales level after the effect of the promotion has passed. In branding
terms, the primary job of effective promotion is to influence this
long-run or base sales level; it is only its secondary role to produce
short-term effects. Tactical short-term promotion decisions should
always be checked against the long-term strategy for promotion of
the brand in general; it is quite possible for short-term promotion
decisions to have long-term effects on the brand.

For these reasons, it is wise to resist pressure to assess promotion
expenditures in terms of sales. There are other problems with such
objective setting:

- **Other variables.** It is almost impossible to exclude other factors
  influencing the level of sales. Variations could be produced
  by, for instance, reaction to competitor activity, the way the
  product is displayed at the point of sale, or the general economic climate. It would be rash to ascribe effects to the
  promotion except where all other variables are known with
  confidence to be constant.
- **Content of the promotion.** There is a creative element to
  advertising that aims at the heart rather than the head and
  provokes responses in consumers that cannot be measured in
  numbers. Cause-effect models necessarily compare all campaigns solely on the basis of what can be quantified—that is,
  the weight of exposures to the audience. In fact, all the money
  spent on an advertising campaign can be worthless if the
  message is ineffective or wrong.
- **Advertising as part of the brand.** Most econometric models
  treat advertising as separate from the product, in order to

model the effect of one upon the other. Clearly, this is hardly a brand-oriented view. Because it conveys intangibles and images, all promotion is necessarily building the brand and therefore the sales level, but never in isolation. The Marlboro cowboy is as much part of the brand as is the tobacco blend or even the paper in which the tobacco is encased, but it is almost impossible to break down the total offer into its component parts in observing normal consumption behaviors.

- **Promotion as a "highlighter."** It is clearly also true that promotion, as a means of communication, exists to reinforce effects from other parts of the marketing mix, as well as carrying its own power. If an advertising campaign features a new product formulation, for instance, it is impossible to say how much of the sales effect is from the new product and how much from the weight of the advertising—the two elements work in conjunction. Promotion should be considered not as an alternative to any other single element of the marketing mix but as a gateway for the customer into the total offer.

So long as these issues are considered, there is a place for econometric models of short-term response to promotional stimuli. But it is vital to understand that anything done to a brand can potentially have a long-term effect as well, and that the two can rarely be separated. A doyen of advertising management, Simon Broadbent of the Leo Burnett advertising agency, firmly believes that the two are interlinked:

> The sales of a brand are like the height at which an airplane flies. Advertising spend is like its engines; while the engines are running, everything is fine but, when the engines stop, the descent starts. The effectiveness of branding is like the aerodynamic design of the plane. Great creative, or better design, means that by spending the same money, or by using the same engines, we can take the brand or the plane higher. If we cut the spending on advertising, or stop the engines, the better brand or plane will stay up longer. But both will come down! Note that, in this analogy, advertising both creates increases in sales (gets the plane up) and is needed to maintain sales (to stay at the same height is an achievement). . . . The brand image is a mass of great momentum which is slow to alter direction, and often we are dealing with unquantified effects. This does not mean that they are unreal. True marketers have the instinctive and correct feeling that the brand is the most

valuable property, that it will evaporate slowly unless supported, and that long-term effects are the main justification for the advertising investment.[5]

This search for a model to explain how advertising generates sales is losing some of its urgency as it becomes clear that there is no single answer. Furthermore, we are becoming more tolerant of uncertainties in the 1990s as we move away from the view of management as a science. Ever since the surge of interest in the last decade in such phenomena as total quality, corporate culture, and high-performing people, companies are less inclined to view the quantified returns on their financial investment decisions as the only source of competitive advantage. The emergence of branding as an important issue for all management, not just the marketing department, is itself indicative of the new acceptance that the company's fortunes may be determined in part by intangibles. Advertising is such an intangible, as is the boom area of management development. Interestingly, accounting methods are beginning to adjust to the importance of intangibles as a measure of corporate health (see Chapter 10).

The growing understanding of the importance of branding, in other words, is influencing our understanding of how promotion works. Most importantly, there is now a general acceptance that consumer reaction to promotion is not the sort of logical information-processing decision suggested by traditional microeconomics or even by most textbook models of consumer behavior.

How Consumers React to Promotional Activity

The biggest single breakthrough in thinking about advertising effects was the idea of selective perception—that the response of consumers to promotion will vary according to their own personal situation. A consumer may be more or less receptive to a promotional message at different times for reasons that the advertiser can neither perceive nor influence. The consumer may be bored with current purchasing and actively seeking a change; the advertisement may contain an image that has strong personal associations. We know from Ehrenberg's work (discussed in Chapter 2) that most brand purchases are repeat purchases from an established repertoire made without much obvious decision process, and so most advertising researchers now agree that the normal situation is indifference or even, as Gordon Brown terms it, "resistance." One authority in the

Figure 8.1 **The "Black Box" of Consumer Choice**

Promotion

Consumer buying behavior

area, John Philip Jones, advocates the view that "advertising operates as a contribution to the maintenance of essentially stationary patterns of consumer behavior."[6]

Consumers, then, rarely buy as a simple reaction to the stimulus of promotion. There is some sort of "black box" that represents consumer decision making (see Figure 8.1, above). The black box is the consumer's learning as a consumer, built up from experience of various products, word-of-mouth reports from other consumers, advertising and promotion memories, and all other experiences unrelated to the product field. Sometimes this vast body of learning is used consciously, but most of the time it is employed in the "shorthand" form of brand perceptions.

Most of the time, then, promotion is reinforcing the existing behavior of existing customers. Only rarely does it inform, persuade, or stimulate different behavior, and management has limited power to identify, let alone to exploit, those rare situations. Practitioners of direct mail or sales promotions would dispute this, claiming that their work can induce behavioral responses, such as returning coupons or even brand switching. This may be true but partly misses the key branding issue: Most purchases are repeat purchases made on the basis of long-term views and attitudes. This type of buying is what brand companies are aiming at; it is, in essence, brand loyalty. To build a brand, therefore, a company has to get into the black box and deal with customer attitudes and brand images.

Promotion can contribute to the development of these attitudes, but it will not be the only contributor. Short-term changes in buying behavior may be caused by promotion, but may be driven by the consumer's own private motives. Where they are induced by promotional activity, Ehrenberg's work seems to demonstrate that it is the subsequent experience of the brand, rather than the initial promotional stimulus, which is likely to shape underlying attitudes. Indeed, Gordon Brown of the advertising research company Millward Brown suggests that consumers will defend these attitudes in the face of promotion:

> Marketing theory does not take sufficient cognizance of the fact that decisions take time and effort, and the habit mechanism is a vital way of freeing the brain by taking repeated decisions in the same way . . . defensive attitudes build around these habitual buying patterns—which is why we see evaluative attitudes swing into line with purchasing behavior. They are partly generated by familiarity and partly by the fact that the decisions you have taken are an aspect of your personality, just like the wallpaper you choose or the curtains you hang. . . . This is why it is not easy to alter brand perceptions quickly on attributes which are obviously important.[7]

To attempt to change attitudes is risky, in the sense that it will take time and money to overcome the consumer's defenses, if it is possible at all. There is the risk of antagonizing consumers by acting against their perceived interests, never a sound route to gaining brand loyalty. The most common example of this is where a reduced price "cheapens" the brand perception, or upsets existing consumers who have already paid a slightly higher price for it.

Promotion as Communication

All promotional activity is a form of communication. Whether it is intended to stimulate certain behaviors or not, any promotion should be undertaken with a clear view of what is being communicated and to whom. In discussing advertising specifically, Gordon Brown suggests three "mechanisms" by which advertising can play a different role in the continuum of communication objectives:[8]

1. **Immediate challenge.** When there is something new to say about a brand, the advertiser can make a specific, tangible claim that may induce the consumer to reconsider. This is a

one-off opportunity, and clearly the claim has to be borne out in experience if long-term attitudes are to shift.

2. **Interest mechanism.** There is a background role for advertising in maintaining interest in the brand among nonusers. Consumers will occasionally reconsider their repertoire for their own reasons, and they may turn to brands they remember. Advertising that is memorable and interesting will implant the brand image in the long-term memories of all consumers, helping the brand to take advantage of any random, experimental brand switching. Research from the Center for Research & Development suggests that there is a link between how much consumers like an advertisement and their subsequent propensity to buy the brand.[9]

3. **Enhancement.** Advertising can provide a criterion for consumers when judging the brand. Brown quotes tests on users of Timotei shampoo, who were converted from a general "good for frequent washing" perception before they had used it to a "I've tried it and it's true!" perception after trial. Advertising has clearly provided a claim whereby consumers can justify their experience of the brand. It is neither the claim alone nor the experience alone but a combination of the two that is shaping the attitude.

The first mechanism is demonstrated in the case study on Radion, a new British detergent brand. Advertising was the key element in positioning the new brand into what is an established market with strongly entrenched attitudes. The advertising worked by challenging consumers to reexamine their habitual preferences. It is one of the rare cases where advertising can clearly be seen to have influenced market shares substantially and in the short term. It worked because there was a real message, delivered in a window of opportunity.

Text continues on page 181, after the case study.

Advertising as a Challenge:
A New Brand Asks New Questions
Radion Detergent

•　　•　　•　　•　　•

In October 1989 Unilever's Lever Brothers launched its first U.K. dual variant (liquid and powder) detergent brand in over a decade: Radion. The product's TV commercials became notoriously disliked. They stridently flew in the face of the accepted advertising trend reflecting the caring 1990s, the new man/woman, the lifestyle ad, and the soft sell. They were, however, strategically sound and highly effective in ensuring the successful launch of the brand.

The performance of Radion must be seen in relation to the other existing Lever brands. The risk of launching a detergent that might cannibalize its stablemates was all too apparent. Radion had to be judged by its contribution to Lever's portfolio.

The Low Suds Detergent Market

The low suds sector represents over 90% of the detergents market. Prior to Radion's launch the market was divided as shown in Figure 8.2 (see page 173). Although the marketplace remained dominated by a few established brands, the introduction of new product variants, such as liquids and powder concentrates, and different package sizes had increased choice for the consumer and competition for shelf space among manufacturers.

Persil and Ariel, the market leaders, are widely trusted and have very distinct characteristics, appealing to homemakers in different ways. Ariel is considered to be a modern and effective product particularly good at removing stains. Although Persil is also an effective cleaner, it is perceived as being used by more caring people and as being softer on clothes.

It would be fair to say that Persil and Ariel tend to characterize the imagery for Lever Brothers and Proctor & Gamble respectively. P&G advertising has historically depended upon a definitive functional platform, while that for Lever products has offered a more emotional appeal.

Figure 8.2 **Low Suds Market Segmentation: Value Share, September 1989**

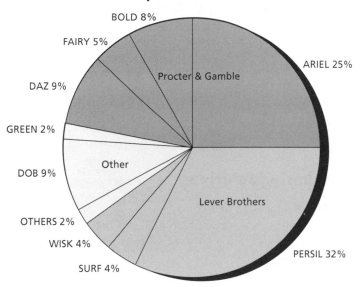

BOLD 8%

FAIRY 5%

DAZ 9%

GREEN 2%

DOB 9%

OTHERS 2%

WISK 4%

SURF 4%

Procter & Gamble

ARIEL 25%

Other

Lever Brothers

PERSIL 32%

Source: Nielsen audit data, 1989.

The Marketing Task

In 1980 Lever Brothers held 61% of the market by value. Its share fell to 43% in 1984 when it was overtaken by P&G as Persil lost 5%, largely to Ariel. By 1988 Lever's value share had slipped below 40%.

International experience from the mid-1980s provided Lever with a possible key to the solution of this dilemma. In 1984 a low suds detergent with a dirt and odor removal proposition was launched in the United States. It was based on a Unilever patented technology, a unique deo-perfume system that deodorizes clothes rather than merely masking odor. This was launched under the name Surf, the claim being that "Surf fights dirt and odors." Exceeding all expectations, it became the second-best selling brand in the United States and has since been successfully launched into eight European countries.

Odor removal, it seemed, could be a motivating proposition, and Lever Brothers believed that its international success could be repeated in the United Kingdom. But Surf was already the name of a British detergent, and it had a distinctive price-based heritage in the United Kingdom from years of "Square Deal Surf" promotion. It was thought that this would inhibit the introduction of the new proposition as Surf, so a new brand name, Radion, was chosen. The task for Lever was to establish Radion Automatic as a major brand in this fiercely contested marketplace.

The first-year objective for penetration was set at 35% and that for repeat purchase at 24%. Two strategic issues loomed large:

1. How was Radion to attract consumers away from long-established brands?
2. How could Lever ensure that sales of Radion were not gained at the expense of its other brands?

The Marketing Solution

The strategy developed to overcome these issues was to position Radion as a *superior* alternative to competitive brands and as a complement to Lever's existing brands. This strategy entailed two distinct but inter-related components.

First, Radion was to be promoted in a very different style from Lever brands such as Persil and Surf. From packaging to advertising, support would be executed in a non-Lever manner.

In direct contrast to the gently toned lifestyle advertising that Persil employed, advertising for Radion would be required to promote modernity, vigor, and uncompromising cleaning power. Similarly, the packaging was designed in bright "day-glo" colors instead of the traditional soap powder bias toward white. Research showed that Radion packages communicated "excitement," "powerful cleaning," and "modernity."

This positioning was designed to ensure that Radion did not cannibalize its Lever stablemates. A brand that competed on the platform of uncompromising cleaning power would complement Persil, "the caring brand." It was intended that this would reinforce Persil's position in the battle for corporate market leadership.

Second, Radion was to redefine the parameters for judging a detergent's effectiveness. International evidence showed that odor removal was a "want" in a large part of the market that had not been met. It needed to be defined as an important part of the cleaning power of a product. Radion needed to be positioned as "owning" this power, thereby offering a tangible benefit to the consumer and a proof of its greater cleaning effectiveness.

The bulk of this task fell to advertising, and TV was chosen to execute this dual communication. The sell line "Removes dirt *and* odors" was reinforced by its appearance on other promotional material and on the package itself. Lever's pricing policy for Radion reflected its positioning. Launch prices for Radion were set at parity with other *premium* brands for both liquid and powder.

The Role for Advertising

Advertising had a critical role to play in defining Radion's positioning and credentials. Three objectives for advertising were laid down:

1. To *create awareness* of the launch of Radion
2. To *communicate the brand's USP*—unbeatable cleaning across the wash with unique odor removal benefit
3. To help *prompt* consumer trial

The primary target audience was defined as homemakers owning front-loading automatic washing machines, especially those currently buying strictly effective detergents. Radion was designed to appeal to those homemakers who were attracted to a functional cleaning promise and responded to a didactic and authoritarian tone in advertising. Radion advertising had, therefore, to confront the traditional cleaning promise head on and to surpass it with the unique odor removal benefit. The following proposition was used:

> "New Radion is as good as any other brand at cleaning and removes lingering odors that they sometimes leave behind."

The Advertising Solution

Advertising for the United Kingdom was not developed in isolation from this proposition. Given Radion's international heritage, executions for the U.K. drew heavily upon experience from the United States and Belgium. Both confirmed the potential of using a very direct creative execution.

The U.S. launch had used a traditional "slice of life" advertising format in which the product was presented in a "real life" family situation. Several executions were developed for the United Kingdom in this mold. Using scenes such as a father and son erecting a new fence or a father and children building a shed, they showed the family's reaction to the father's smelly working shirt, followed by approval of the clean shirt once it had been washed using Radion. The odor removal message was reinforced by the use of a computer graphic representation of the shirt and a demonstration of Radion's deodorizing action.

The commercial was introduced by loud "new style" music that, followed by the commanding tone of the presenter, made the advertising difficult to ignore. Again, the presenter conveyed authority and validity. The message was delivered by the simple line "Radion removes dirt *and* odors." The news style presentation added an urgency to the message and finished with the line "New Radion. Try it."

Executions developed for radio followed the same format. They capitalized upon the pervasive "Radion news" music used in the TV commercials and to add urgency to the message.

Posters supporting the launch featured simply a package shot and the line "Radion removes dirt *and* odors" printed large in Radion's day-glo orange. The color was eyecatching and an important branding tool for Radion, which the posters were designed to reinforce.

The Radion Launch

Radion was launched on October 2, 1989, supported by advertising, promotions on packages, and product sampling. The brand accounted for over one-third of total detergent market TV activity between October 1989 and March 1990 and consistently outrated all other brands.

Radion's market share grew to 7% (value) by March 1990. After just six months it had overtaken smaller brands such as Fairy, Wisk, and Surf and was only 0.7% (value) behind both Bold and Daz.

By April 1990 cumulative penetration had reached 25% of the market, on target for its first-year objective, and the brand has performed well by comparison with the other new detergent launches of 1989. Figure 8.3 (see page 177) shows the cumulative household penetration built by Fairy, Ariel Ultra, Bold Liquid, and Radion at equal intervals following their respective launches. It demonstrates that Radion reached more households faster than any other new brand in 1989. Radion has also outperformed these brands in building market share. This is clearly demonstrated in Figure 8.4 (see page 177).

The success of Radion was achieved despite significant adverse factors. First, distribution levels were limited because Radion was not stocked by Tesco, one of the two major U.K. retail chains, until the end of March 1990. Second, P&G attempted to preempt Radion's odor removal

Figure 8.3 **Cumulative Household Penetration for 1989 Detergent Launches**

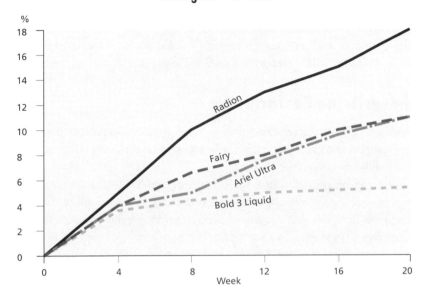

Source: AGB data, 1989.

Figure 8.4 **Monthly Market Share (Volume) for 1989 Detergent Launches**

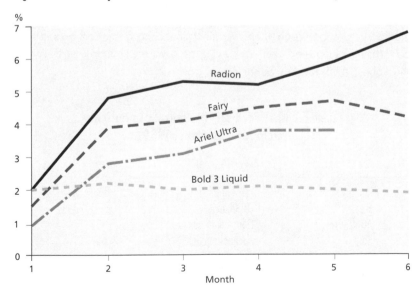

Source: Nielsen audit data, 1989.

claims by screening an Ariel odor removal commercial before and during Radion's launch.

Radion's success has not been in isolation; it has also met Lever's more fundamental objective of contributing to the company's portfolio. Over the period of Radion's launch, Lever's volume share of the market rose from 41.7% to 44.8%, overtaking P&G in the process.

Advertising Performance

Radion's advertising was certainly noticed. The combination of generous budget and branded memorability led to Radion obtaining 82% awareness within two months of launch.

It could be argued that Radion's advertising success was entirely a function of media weight. Indeed, generating this level of awareness involved considerable media expenditures. However, in such a high-spending market Radion's budget of £8.9 million (October to January) was not unusual. It represented approximately half the annual budget of Ariel or Persil.

The requirement for such a budget and the evidence that it was employed efficiently is provided by the Millward Brown awareness index. This is a measure of the extra advertising awareness (i.e., that above base awareness) generated per 100 TV rating points. Using a modeling process, researchers can compare the effectiveness of campaigns, having allowed for, among other things, the difference in sheer media weight between them. Against these criteria, Radion's launch advertising performed well, achieving an awareness index of 8, by far the highest in this market, as shown in Table 8.2.

Table 8.2 **Millward Brown Awareness Indices (October/November 1989)**

	Advertisement	Index
Radion	"Presenter"	8
Persil	"Oil Change"	3
Ariel Auto	"Odor Campaign"	1
Bold 3	"Michael Elphick"	1
Ariel Ultra	"Greener"	2
Daz	"Spiderman"	3
Fairy	"Sumo"	2

Advertising, however, has not worked simply to achieve success for Radion. It has also positioned Radion to complement other Lever brands. Furthermore, the advertising has introduced the concept of odor removal as an ultimate test of a product's cleaning power and has conferred ownership of this property on Radion.

Advertising's contribution to this positioning is demonstrated by a Millward Brown finding that of all those recalling the "Presenter" advertisement, 70% stated spontaneously, "Radion gets rid of smells." The comparable figure for Ariel's odor removal ad was just 19%, despite the fact that its own ad had been running since before Radion's launch.

The impact of Radion's launch upon brand images in the low suds sector is illustrated in Figure 8.5 (see page 180). Based upon the images attributed to brands by consumers, the map shows how Radion is perceived relative to its competitors. The communication of odor removal as a vital part of the cleaning process has placed Radion in the modern/efficient quadrant of the map. It is clearly differentiated from the Lever portfolio, Persil in particular.

Consumer panel data over 30 weeks pre- and post-launch clearly show that Radion has not cannibalized the Lever portfolio. It gained 15% more volume than expected from the Ariel brand, without encroaching on Persil's franchise. Radion's source of volume from Persil was in fact lower than expected, by a margin of 7%.

How the Advertising Worked

It is rare to find anyone who would admit to liking the Radion advertising, yet the product has already been used by over 21% of households. Qualitative research has revealed that this unusual result has been achieved *because* of the bold and even authoritarian style of the advertising. The news style presentation of Radion was extremely striking and authoritative. The message was clear and forceful: Radion is new, different, and much more effective—it removes odors.

The research concluded that this communication worked by challenging homemakers' confidence in their wash and daring them to try Radion. The loudness of the approach prompts some recoil, but this only serves to strengthen Radion's position as a challenge to be met. The authoritative tone makes Radion more credible to the homemaker who seeks perfection. This challenge is neatly summarized by the woman who said: "That dreadful ad made me buy it." The research also discovered that the advertising polarized homemakers' attitudes. The person who seeks

Figure 8.5 **Detergent Brand Image Map**

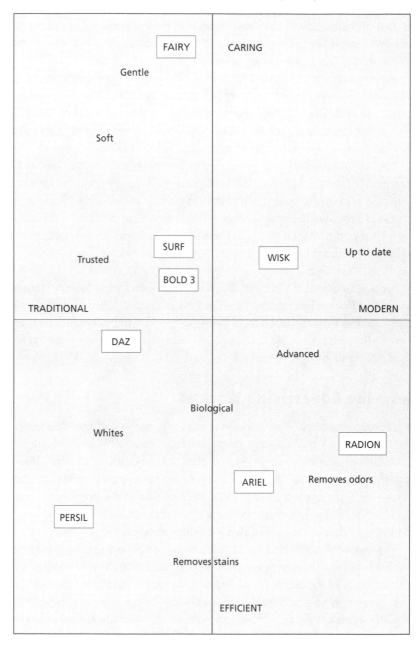

Source: Millward Brown tracking study, 1990.

gentle, caring values in a detergent brand ignores the challenge. In this way the advertising has tended to attract the competitor franchise to Radion but has repelled those who would constitute the core buyers of a "caring" brand such as Persil.

This effect demonstrates the appropriateness of Radion's advertising. Radion advertising can be seen, therefore, as an accurate translation of the core marketing strategy into a creative execution.

CONCLUSION

Promotion works in different ways. Long-term effects are possible, influencing the customer perception and building brands. Short-term behavioral effects may be independent of these. The manager must be quite clear about which objective is to be set for any given promotion. Good brand management will also involve careful monitoring of the effect of one type of promotion on the others.

Text continued from page 171.

Setting Objectives for Promotion

So what are suitable objectives for promotional expenditure?

The Hierarchy of Effects Model

Common practice is to target a stage from what is known as the "hierarchy of effects" behavioral model of Lavidge and Steiner (Figure 8.6 on page 182).[10] This is a hierarchical model—that is, the consumer must progress through one stage before moving on to another. In particular, it reflects the common behavioral science premise that behavior (in this case, purchase) is the output of attitude and an intention to act. In marketing terms, it means that direct incitements to buy would be a waste of money if efforts had not been made to help consumers through the previous stages.

The hierarchy of effects idea is immortalized in the advertising world as DAGMAR—"Defining Advertising Goals for Measured Advertising Results," the name of an influential essay written by Colley in 1961—which argued that the intermediate stages of communication made valid measures for advertising. Different types of

Figure 8.6 **The Hierarchy of Effects Model of Consumer Behavior**

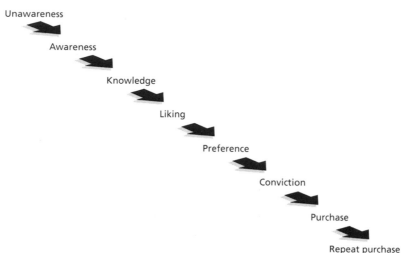

Source: R.J. Lavidge and G. Steiner, "A Model for Predictive Measurements of Advertising Effectiveness," Journal of Marketing (October 1961).

promotion are directed at different stages in the hierarchy, and results are increasingly measured against awareness levels achieved, or attitudes toward a brand, as well as against sales. It is still true, of course, that all promotion is directed at generating sales in the long run, but money may be spent to help consumers progress through intermediate stages on the way to a purchase.

This approach is certainly in line with a branding orientation, as it recognizes that customers may come to the point of purchase with perceptions already well formed, and that it is a key task of marketing to understand and manage those perceptions. The hierarchy of effects model must nevertheless be treated with caution. Customers do go through some sort of process, but that process is unpredictable. The model assumes that a lot goes on in the customer's mind before the purchase decision is made (it is what is known as a "high involvement" model). In a business-to-business purchase such as a new item of manufacturing plant, this may be true: The process is likely to be explicit and deliberate, with extensive searches for information, published criteria for assessing alternatives, and defined roles for the various people involved. The customer will edge very gradually toward a purchase.

But research evidence indicates that customers often do not go through any form of information processing before they make a purchase. Indeed, Ehrenberg's research into repeat purchasing (which is discussed in Chapter 2) tends to the opposite conclusion—that attitudes are formed by experience of the product—that is, after purchase. Ehrenberg's work suggests that the main role of promotion is in reinforcing attitudes among users. A subsidiary role is the creation of awareness, which may help induce trial (first purchase) and therefore improve the penetration of the product in the market. It follows that any stage in the model can be targeted on its own, as long as the stage of consumer knowledge and attitude about the brand is known.

A Continuum of Objectives

Stephen King has suggested that there is a continuum of suitable objectives for promotion:[11]

Most direct	Direct action
	Seek information
	Relate to own needs/wants/desires
	Recall satisfactions/reorder/short-list
	Modify attitudes
Most indirect	Reinforce attitudes

Much promotion, and certainly most advertising, would fall into the most indirect category of reinforcing attitudes. In this context, the vast advertising expenditures of brands such as Coca-Cola and Pepsi make a new kind of sense: They are not spreading awareness, which is pretty well universal anyway, and they do not convey much information, but they do reinforce the image and perceptions of the brand that have existed for years.

Three Categories of Objectives

In practice, objectives tend to fall into one of three categories, which are treated independently.

Awareness Objectives.   Awareness consists essentially of memory. It is therefore relatively easy to measure and is commonly used as an objective for advertising. The awareness need not relate just to the brand; researchers can measure awareness of specific elements of the mix, such as a particular advertisement, new packaging, a new feature, or a price level. This is particularly useful when the brand company has made some changes to its offer, because it can measure the rate at which the market is being reeducated. Awareness is also an important aspect to measure in relation to competitor brands.

In any of these cases the promotional activity is required only to expose the brand to the target audience as cost effectively as possible.

Attitudinal Objectives. Objectives in this category most commonly consist of rankings against brand "personality traits" in order to assess the brand's position in the market—that is, what customers think about a brand, what they know about it, and how they see it in terms of quality and propensity to purchase. This area is essentially concerned with long-term effects. The first stage is to inform consumers of all aspects of the brand offer. Thereafter, most promotional activity is aimed at reinforcing or making fine adjustments to perceptions of brands that are already well known. The full range of promotional options may be suitable for attaining such objectives, although the balance between short- and long-term effects needs watching in areas like personal selling and sales promotions where the design is usually geared to immediate results. The only way to measure results against these sorts of objectives effectively is to use tracking studies (the same study repeated at intervals over a long period) to show up any long-term shifts in attitudes toward a brand. It is also vital that the whole market is researched, because consumers' attitudes to brands are always comparative.

Behavioral Objectives. This category of objectives is concerned with observable changes in behavior—notably sales, but perhaps also the composition of the customer base (who is buying?), or the form in which the product is bought (a switch to multipacks, for example), or the channel through which the product is bought. To measure any of these factors, the company must be sure that all other variables are reasonably static, and must also know the base level from which variations are to be measured.

This type of promotional objective is most common in controlled experiments such as test markets. However, the controlled conditions of a test market are impossible to maintain over the longer term, so the limitations of promotion-to-sales measurement already discussed apply. This is not to discount the need that arises from time to time to undertake some tactical activity to produce behavioral changes—a sales promotion or discounting offer, for instance, to produce a short-term boost in sales. In such cases the only necessary constraint is to check that nothing is being done to undermine the long-term positioning of the brand. It is common to see "suboptimizing" decisions in this area, such as a brand manager running a sales promotion near the end of the budget year to ensure that sales budgets are met and in the process altering the market perception of the brand.

The most common behavioral objective is concerned with trade management in industries where there is an important distributor link in the supply chain—for example, an FMCG company running a trade promotion to influence the supermarkets. Specific objectives in such cases may be to get the brand stocked by a certain retailer, to get it a better position on the shelves or in the store, or to get a certain price.

Target Levels

It is almost impossible to generalize about the exact scale of the desired effect of any promotional exercise—that is, at what level to set the target. Common sense would tell a marketing manager that for a newish brand, especially in a growing market, more sizeable effects should be possible than with an established brand in a "closed" market with entrenched attitudes. The only way to get anything like reliable information is to dig deep into what seem to be the norms for the particular industry or product category. Of course, future changes in consumer attitude or competitor activity cannot be predicted.

Selecting an Objective

The real management challenge is selecting an appropriate objective in the first instance, for which there are no models. Usually, the two levels of customer, end consumer and trade distributor, are treated separately.

For the end consumer, something like the hierarchy of effects model generally applies, with awareness objectives for a new offer of any sort, followed by more informative and attitude-building promotions. Objectives for established brands may polarize into either behavioral objectives for tactical short-term promotions, or very general and emotive promotions to reinforce long-term attitudes.

For trade promotions, behavioral objectives are more common and are certainly the starting point for anything new.

SUMMARY

Promotion will continue to be the heart of brand management. Advertising will not enjoy its previous dominance, as alternative methods, such as direct mail, telemarketing, and sales promotions, grow in sophistication; this will lead to more varied portfolios of promotions for most brands. While it is known that good promotion does eventually result in higher sales levels, not enough is known about the exact communications process to justify cause-effect econometric models of advertising effects. It appears that, in most cases, promotion reinforces existing perceptions and behaviors, and only rarely persuades or incites to action. There is a spectrum of possible effects from short-term actions, such as sales, to long-term image building in the "long-term memory" of the consumer. The promotion method must be chosen accordingly, and management must be prepared to invest in building intangible brand perceptions over the long term as well as stimulating specific short-term responses.

CHECKLIST

The following questions should be answered as the basis for all decisions on specific promotions:

- What is the underlying sales level for the brand?
- What is the target underlying sales level for the brand over the next planning period?
- In current promotion activity, what proportion is attempting to reinforce consumer perceptions and behavior, and what proportion is attempting to change them?
- What specific communication objectives are appropriate for the brand in the context of the brand plan?
- What are the best promotion methods to achieve these objectives?
- Are the planned promotions consistent with the brand strategy and the other promotions—that is, will each promotion reinforce the others?
- What is the financial value of the responses being sought? Does this justify the promotion expenditure?

REFERENCES

1. Regis McKenna, "Marketing Is Everything," *Harvard Business Review* (January/February 1991), p. 74.

2. "The Advertising Industry," *The Economist* (June 9, 1990).

3. John Philip Jones, *What's in a Name? Advertising and the Concept of Brands* (New York: Free Press, 1986), p. 262.

4. Alexander L. Biel, "Strong Brand, High Spend," *ADMAP* (November 1990), pp. 35–40.

5. Simon Broadbent, *The Advertising Budget* (London: IPA/NCT Publications, 1989); *The Advertiser's Handbook for Budget Determination* (New York: Free Press, 1988).

6. Jones, *What's in a Name?*, p. 262.

7. Gordon Brown, "Big Stable Brands and Ad Effects," *ADMAP* (May 1991), pp. 32–34.

8. Brown, "Big Stable," pp. 32–34.

9. Alexander L. Biel, "Love the Ad. Buy the Product?" *ADMAP* (September 1990), pp. 21–25.

10. R. J. Lavidge and G. Steiner, "A Model for Predictive Measurements of Advertising Effectiveness," *Journal of Marketing* (October 1961).

11. Stephen King, "Practical Progress for a Theory of Advertisements," *ADMAP* (October 1975), pp. 338–43.

Spending Money on Promotion

· · · · · · · · · · · · · ·

How Much to Spend on Promotion

This is perhaps the most difficult question of all from a managerial viewpoint. Without a clear idea of the relationship between investment and return, it is hard to work out how much to invest. There is no one correct answer.

Broadbent's Model Process

In the words of the world's authority on the subject, Leo Burnett agency veteran Simon Broadbent, "The amount to spend on advertising is determined by a process, not by a formula." He states quite categorically that there is no method that can be employed to work out a promotion budget that will produce an optimal figure. In his authoritative book on the subject Broadbent stresses that, in the absence of good data on the effects of expenditure, budgeting becomes a political process internal to the organization; it is determined in part by personalities, power bases, timing, the general company situation, and so on. So, as in other areas of marketing, the process is the important thing, the sequence of decisions vital, and common sense the main criterion.

Broadbent suggests a model process, which consists of six steps:[1]

1. **Review the brand objectives**. Assess the importance of the brand to the company, and what is expected of the brand in terms of its competitive or financial targets.
2. **Review the brand budgets**. Current as well as future budgets will provide information on how the brand has behaved in the market in the past.

3. **Review market history and forecast**. Review historical market data in terms of marketing activity, and assess how competitors are likely to behave in the immediate future.
4. **Assess advertising effects**. Assemble from previous stages some scenarios of the results of promotional expenditure. This will require market experience and wisdom as well as deductions from past experience.
5. **Set budgets**. Broadbent recommends trying out a few of the standard methods of budget determination (see below) to help determine the budget after the strategic review of the brand's performance.
6. **Check for feasibility**. The proposed budget will have to be checked for feasibility against other performance objectives, and against budgets for other brands and the company as a whole.

Broadbent's model process is a balanced and realistic one, and the reader is referred to his book for a full-length exposition. It incorporates what can be measured about brand image and advertising weight, without relying on the absolute validity of any of it, and as such is an exemplary approach.

Standard Methods of Budget Determination

Most discussion of budget determination is centered on certain methods or formulas. While these may be useful starting points for discussion, their apparent objectivity is illusory, because most are based on ratios and offer only the possibility of benchmarking with past experience or competitor activity.

Ratios. Perhaps the most common ratio is *advertising-to-sales* (or A/S), based on the ratio of the promotional budget to the brand's turnover. This does provide a useful benchmark, especially in industries (mainly FMCG again) where a market norm or average is available from advertising associations. It should not need pointing out, however, that there is no such thing as a correct ratio—even though it is easy to lose sight of this in the budgeting process. Another problem with this method is that it is the wrong way round, in that it suggests that sales drive advertising, and denies any possibility that advertising might influence the level of sales. The same is true of other ratio methods such as *advertising-per-case*.

Another common ratio is *share of voice* (SOV), the proportion of all the promotion in a given market that is accounted for by a given brand. (Published data on advertising expenditures by the various players tend to be limited to FMCG markets). A management team might decide that, as it has 20% market share, it should have a minimum of 20% SOV, and up to 30% if it wants to make a major push on the brand's sales.

SOV is still widely used as a basis for models of various kinds, attempting to measure the elasticity of campaigns or the success of brand teams that achieve a higher market share than SOV. Enlightening though they may be, their mechanical view of brand building will never tell the whole truth.

Objective and Task Method.   The reason that ratio methods predominate is that they are relatively easy to use, and that there are no better alternatives. The other obvious way to approach the issue is to establish a desired effect and to take a view on the resources required to achieve it. Clearly, the objective has to be something that can be measured before and after the promotion; typical examples might be to raise awareness from 55% to 70%, or to increase to 50% the proportion of the population associating Brand X with durability. This is what might be taken as a commonsense approach, and is the basis of DAGMAR (see pages 181–82). This method has several virtues: It emphasizes the need to measure results, and it has a wider view of appropriate objectives, embracing awareness, knowledge, attitude, and anything else that can be measured. It falls down, however, on the same block as all other methods: The right amount to achieve the task can never be stipulated with accuracy because of the impossibility of isolating and measuring cause and effect.

> *There is no formula for determining a promotion budget. It should be managed as a process, drawing on industry experience and using quantitative methods as checks and balances.*

How to Allocate the Promotion Budget

One area where brand expenditure can be well monitored is in measuring the number of consumers who see any promotion. Because audience research is such a well-developed sector of the research industry, a quasi-scientific assessment can usually be made. This is especially true of TV and radio, where minute-by-minute ratings are now readily available. It is also the case with the press, where circulation and readership statistics are easily available; with movies, where admission figures are gathered; with billboards and posters, where the number of people passing a particular site is measured as "passage figures"; and, of course, with direct marketing, by telephone, facsimile or mail, where individual targeting has been made possible by the rise of sophisticated information technology for holding customer data bases. Sales calls have always been well recorded. Media planning is therefore one of the most accountable activities in brand marketing, and anyone managing a brand in the 1990s should be able to find out who has had an opportunity to see the brand promotion.

Media planning cannot go beyond the "opportunity to see" (OTS), and does not deal with the "creative" content of the promotion and how the consumer reacts to it (although clever media planning can do something to enhance "stand-out value" by creative placing of the promotion). What we do learn from the dynamic difference model and others is that over the long term the weight of promotion is an important factor when the content of the promotion is not changed significantly. This should be the usual situation in managing brands, as consistency of positioning is vital in building a brand equity. It follows that the control of promotional expenditure is not just an area offering a high level of accountability, but one where good management can contribute to cost-effective brand building.

Because of its quantitative basis, this is an area of marketing activity where most of the people employed are highly numerate and scientific by inclination—rather different from the stereotyped seat-of-the-pants marketer. This "specialist" culture, and the changes in the agency world, have led to a distinct trend towards media departments buying themselves out of advertising agencies and setting up in their own right. The discounts these "media shops" can achieve from media owners once they pass a critical mass of clients from several agencies (and are therefore buying huge amounts of media space and time) are well worth having, and so the trend would seem likely to continue toward fewer, bigger, more dedicated media buying and planning companies.

The Objectives of Media Planning

The objectives of any media plan are clear:

- To reach the target audience as defined by the brand management team.
- To contact them through a medium that maximizes the probability of the communications objectives being achieved (for instance, TV might be used to reinforce an advertisement with an emotional appeal, whereas the press might be more suitable for a detailed explanation of changes made to a service offering).
- To reach them at the right time and in the right place (for instance, it is best not to show ads targeted at women in the middle of a hockey game on TV).
- To achieve this at minimum cost.

Measurement Mechanisms

The language of media planning is still that of the mass-media advertising industry. The total weight of a promotional campaign will usually be expressed in rating points. A single rating point is reached when 1% of the target population has one opportunity to see (OTS) the promotion. Some broad classification of the consumers reached in a given exposure will usually be provided, such as age group or social grade. Although there will be some overlap, different consumers will be involved in different showings of the advertisement, and so only an average OTS figure will be possible. The ratings from each exposure or "spot" will be totaled to reach a total number of GRPs (Gross Rating Points) in the United States or TVRs (TV Ratings) in the United Kingdom. Given that the number of consumers exposed to the promotion is known, figures can then be calculated for CPT or cost-per-thousand (the cost of reaching 1,000 consumers) or CPH or cost-per-hundred (the cost of buying 100 ratings).

There are problems in defining these terms, such as an opportunity to see. A person in a darkened movie theater is far more likely to pay attention to an advertisement than somebody who buys a 200-page newspaper and flicks through it for five minutes, yet both are considered to have had an opportunity to see. There are even high-tech problems, such as "zipping" (fast-forwarding through advertisements when watching a video recording) or "zapping" (using remote control to avoid TV advertisements by changing the channel).

Technological developments are always refining the measurement mechanisms, but even so the information that is available is far more detailed and more accurate than in any other aspect of brand marketing, and it provides management with a valuable tool. Advertising has paved the way, but other promotional sectors are still lagging behind. In some, such as direct marketing, there is the potential to provide even greater detail on the individual consumer. In other sectors, such as PR or sponsorship, information is always likely to be fairly vague because there is no single channel of communication to provide a point of measurement. The sophisticated mass-media systems can always be used as a benchmark for what could be achieved with a given budget.

Implementing the Media Plan

Despite all this information, the critical decisions are still made by managerial judgment rather than number-crunching. In implementing the plan, there are two vital tactical decisions where trade-offs have to be made:

- **Coverage versus frequency**. Coverage is the proportion of the target population who have the opportunity to see the advertisement (or other promotion) once. Frequency is the number of exposures each consumer has to the promotion. A trade-off will have to be made between a campaign with wide coverage but single or relatively few exposures, and a concentrated campaign where a smaller proportion of the target population is more repeatedly exposed to the promotion. The trade-off will depend upon a view on the optimum number of exposures to achieve the communication objectives (and possibly some financial considerations from variable buying conditions).
- **Intensity versus continuity**. The campaign can either be concentrated into a short period for maximum intensity (known as a "burst" campaign), or spread out so that some continuity of contact is achieved with the consumer (known as a "drip" campaign).

This is another area where some former common wisdom is now being questioned. It used to be assumed that several exposures were necessary to influence consumers—advertising agencies sometimes still talk of "effective cover" or "four-plus cover" (referring to the need for schedules that offer at least four OTS to the target consumers). This in turn is based upon the idea that at fewer than four OTS consumers will still be familiarizing themselves with the ad and learning more of the message, and that at above four OTS

Figure 9.1 **Traditional Consumer Response Curve to an Advertisement**

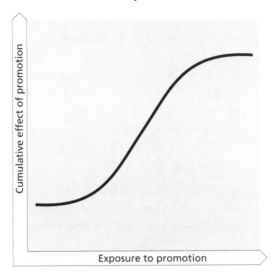

the learning tails off and the advertiser is getting diminishing returns. The response curve looks something like Figure 9.1 (above).

New views are beginning to emerge, however. First, alternative forms of promotion that operate on different assumptions are increasingly important. In direct mail, for instance, the accepted wisdom is that the consumer accepts or rejects the message at the first exposure, and even that the first few seconds are when the decision is made. This assumes a quite different response curve (see Figure 9.2 on page 195).

Second, more enlightened views on the role of branding in consumer behavior indicate that there is less point in making strenuous efforts to solicit a quick response, and more point in offering repeated reminders. This will work only if single exposures are effective, in line with the second of the two response curves above. As John Philip Jones of Syracuse University argues:

> There are . . . cases in which it is only possible to measure an effect on sales within the purchase cycle after the exposure of a minimum of two, or more commonly three or more advertisements. In explaining this phenomenon, the theory that three insertions are necessary to penetrate the consumer's psyche is the best explanation of how advertising communicates for unfamiliar new brands. With ongoing brands, however, single insertions operate as a reminder . . . and each can perfectly well work on its own.[2]

Figure 9.2 **Typical Consumer Response Curve to a Direct Mailing**

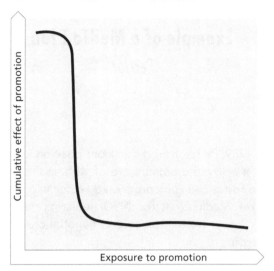

Usually, managers are too tempted by the idea of dominance and tend to waste money:

> It is universally agreed that diminishing returns set in when we pass a threshold level of advertising pressure, and this argues strongly that media schedules should be more dispersed as budgets are increased. In my judgment there should in fact be more dispersion than at present in the majority of schedules, although the Americans are not as great offenders as the British in this regard.[3]

This dispersion can be achieved over time, by a "drip" campaign, or over the population, achieving higher coverage figures. It could also, of course, be achieved by dispersing expenditures through different promotion mechanisms, such as some PR or sponsorship activity. Only when there is some news to be conveyed or some novelty in the communication is a more concentrated campaign with higher average OTS appropriate.

Such was the case with the relaunch of Perrier in the United Kingdom after its withdrawal over the benzene scare. The case study shows the media plan for the year and explains the media strategy that drove it.

Text continued on page 200, after the case study.

Example of a Media Plan
Perrier

•　　•　　•　　•　　•

At the end of 1989, Perrier held a dominant position in the U.K. mineral water market. It enjoyed a brand share of 48% in the sparkling sector and, taking the fast-growing uncarbonated sector into account, 25% of the total market. Media plans for 1990, featuring the award-winning "Alphabet" TV copy, were in place and negotiations with key media owners had begun.

Then came the infamous benzene incident. On February 14, 1990, traces of benzene were found in the water during a regular U.S. Food and Drug Administration check; minute though the traces were, they exceeded the FDA's maximum. The brand was immediately withdrawn from sale while investigations took place at the Perrier spring in Vergeze, France.

The withdrawal of the brand in the United Kingdom and its immediate disappearance from the nation's stores naturally had a dramatic effect on the annual advertising plans. The 1990 media plan, created by Leo Burnett Advertising, was scrapped, and the agency began implementing a new plan for the relaunch a few weeks later (though the final plan evolved in response to the changing circumstances in which the Perrier Company found itself).

Different media had to play different roles throughout the year. The only elements of the original media plan to survive the benzene incident were the large electronic "superlite" posters in London scheduled for May—which were booked by early January to secure the best possible terms given the heavy demand on these sites—and the traditional Christmas billboard, a single site taken each year in London at the junction of Warwick Road and Cromwell Road, one of the busiest traffic junctions in Europe.

The final 1990 media plan is reproduced in Figure 9.3 (see page 197). The rest of this case explains the various elements of the plan.

Figure 9.3 Perrier's Revised 1990 Media Plan

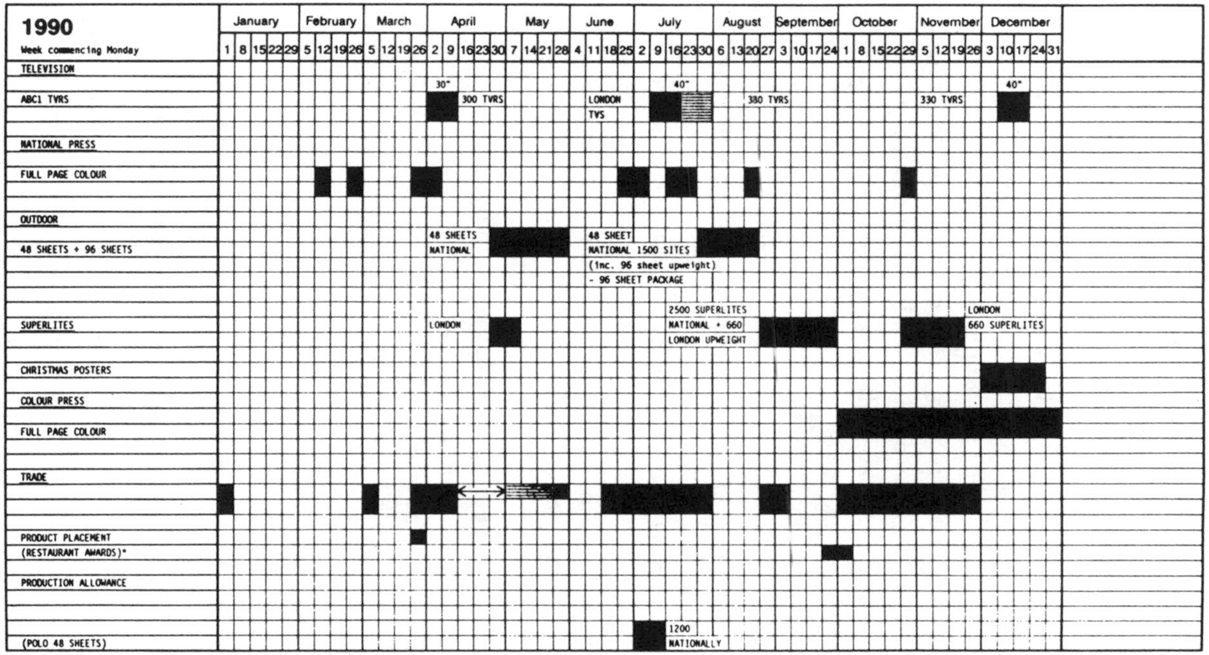

Source: Leo Burnett, London

Target Audience

The television audience measurement system leads to a bland description of the target audience for Perrier. ABC1 adults, a wide social grade categorization on the basis of occupation, is the closest audience research comes to the lengthy attitudinal and behavioral description of the Perrier user which, together with the more usual demographic descriptors, forms the media planning and creative target audience.

Media Rationale

This falls into two parts—immediately after the brand's withdrawal, and the brand's subsequent comeback and reappearance on the shelves.

At the withdrawal stage, the media rationale was to inform the consuming public and the trade what was going on. Leo Burnett used both national and trade press for this task. National press meant very short copy deadlines, essential given the fast-changing nature of the crisis, and the opportunity to strike the right tone. The agency also had to consider the very large amount of press coverage generated by the crisis. Putting Perrier's message into the medium carrying the continuing editorial story gave added impact. As every national paper had carried the story, advertisements were placed in every paper—with the ads all appearing on the same day to ensure maximum impact.

The use of trade press allowed the various critical trade sectors to receive a message tailored specifically for them. Naturally, the trade would be exposed to the consumer message as well, but that did not, in the agency's view, negate the use of the trade's own media vehicles.

The brand's comeback was to take place in early April. Again, the aim was to *inform* consumers and the trade that Perrier was back. A key objective from now on was to be ubiquitous. Perrier advertising had to be everywhere. It had to come back with style, and with confidence, as befits the brand leader. The comeback activity began with a teaser campaign in the national press and announcements in the trade press. This was followed by a 300 ABC1 adult TVR campaign on the ITV network, compressed into just five days. This "burst" was to leave no doubt that Perrier was back.

The advertising ("Helleau Again") broke Perrier's long-standing tradition that people should not feature in the ads for the brand. The media plan also broke with convention in its intensity. Perrier enjoys such a high awareness level and the advertising has such a reputation as being enjoyable that normal TV bursts have spread 300 to 400 TVRs over approximately four weeks. Given the 1990 circumstances, a far heavier weekly strike rate was decided on.

Outdoor advertising was selected to continue the TV campaign through large (48-sheet) sites, supported only in London by the prebooked superlite campaign. This activity targeted the key sales region with a message ("Eau 71, Eau 81") both topical (it coincided with the splitting of the "01" London telephone area code into 071 and 081) and pertinent to the capital.

Perrier's (and the market's) key sales period in any year is the summer. Pressure was maintained by using national newspapers and national posters throughout July and August, supplemented by television, this time in the vital London and TVS regions only.

Newspapers allowed the flexibility to run topical messages linked in to major events (Wimbledon: "Eau, I Say"; the British Open Golf Championship: "The Eaupen"). Outdoor posters provided ubiquity. Perrier advertising was everywhere. The large-size (48-sheet and 96-sheet) campaign was followed throughout September by the smaller superlites, this time nationally, although more weight was put on London.

Ubiquity was maintained through a heavyweight color press campaign—by now using more familiar and less topical Perrier imagery. The long copy dates of these titles, and a determination to reflect Perrier's status and image by buying only prime positions such as covers, whatever such a policy did to delay the start of this phase, meant that this element of the plan did not commence until October. It continued for six months into 1991.

Three further elements of the plan warrant comment. First, during the early part of the year the advertising agency was approached by several film companies offering "product placement" deals to ensure the brand's exposure during feature films. Most were rejected as too expensive for the visibility offered. One, with modest demands on the budget, offered enough quality to warrant proceeding.

Second, throughout the February/March crisis, and beyond, the agency's media department had worked very closely with Infoplan, Perrier's PR agency. The Perrier Restaurant Awards, which were supported by a limited amount of above-the-line advertising, are a good example of this cooperation.

Lastly, the confectioner Rowntree had approached Perrier for permission to run a pastiche of the Perrier "Eau" campaign for its brand Polo (or "Poleau"). The ads were to appear on 48-sheet posters in the summer. Leo Burnett believed this activity would have some beneficial effect on Perrier (which was happy to give permission) and it was included on the media plan for information only. As it happened, the Rowntree activity fitted very well into the overall Perrier plan.

CONCLUSION

The Perrier 1990 media plan is unusual in that it evolved out of very specific circumstances. For all that, it is a good example of a task-based media plan, using many media in combination to fulfill a number of key objectives:

- National press allowed advertising first to inform, then to entertain through highly topical treatments.
- Television gave impact to announce Perrier's comeback, and then reverted to its proven business-building role for the brand in its key sales regions. Thus the medium's key properties of impact and regionality were utilized to the full.
- Outdoor advertising extended the campaign over time, while literally putting the brand on to the streets.
- Magazines also added longevity, with the style and imagery that comes from a careful selection of both the most appropriate titles and the most appropriate positions within those titles.
- Trade press allowed contact with key customers in their own medium—keeping them informed of the brand's progress following withdrawal and then, as usual, promoting Perrier's many unique properties.

With clear objectives drawn from an overall strategy, the money spent in supporting brands can be thoughtfully deployed and very closely targeted.

———

Text continued from page 195.

Evaluating Promotional Expenditure

The last piece in the jigsaw is to monitor performance against objectives. There is no such thing as a good advertisement or brochure. Any promotion is worth only what it achieves against its specific objectives. This is not to play down the role of creativity in promotion—indeed, this is becoming more important to engage consumer attention. But creativity must always serve brand strategy, and not vice versa.

It follows that the promotional objectives are the base for all evaluation of promotion. The possible forms of evaluation divide into two basic phases, before the promotion is run (pretesting) and after (posttesting).

Pretesting

The purpose of pretesting is to determine whether the promotion solicits the desired response from a sample group of the target population. The testing tends to fall into two categories: checking the message or checking the impact. Ideally, both aspects are tested, because a promotion is clearly useless without both qualities.

Testing the message is usually done through qualitative discussion or "focus groups," facilitated by a skilled qualitative researcher. The consumers are shown the promotion, and then asked to discuss their reaction to it. The main purpose is to identify the consumers' "take-out"—that is, the single message that most struck them—which should clearly be in line with the communication objectives for the promotion. At this stage, the promotion will be presented in some form of mock-up, such as a storyboard (large hand-drawn visuals of the promotion) or animatics (simplified cartoon versions of film advertisements).

Testing the impact of the advertisement will help management assess how effective the promotion will be at cutting through the "noise" of commercial messages with which it will eventually have to compete for the consumer's attention. This is usually done through some sort of "folder test." The promotion is shown to the consumer as one among a series of promotions. A test is then run to see how many consumers can recall the promotion, and if so what they remember about it. This can be done quantitatively to produce ratings of impact effectiveness.

The problem with all pretesting is that in everyday life people do not often study a promotion and deliberate on it, nor do they flick through a series of promotions. Indeed, consumers often only half-notice promotions when they are really engaged in some other activity. The research community is divided over whether the inherent artificiality of pretesting invalidates the results. Another objection is that pretesting probes only conscious or "top-of-mind" responses, whereas we know that brand images are often stored in the subconscious or long-term memory.

Pretesting is nonetheless a valuable form of "exception testing" —that is, it will highlight obvious errors before they reach the wider market. Used discriminatingly, pretesting is bound to be better than guesswork.

Testing Afterwards

Testing after the promotion has run is much more common than pretesting, but it relies entirely on management having clear communications objectives against which to evaluate the promotion.

The most direct form of testing is to evaluate some form of *behavioral response*, such as sales, the return of a coupon asking for information, or entry into a competition. The research is either drawn from established market auditing mechanisms, such as those discussed in Chapter 4, or desk research at the point of response, such as the address for coupon mailings. These measures are most appropriate to forms of promotion with behavioral objectives, such as direct mail. The results can be clear, and reasonably reliable, as such promotions are often one-offs and other variables are unlikely to be interfering with the results. The problem, as already discussed, is assessing why consumers responded: Have their brand perceptions been influenced, or are they merely taking advantage of the promotion, with no intention of altering their long-term buying patterns?

Perhaps the most common forms of evaluation are those connected with awareness (usually referring to awareness of the brand) and recall (usually meaning recall of the promotion).

In FMCG markets in particular there are well-established systems for measuring *recall*, including so-called "reading-and-noting" research or DART (day after recall tests), where consumers are regularly asked which advertisements they remember. The results can be bought by any producer. The most thorough example is the idea of "adstock," a theory developed by the Leo Burnett agency. Adstock is the extent of recall of an advertisement in the target market; the effectiveness of any new bursts of advertising can be measured by their effect on adstock. The term "half-life" is used to denote the period it takes for the adstock to reach half its level after a burst of advertising; decay rates can then be modeled.

The principle behind such testing is that, if consumers remember the promotion, then there is an enhanced probability that they will purchase the brand. However, the value of recall testing is now being questioned for two reasons: First, there are contentious issues of research methodology, such as discrepancies between claimed and actual recall; second, our changing view of how promotion works is calling into doubt the link between recall, attitude, and purchase.

There are clearly circumstances in which recall will be an important measure. In a new brand launch or repositioning, a vital communication objective is bound to be the building up of familiarity with the brand. It could also be argued that recall is important in a "high involvement" purchase, but in such situations a direct form of promotion such as a mass mailing would probably be more appropriate than advertising.

A direct problem with recall as an evaluation mechanism is that a company really wants the consumer to remember the brand, not the promotion. This is overcome by measuring brand *awareness*. This requires special research to produce figures for either "spontaneous awareness" (where the brand is recalled when the only prompt given is a mention of the product category) or "prompted awareness" (where the consumer is shown a list of all the brands in the category and asked which they know). Spontaneous awareness is more desirable, as it means the brand is at "front of mind," but the wise manager will realize that front of mind is often not what drives purchase decisions; indeed, a brand could be front of mind because it is actively disliked. The same caveats apply to measurement of awareness as to recall—it is undoubtedly useful but will not explain the full picture of brand images.

From all that has been said about the way promotion works, it follows that *image* measurement is the best way of evaluating promotions other than those directed at behavioral responses. The problem in the eyes of many managers is that image is a long-term measure. The results of a promotion take a long time to show through, and when an image shift is detected it cannot be ascribed to the single variable of the promotion.

In recent years there has been significant development in the measurement of image attributes over long periods. *Tracking studies*, which run at regular intervals, were pioneered by the British advertising research company Millward Brown. Clearly, such studies must begin with a detailed knowledge of the important brand attributes, which requires some initial research into the nature of the brand and its competitive positioning. The tracking study results can then be compared with patterns of promotional activity, as well as with norms for particular markets or segments, and some idea of the brand's standing in the long-term memory of the consumers gained.

Image measurement is produced in the form of either perceptual maps (see the case study on Midland's Vector account in Chapter 6 and the discussion on mapping in Chapter 5) or ratings on specific variables. The Visa case study shows how in the advertising-sensitive credit card market the brand position is measured by tracking responses to simple rating questions. By plotting results against bursts of advertising, Visa can begin to evaluate its new advertising approach.

However thorough the evaluation program, the results should not be mistaken for fact—they will always be only best estimates of what is happening, and causes and effects can never be linked beyond the status of probability.

In summary, the evaluation of promotion activity is probably best divided into three catagories:

- *A straightforward check on how the money was spent in terms of media planning: Who saw the promotion and how many times.*
- *Simple behavioral measures, especially where the promotion is likely to provoke this type of response. It must be remembered that behavioral responses do not necessarily indicate any shift in the image or attitudinal aspects of brand-building.*
- *Long-term measurement of image and attitude attributes.*

Text continues on page 209, after the case study.

Tracking Studies and New Lines of Credit
Visa

● ● ● ● ●

The credit card industry, with its intangible products and service orientation, is heavily dependent on consumer perception. The role of the advertising agency in portraying the correct consumer imagery, and in positioning the entire brand, is particularly crucial. In 1985 the three major competitors—Mastercard, Visa, and American Express—were aggressively vying for the biggest share of consumer usage with different advertising campaigns that produced varied results:

- Mastercard's "So Worldly, So Welcome" campaign was successful in providing upscale international imagery.
- Visa's "All You Need" failed to provide a focused image with strong impact.
- American Express's advertising continued to portray prestige (recognition) via "Do You Know Me?"

To assess Visa's performance, management utilized tracking studies. These measured Visa against both Mastercard and American Express on certain attributes: best overall card; accepted by more merchants; and best card for personal and family shopping, personal travel and entertainment, international travel, and business travel and entertainment. The results of the studies are shown in Table 9.1.

Figure 9.4 exhibits the exact percentage of consumers who responded to each card as the best overall. Although some companies would have been satisfied that they were judged as the best overall, management at Visa looked at the less positive ratings from Table 9.1 and concluded the following:

- Visa and Mastercard were viewed by consumers as functionally identical with retail orientations.
- American Express was seen as more appropriate for business and international travel; it was the "gold standard" in terms of prestige.

Figure 9.4 **Cardholder Tracking Study: Best Overall Card, 1985–1990**

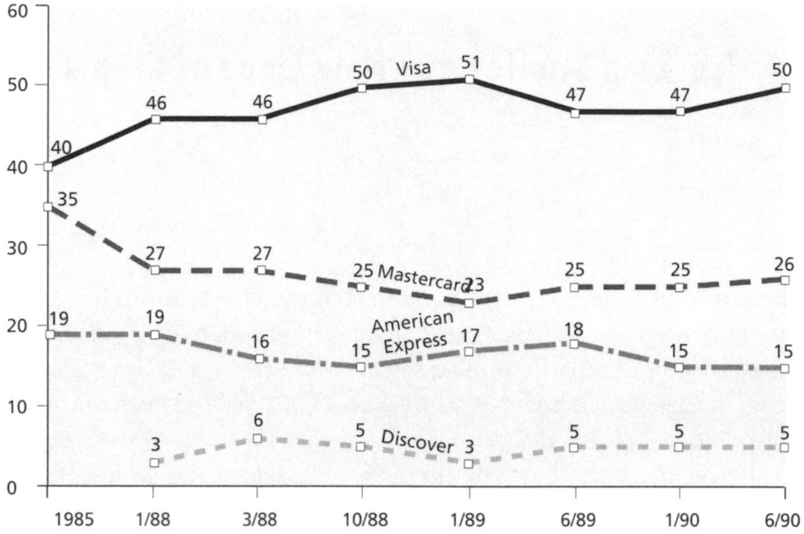

Source: Silney, Rosenberg & Associates.

Table 9.1 **Visa's 1985 Tracking Study**

	Visa vs. Mastercard	Visa vs. Amex
	% POINT DIFFERENCE	
Best overall card	+5	+21
Accepted by more merchants	+7	+7
Best card for . . .		
Personal and family shopping	+1	+38
Personal travel and entertainment	+4	+9
International travel	+1	−59
Business travel and entertainment	+2	−34

Developing a New Advertising Strategy

These conclusions led Visa management to seek a new advertising strategy. They went to BBDO Worldwide, one of the world's largest advertising agencies, to develop advertising that would separate Visa from Mastercard in regard to (a) user imagery and (b) performance imagery. To establish the correct advertising message, a strategic analysis of Visa's retail characteristics and imagery had to be made. The results of this study pointed the way forward.

Visa's retail characteristics were viewed as both an asset and a liability:

- Guaranteed strength of daily transactions
- Limited opportunity to upgrade image
- Vulnerable to competition with more desirable images in retail

It was decided that a unified image was necessary in order to accomplish the following:

- Break parity perceptions
- Increase the impact of advertising dollars
- Make Visa less susceptible to technological changes
- Build brand loyalty and insulation

With the strategic considerations in place, BBDO devised a new Visa advertising campaign. The campaign was introduced in October 1985 and featured merchants (i.e., retail establishments, restaurants, etc.) that the viewer would expect to accept American Express, but in fact did not. In every case, the advertisement praised the establishment but finished with the line ". . . but they don't take American Express." The sign-off was "Visa. It's everywhere you want to be."

Campaign Results on Visa's Performance

To measure its advertising effectiveness, Visa utilized specific advertising tests and continued tracking studies through the research firm Silney, Rosenberg & Associates. Figure 9.4 (see page 206) exemplifies how Visa increased its rating as best overall card from 40% to 50% in the years 1985 to 1990. During this same period, Mastercard's and American Express's ratings decreased from 35% to 26% and 19% to 15%, respectively, owing to Visa's improved image via advertising and to new entrant Discover. Quite impressively, Visa commanded a 2:1 lead over Mastercard and more than 3:1 over American Express in this category, and Visa's card volume market share moved from 45.7% in 1988 to 49.5% in 1990.

Figure 9.5 **Tracking Study Comparison: Visa vs. Mastercard, 1985 and 1991**

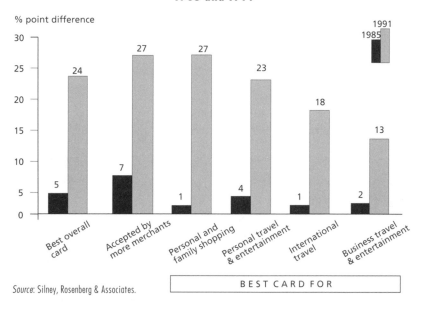

Source: Silney, Rosenberg & Associates.

BEST CARD FOR

Figure 9.6 **Tracking Study Comparison: Visa vs. Amex, 1985 and 1991**

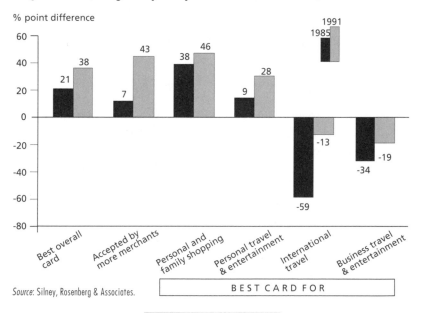

Source: Silney, Rosenberg & Associates.

BEST CARD FOR

The most recent tracking study by Silney, Rosenberg & Associates, conducted in 1991, reveals noticeable improvements in each category compared with the 1985 study. Figure 9.5 (see page 208) graphically illustrates Visa's dramatic improvement compared with Mastercard, while Figure 9.6 (page 208) represents Visa's perceptual gains over American Express. Although Visa still lags behind American Express in the areas of international travel and business travel and entertainment, it nevertheless improved greatly in these areas from 1985 to 1991.

CONCLUSION

In 1990 statistics indicated that Visa's overall transaction volume was $158 billion. This was 70% higher than that of either Mastercard or American Express. Visa was clearly the market share leader with 225 million cardholders, 8 million merchant locations, and 22,000 member financial institutions.

Visa's advertising strategy has successfully elevated the brand's image on key dimensions. As a result, Visa's business has been insulated from both current competitors and new entries into the category.

Text continued from page 204.

SUMMARY

Spending on brands mainly consists of promotions. It is not possible to use any of the well-known formulas available to decide optimum expenditure. Most of these are ratios between expenditures and some other market indicator, and trends in the ratios will not yield specific information.

Once the budget is determined, quantitative measurement techniques can measure the weight of the campaign that is being purchased. This enables informed decisions to be made on the strategy and structure of any promotional campaign. These measures deal with the quantity of promotion. To assess the quality (the effectiveness of the message), there are well-established pretesting services. Image tracking studies are also becoming more common and enable companies to correlate changes in the images of their brands with bursts of promotional activity.

These measures are useful managerial aids, but they are not accurate diagnoses. The evaluation of brand expenditure still depends partly on the judgment of those who know the brand, its owners, and the market.

REFERENCES

1. Simon Broadbent, *The Advertising Budget* (London: IPA/NCT Publications, 1989), pp. 73–84.

2. John Philip Jones, *What's in a Name? Advertising and the Concept of Brands* (New York: Free Press, 1986), p. 239.

3. Jones, *What's in a Name?* p. 188.

Brand Valuation

. . . .

Brand marketers in FMCG markets have long referred to their "brand equity," using a financial term to indicate their certainty that the brand is one of the company's principal assets. The "equity" in question is the perception in the minds of customers that any established brand builds up through years of use, advertising, and distribution. Marketers are well accustomed to the fact that an established brand's chief defense against new competitors is its familiarity. This residual image or personality will not disappear quickly, any more than memories of real people or events will, and it can therefore be treated like any of the company's more tangible assets, such as money or manufacturing plant. It is the result of past investment and if well managed is almost certain to continue to produce revenue in the future.

In recent years, the idea of brand equity has been taken literally, and the value of brands has started to appear in company accounts as an intangible asset. This is the issue that has done most to bring brands into the headlines in the 1990s.

> Valuing "intangible" items such as brands is set to become an uncontrollable craze in the coming months. . . . Many more examples of this accounting fashion are set to appear—and they will push the boundaries of companies' accounts, and readers' credulity, far further than at present, the accountants believe. . . . Companies may choose what intangible assets they value and how they do it, but they should at least be aware that they may be opening a Pandora's box in the process.[1]

The fuss was triggered in 1988 by a series of acquisition battles. The contentious issue was the inclusion in the valuation of the whole company of a monetary value for its established brands. From a strategic viewpoint, it was quite clear that the would-be acquirers were chasing these brand names as the best way of achieving growth in maturing markets. They took the view that it would be either impossible or prohibitively expensive to launch new brands into these markets, because of the strength of established brands. The debate over how this should be reflected in the financial statements of a company has indeed opened up a Pandora's box. American regulations discourage brand valuation, but because of different accounting standards the issue has been thoroughly aired in the United Kingdom. In the coming years it will be an important issue in brand markets around the world.

The Development of Brand Valuation Practices

In the mid-1980s a few companies outside the United States began to include brand valuations in their balance sheets, without attracting much attention. Possibly the first was Rupert Murdoch, who in 1984 included a valuation for "publishing titles" in the balance sheet of his Australian-based News Corporation. News Corporation was paying a substantial premium for companies over and above their tangible assets, which represented the almost guaranteed earning power of established media titles, licenses, or franchises. At the time, the premium was classified as an intangible asset described as "goodwill," which had to be written off in the profit and loss account of the single year of purchase or over several years as depreciated goodwill in the balance sheet.

Given that News Corporation made several such acquisitions in the year, the writing off of all these premiums was drastically distorting the balance sheet and profit and loss accounts; in particular, it was producing a bottom-line loss and failing to increase the asset base of the company by the amount it had invested. News Corporation's argument for including the premiums as an asset on the balance sheet was that the assets it had bought would produce revenue for more than one year, and so the cost should be regarded as an investment, not as a single expense item. It argued that newspaper titles and television licenses were identifiable assets, capable of producing revenue in their own right. Furthermore, they passed the acid test of "separability," another key element in defining an asset—they could be transferred to other parties independently of the other assets of the business, "produced" by the fixed assets of another owner, and still retain their earning power in the market. By treating these titles and licenses as assets on the balance sheet at their true current (1984) value, they strengthened the balance sheet, increased shareholders' funds, and provided a more accurate representation of the total assets of the company.

In 1985 the food, toiletries, and household brands group Reckitt & Colman was one of the first U.K. quoted companies to incorporate a value attributable to brands in the balance sheet, following the acquisition of the Airwick Group from Ciba-Geigy. Of the price paid of £165 million, Reckitt & Colman took £55.8 million of assets to its 1985 balance sheet in recognition of the Airwick brands. Then in 1988 Grand Metropolitan decided to include £558 million in its balance sheet, recognizing that a large part of the sum paid for Heublein was attributable to the Smirnoff vodka brand. Its balance sheet was thus strengthened, something which proved vital in the following year when it successfully acquired Pillsbury for $5.5 billion.

So far, the figure shown on the balance sheet reflected the actual purchase costs of newly acquired brands, and the acquirers had merely sidestepped the requirement to write off goodwill in the year of purchase (which in some cases was a new requirement). This had taken place mainly in Britain. In the United States, accounting regulations prohibit the revaluation of assets on the balance sheet; although American companies write off the goodwill of a brand name over 40 years, the IRS ignores such amortization. In other countries goodwill had been regularly capitalized and depreciated over fixed periods.

The event that brought the issue of brand valuation into the public arena was the publication of the 1988 accounts of the British food brands company Rank Hovis McDougall. This was a first in two ways. First, the valuation included brands that the company already owned, and in some cases had built up itself over several decades. Second, the valuation of these brands was carried out independently, by the consulting company Interbrand (more details on their method of valuation are given later in this chapter).

At the time, RHM was the subject of a hostile takeover bid of £1.78 billion (15.5 times RHM's 1988 earnings) from Goodman Fielder Wattie, an Australian baking group. The bid came at a time when RHM's balance sheet (i.e., its net assets figure) was relatively weak, after having itself acquired a major food company and written off much of the goodwill. Therefore RHM took the opportunity to include its brands in the balance sheet, in effect treating them as a capital item that would be depreciated, with the figure of £678 million being shown as an intangible asset. The defense document detailed the strength of RHM's brands in their various sectors; the weight and consistency of marketing support that had been deployed; the buoyant sales and profit trends, etc. RHM concluded by stating that Goodman Fielder Wattie had, in its opinion, failed to offer shareholders full value for its brands.

The effect of capitalizing the valuation attached to RHM's brands was to transform RHM's balance sheet. The figure of £678 million for intangible assets compared with £463 million for tangible assets, and net assets rose from £265 million in 1987 to £979 million in 1988. RHM managed to see off its hostile bidder and very shortly afterward used its new balance sheet strength to purchase Nabisco's U.K. breakfast cereals brands.

This pioneering move by RHM drew attention to the off-balance sheet valuation of brands that was continuing in the mergers and acquisitions field on both sides of the Atlantic. In Europe, the bitter takeover battle for Britain's Rowntree confectionery company contributed to the interest. Two Swiss-based giants, Nestlé and Suchard, wanted to strengthen their position in the important U.K. confectionery market and reasoned that the only strategy was to acquire existing brands. Eventually Nestlé won the day, but it had to pay £2.5 billion for Rowntree, even though it had a net asset value of only some £300 million. Rowntree's market capitalization (the value of all the shares in the company) was only about £1 billion when the bid was first launched, even though the shares should reflect the current market value of the company. Clearly, Nestlé took a different view of the value of the company's brands from that of the financial community.

Most cases of brand valuation are being used for the purposes of valuing companies, with the balance sheet adjustments restricted principally to the United Kingdom and Australia because of accounting regulations. In these countries, it is almost becoming normal practice to show brands on the balance sheet. The biggest company to take this step so far is the liquor company Guinness, which since 1989 has included on its balance sheet a figure of well over £1 billion for recently acquired brands such as Johnnie Walker, Gordon's, Bell's, Dewars, and White Horse, as well as valuations for its 20%

stake in the French brands company Louis Vuitton Moët Hennessy, which includes brands like Christian Dior, Givenchy, Hennessy, and Dom Perignon. Perhaps the most controversial was the £175 million valuation placed by marketing services group WPP on its J. Walter Thompson and Hill & Knowlton names (agencies in the fields of advertising and publicity).

In the United States Philip Morris was prepared to pay four times the book value of Kraft when it purchased the company for $12.9 billion and later paid a similar premium for Suchard, the loser in the battle for Rowntree. As an American company, however, it cannot alter its balance sheet but must write off the goodwill over a period of 40 years. Pressure has begun to grow on the U.S. government to change these requirements so American companies face the same conditions as other corporations when acquiring brand companies.

New accounting approaches to brand valuation on the British model look set to spread to the United States. Current American accounting standards discourage the inclusion of brand valuations in financial statements, but in late 1990 legislation was proposed to allow companies to offset advertising and some other marketing expenditures against tax over several years, a move that recognized the relationship between brands building and long-run returns on investments. While the brand marketer might be delighted that the brand value is at last being recognized for its huge potential, the whole issue raises as many problems as it solves.

Reasons for Brand Valuation

It can be seen that brand valuation started almost by accident, as a defensive reaction to weakening balance sheets. Very quickly, however, it was realized that brands do indeed have a significant value, and that valuation in fact benefits everybody by giving a true picture of a company's worth. Any brand company might now find itself wanting (or being forced) to undertake a full valuation of its brands. Initial enthusiasm for such a project may well focus on the benefits to the company.

Balance Sheet Benefits
Bank lending criteria and stock exchange rules still rely on balance sheet strength. By capitalizing brands, and reducing the goodwill write-off to reserves, company balance sheets are left in a much stronger position. One obvious effect is that gearing ratios (borrow-

ings expressed as a percentage of a company's net assets) are much reduced. As a result, banks may agree to larger loans based on a more favorable view of the security of the assets.

The benefits of balance sheet strength in relation to the mergers and acquisitions field have already been discussed. In a company where the majority of the shareholder value (as assessed by a potential acquirer) is in "hidden" or intangible assets like brands, a brand valuation on the balance sheet can be of enormous defensive value (raising the price for the potential purchaser) and a potential lever when the company is on the acquisition trail itself and comparative company values are vital.

Financial Market Information

The Nestlé bid for Rowntree raised questions about whether the London stock exchange understood branding well enough to value the company properly. One possible benefit of brand valuation is therefore that the financial markets gain a more accurate picture of the value of companies. This would allow more efficient transactions in the areas of investment in companies, trading in their stocks, and mergers and acquisitions, where a suitable price could be better determined in advance.

Using Brands as Separate Financial Entities

There is an increasing trend toward separating a company's brands from its other assets, and using them as financial entities to be traded. Applications include the licensing of a brand, either internally or to third parties, so that its trademark or identity can be used elsewhere. This will obviously be of benefit in growth initiatives implemented through joint ventures, such as franchising arrangements, or more specific line extensions or entry into new geographical markets. Increasingly brands are also used as collaterals on loans, or are even employed in sale and lease-back arrangements to achieve tax benefits. In the words of one of the experts in this area, John Murphy of the consulting company Interbrand, it "seems quite certain that the major long-term impact of brand valuation will be in these areas rather than in the specialist area of balance sheet repair."[2]

Management Information

Although brand valuation began as a balance sheet exercise, it soon became clear that the information generated in the process of valuation was of enormous value to both marketing and general management. Many companies have never made a wide-ranging assessment of their full portfolio of brands simultaneously, and brand valuation is therefore a desirable exercise in its own right. The very nature of brand valuation, in that it needs to assess brand profits and the prospect of future profit earnings, means that markets, positioning, trends, market share, and all other relevant factors are inevitably taken into consideration.

By identifying brand profits, a detailed brand-by-brand comparison can be made. Brand strategy decisions can be sensibly made only by taking a view of what the brand stands for and how this may be translated into future profit-earning potential. Brand valuation can help in resource allocation between competing brands in a portfolio by assessing the effect of various brand strategies on the resulting "worth" of the brand. Differing strategic options, such as whether to spread marketing resources equally among all the brands or to focus on one or two key brands in the short term, can be assessed against the current brand valuation and some attempt can be made to model the impact of these strategic decisions on future brand values. Brand valuation thus aids management to focus on just these issues and reduce "wasted" advertising expenditures.

Internal Management Benefits

One benefit has gone largely ignored; it has been highlighted only by brands guru Stephen King:

> In my view much the most important reason for putting a value on brands . . . [is] . . . *to proclaim the purpose of the company*—a signal that the health and development of the company brand and its product brands is the key long-term objective. This signal is partly to outsiders—analysts, shareholders, journalists, government, etc.—but more important maybe to employees at all levels—a sort of mission statement, one of several signals that company leadership can use to inspire people and help them understand the corporate ethos.[3]

This internal management benefit will be of value only if it adds to the existing knowledge about a brand, and in many cases this may be so. It is possible that a complete brand valuation or "brand audit" will bridge the gap between two forms of analysis, or two sets of information, which have traditionally never met in many companies: short-term financial assessment and long-term strategic analysis. David Allen, a British finance professor who was previously finance director of Cadbury Schweppes, holds out hope that brand valuation can move financial statements away from what he calls "steward-ship reporting" to "pro-active financial management, which involves forward-looking subjective judgements, often based on intangible values, i.e., on gains which are as yet unrealized and thus do not find their way into a set of financial accounts."[4] He suggests that such a system would be able to relate short-term financial perfor-mance to long-term brand strategic health.

The many benefits to a company of a brand valuation seem bound to help the practice become more widespread. However, there are many critical issues on which commentators are fiercely divided.

Issues in Brand Valuation

Much of the debate about brand valuation is not about brands at all but about complex accounting issues. The biggest issue, and the most obvious, is how a brand should or can be valued, if at all. Closely related, though, are a host of other questions, many of them fundamental in their own right. These will take many years and many people to resolve; the purpose of this brief discussion is to raise awareness of some of these problems in brand valuation.

What Is the Function of the Balance Sheet?
The balance sheet's traditional role is to give a snapshot of the investments (or equity) that have been put into a company, and how they are currently tied up. This places the emphasis on objective reporting. Valuation, on the other hand, is subjective, being deter-mined by what anybody will pay for something. The accounting profession is by no means agreed that balance sheets should be redefined to include subjective elements and become *ipso facto* a statement of their valuation.

Current versus Historical Cost in the Balance Sheet
Related to the first point is the issue of how costs should be shown in the balance sheet. Assets have traditionally been shown at the historic cost of acquiring them (which is fact) rather than at the current costs of selling or replacing them (which is judgment). If assets were decreasing in value, an amount was taken off every year for depreciation, whereas nothing was added by way of revaluation if the assets appreciated (in line with the accounting principle of

conservatism). In recent years, this has been upset in particular by property, which has appreciated considerably over short periods, and many companies have adopted current cost accounting for their balance sheets. The brand valuation debate confuses this matter further on two counts. First, any brand valuation will make the balance sheet more likely to be an unsatisfactory mixture of costs and values. Second, the valuation can be based on costs only if it has been acquired; if the brand has been nurtured by the company over more than a few years, it will probably be impossible to calculate the costs that went into building the brand, in terms of advertising, production, staff time, etc.

Consistency of Balance Sheets

One of the prime purposes of a balance sheet is to help financial markets compare one company with another. For this, consistency is required, both over time in the same company and between companies. At present, there is total inconsistency in whether companies include brand valuations, and if so how the valuation is calculated. This clearly diminishes the value of the balance sheet.

Handling the Depreciation or Appreciation of Brands

Goodwill has traditionally been written off on balance sheets, either over an extended period of up to 40 years (as in the United States) or in one year (as in the United Kingdom). This implies that brands, like more tangible assets, tend to depreciate over time and will eventually lose all their value—that is, they have a finite life. This argument could be upheld using the product life cycle (although it would be impossible to determine the correct time span for the brand's life in advance), but in fact all the evidence points toward the longevity and perhaps immortality of well-managed brands. If they are more likely to appreciate, then they will clearly need to be revalued periodically and the revaluation premium shown on either the balance sheet or the annual profit and loss account. Again, practice differs: RHM declared that its brands were not to be revalued in either direction in its financial statements, whereas Guinness has declared that it will review the value of its brands annually and take any provision or amortization through the profit and loss account.

Separability

For a brand valuation to be meaningful, a boundary must be drawn between the brand and the rest of the company's assets. The issue of separability is a complex one in the case of a brand. Clearly, the brand is dependent for its existence upon the plant in which it is produced, the advertising that helps shape consumers' perception of it, the people who manage it, the trucks that distribute it, and even the retailers (in another company) who display it in their stores. How many of these should be included in the valuation? The question is almost impossible to answer, although some attempts are made—as, for example, when a brand is licensed for franchising purposes. The most problematic valuation to date is the £175 million value placed by WPP on its J. Walter Thompson and Hill & Knowlton brand names. It is arguable that these companies are reliant upon people, assets that can disappear within a few months. In the words of the leading academic in this area, Patrick Barwise, "It is not presumably suggested that anyone would pay £175 million merely for the use of these brand names. . . . Nor is it presumably suggested that the economic value of WPP without these names would be £175 million less than with them."[5]

How to Include the Management of Brands?

Brands are not just perceptions in the marketplace; they are also the output of skilled and experienced management within a company. To some extent, this is a powerful factor in the resistance of established brands to attack from new entrants. Stephen King describes two types of "strategic value" of a brand: first, "barriers to entry values depend critically on the continuity and skills of the people in the company and on the leadership and company ethos that keep them there"; the second type he describes as "competition values . . . a judgment of the market strength that Nestlé would have in the longer term if combined with Rowntree, and conversely their vulnerability if Jacobs Suchard were allowed to buy the company."[6]

Such factors are clearly important in determining the strength of a brand, but they are almost impossible to value quantitatively in anything but the most subjective manner.

It should now be clear that the benefits of brand valuation to a company are derived only at considerable cost to those who need to gather information from the company's financial statements. In the words of Patrick Barwise:

A successful, established brand undoubtedly has economic value, in the sense that a company is worth more with such a brand than without it. . . . However, there are very major practical difficulties in establishing what a brand is worth. In most cases the value of the brand is impossible to separate from that of the rest of the business. . . . Any valid assessment of the brand's future profitability involves many inherently subjective judgments about marketing factors such as competitive market position, overall market prospects, and the quality and value of marketing support. . . . These subjective judgments mean that there is a fundamental conflict between economic validity and the degree of objectivity needed for financial accounting.[7]

Methods of Brand Valuation

By its very nature, the whole topic of the best way of valuing brands remains very subjective. The usual accounting methods of identifying values can be employed, but each has its drawbacks.

Historic Cost

One obvious basis for valuation is the sum of all the investment that has gone into a brand: promotion, R&D, distribution, etc. In the case of recently acquired brands, where the purpose of valuation is to bolster reserves depleted by writing off of goodwill, this is fairly straightforward. The problems here lie principally in identifying which costs should be allocated to a brand already owned by the company—should management time be allocated, and if so how? It is quite clear that a brand's success is the output of all sorts of combined efforts within the company, which could never be accurately costed. Even if they could, the historic cost method suffers the drawback that it does not necessarily reflect the current value, because it takes no account of the quality or output of past investment, only the quantity. By this method, failed and less successful brands can be attributed a high value even though the future potential earnings do not look healthy.

Current or Replacement Cost

Current cost is equal to what a third party would pay for a brand, which is in turn theoretically equivalent to what it would cost to establish the brand from scratch. However, brands are rarely traded, and there is no useful market for brands that would help in identifying the correct value. A more realistic view would be to look at the current value of the brand in terms of the profits it generated over the previous year (or perhaps a weighted average of the last few years). While this may give some indication of its current value, it does not begin to address issues related to its future profitability. Because current cost accounting is inherently subjective, being concerned with value rather than costs, it epitomizes all the problems inherent in brand valuation.

Market-based Valuations

A theoretical answer might be to assess a brand's strength on the basis of market-derived data such as market share, awareness, or performance in image or preference surveys. This would be almost impossible to implement and would produce unreliable data. One could always question a market share figure on the grounds of market definition, and there is no consistent evidence on the relationship between profitability and factors such as market share, penetration, or repeat purchase rates, as has been observed earlier in this book. Valuable though all these market data are, they are not of any worth in calculating a financial value for a brand.

Future Earnings Potential

It is tempting to attempt to calculate the future earnings or cash-flow stream of a brand, since this is its actual value to its owner. This has been the most widespread method to date, usually taking the form of an extrapolation of current earnings, discounted to present values. One of the drawbacks with this method is that an assumption of future cash flows does not take into account any changes in the market that might occur. A new competitor might enter the arena, or there might be a health scare (as in the case of Perrier), which would dramatically, albeit temporarily, reduce the brand's cash-generating capabilities. Furthermore, cash flows may rely not solely on the brand, but on the marketing and management skills of the brand guardians and also on the distribution system for the brand. Changes in market conditions and technologies can easily wipe out brands altogether. Lastly, there is a problem in separability, in that cash flows derived from the brand are inextricably tied up with the cash flows derived from other brands within the same company's production, marketing, and distribution system.

Incremental Value of a Brand Against Generic Competitors

A common internal measure of brand equity is the price premium a brand commands over one competitor, and it has been suggested that this extra margin could be the basis of balance sheet valuation as well.[8] While the added value of a brand is often reflected in a superior margin, the size of that margin is not a reliable indicator of long-term profitability, let alone of strategic position. This method also undervalues mass-market brands that profit mainly from the volume of sales and could overvalue niche brands with small market share.

The Interbrand Method

These various valuation techniques are unsuitable largely because they omit some of the key factors contributing to a brand's strength, and they fail to accommodate the uncertainty inherent in any market situation. The consulting firm Interbrand has produced and publicized a valuation method that attempts to balance all the factors involved and to recognize both factual and subjective inputs. This valuation method was employed by RHM in its mold-breaking 1988 valuation, and it is now being more widely employed than any other approach.[9]

Interbrand's methodology combines hard factual information such as market share, sales, and profits with more subjective judgments about a brand's "strength" in order to determine brand-related profit. The basis is the brand's current level of profitability, expressed as a weighted average of earnings over recent years. An earnings multiplier based on the brand strength assessment is applied to a brand's profitability in order to determine the brand's value. The stronger the brand, the greater the multiplier, as a stronger brand is expected to generate more years of future income. The maximum multiplier is 20, as 20 years is assumed to be a reasonable time horizon. The valuation assumes that the brand will continue in its "existing use"; change of ownership or major line extensions would be excluded from the valuation.

The multiplier to be applied to brand profit is made up from a composite of seven weighted factors, against each of which the brand is scored:

1. **Leadership** inevitably depends upon how the market is defined, but its inclusion reflects the commonly held view that

a leader is more valuable because of its "market power" (as discussed in Chapter 1).

2. **Stability** (or longevity) is often related to leadership.
3. **Market** gives preference to markets that are large and stable, such as food and drink, and are less prone to turbulence driven by either fast-changing fashions or technological innovation.
4. **Internationality** gives brands more power both globally and in their home markets because of their perceived international status (see Chapter 11). Obviously, a global presence also offers some economies of scale in either production or marketing, and an insulation against regional upsets in markets.
5. The long-term **trend** for the brand in terms of its relevance to consumers is assessed, with the view that those that remain contemporary in the eyes of the consumer have the most value.
6. **Support** for a brand is equally significant. Not just the total expenditure and consistency of that investment is measured; some attempt is made to assess the quality.
7. A registered trademark or some other **protection** in common law would count toward a brand's strength.

Table 10.1 shows the seven criteria, the maximum that can be scored for each factor, and a hypothetical valuation of Kellogg's and Budweiser.[10] The figure for brand value which this produces is as satisfactory as any. Given the method that is employed, management should use the valuation as a guide and comparative measure, rather than as an absolute truth. With such qualifications, the worth of the valuation exercise should be substantial.

Table 10.1 **Brand Strength Profiles for Familiar Brands**

Criteria	Maximum score	Kellogg's score	Budweiser score
Leadership	25	22	18
Stability	15	14	12
Market	10	8	8
Internationality	25	22	15
Trend	10	8	7
Support	10	8	8
Protection	5	5	3
TOTAL	100	87	71

Source: Interbrand.

Conclusion

The brand valuation debate will continue for some years, especially as American brands companies feel increasingly disadvantaged relative to their European counterparts in terms of balance sheet adjustments made possible by the inclusion of brand values. That brands have a value, realizable in economic terms, is not an element in the debate; the earning power of brands over the long term and the "sales momentum" and "market power" of an established brand are now widely appreciated. The contentious issue is how this value should be calculated and how it should then be used.

To most informed but nonspecialist observers, the inclusion of brand valuations on balance sheets seems something like a finance director's trick. While brands are a real part of a company's value, their valuation remains particularly subjective for two reasons: First, brands are enormously complex and intangible items, with no fixed base from which a value can be calculated; second, there is no established market for trading brands, as there is for property, and there are therefore no norms in terms of valuation. Once balance sheets include brands, they may as well include valuations placed on other intangibles such as human resources; objectivity will soon disappear altogether, rendering them useless for comparison through time or between companies. The key players in this public debate are the accountancy bodies, and their response to pressures and arguments on inclusion and valuation method will eventually settle the argument.

If brand valuation does have a future, as it surely must, it is mainly outside the formal financial reporting system, and within the management information system. As an analytical tool akin to market research, contributing to managerial decisions but not replacing them, it may well prove invaluable.

SUMMARY

In recent years, the balance sheets of several companies have included valuations for a brand's intangible assets. The objective in most cases has been to strengthen the balance sheet, often for acquisition battles, but it reflects the fact that brands are often the major part of a company's intangible assets or goodwill, more usually only valued when a company is purchased. The practice is beleaguered by debate on accounting principles. Should a balance sheet include valuations based on judgment rather than costs? Should brands be revalued and appreciated or depreciated like other assets? What is the best valuation method for brands? The debate will be prolonged, but the practice of valuation would appear to be here to stay for the following reasons:

- Brands are significant intangible assets, and a realistic appraisal of the company needs to include them.
- The exercise of brand valuation has internal management benefits, allowing the company to audit its brands as a starting point for strategy formulation.

REFERENCES

1. *Financial Times*, (December 5, 1988), p. 7.
2. John Murphy, *Brand Strategy* (Englewood Cliffs, N.J.: Prentice Hall, 1990), p. 152.
3. Stephen King, "Brands on the Balance Sheet," in *The Brand Is the Business*, Economist Conference Report, London (March 1989).
4. David Allen, "The Value of Brands: Wrong Figures Lead to Wrong Decisions," *Financial Times* (December 18, 1990), p. 12.
5. Patrick Barwise et al., "Brands as 'Separable Assets,'" *Business Strategy Review* (Summer 1990), p. 51.
6. King, "Brands on the Balance Sheet."
7. Barwise, "Brands as 'Separable Assets,'" p. 51.
8. M. Mullen and A. Mainz, "Brands, Bids and Balance Sheets: Putting a Value on Protected Products," *Acquisitions Monthly* (April 1988), p. 27.
9. For a fuller description see John Murphy, *Brand Valuation* (London: Hutchinson Business Books, 1989).
10. Tom Blackett, "The Valuation of Brands," *Market Intelligence and Planning* (January 1991), p. 33.

The Globalization of Brands

•　•　•　•　•　•　•　•　•　•　•　•　•　•

Major brand companies frequently inform the media that globalization is their most pressing challenge. The year 1990 saw a series of acquisitions and (more commonly) mergers because companies felt the need to expand in order to compete in a global market: Hoffman La Roche and Genetic or Merck and Du Pont in pharmaceuticals; AT&T and NCR in computers; Matsushita and MCA in entertainment electronics; Whirlpool and Philips in white goods; Asahi and Elders IXL in beer. Procter & Gamble's chairman Edwin L. Arztz offered these words at the company's general meeting in 1990: "The acquisition strategy will be driven by globalization, which will be the principal engine of growth in sales. It's not optional. That's the way business will be done."[1]

In all areas of business, small and medium-sized companies are being extinguished by the large multinationals. The world of brands is no different. Behind all the decisive talk, however, the issue of globalization is far from clear.

Is the World Becoming One Big Market?

Globalization became big news after the 1983 publication of an essay in the *Harvard Business Review* by Professor Theodore Levitt. It began with some contentious assertions:

> A powerful force now drives the world towards a single converging commonality, and that force is technology. . . . The result is a new commercial reality—the emergence of global markets for standardized consumer products on a previously unimagined scale of magnitude. Corporations geared to this new reality benefit from enormous economies of scale in

production, distribution, marketing, and management. By translating these benefits into reduced world prices, they can decimate competitors that still live in the disabling grip of old assumptions about how the world works. Gone are accustomed differences in national or regional preference. . . . Ancient differences in national tastes or modes of doing business disappear. The commonality of preferences leads inescapably to the standardization of products, manufacturing, and the institutions of trade and commerce.[2]

In Levitt's new world order, "homogenization" of wants is driven by new technology, mass communication, and travel. No one disputes that these phenomena are leading to the emergence of a new world culture—but is global standardization of brands the correct business response? Levitt cites Coca-Cola, which he argues is sold everywhere and welcomed by everyone, as are Revlon cosmetics, Sony televisions, and Levi's jeans. He suggests not only a new type of company ("global" rather than "multinational") but a new way of approaching marketing. Multinational companies, according to Levitt, mistakenly think that local preferences are fixed and that marketing means giving customers what they claim to want. In fact, he argues, the emergence of global brands demonstrates that standardized brands at acceptable quality levels and ever-decreasing real price levels will always win the day. The Japanese have sought for commonalities and similarities around the world—reliable, standard products at competitive prices—and they have infiltrated Western markets on this platform.

Many corporations embraced the idea of globalization with enthusiasm, using it as a rationale for expansion into foreign markets as their home markets matured. Some, such as marketing services group Saatchi & Saatchi, loudly proclaimed the gospel of a global uniformity of demand, and the need for global players to meet it. In reality, however, most corporations were (and still are) adapting their marketing mix to local conditions. Marlboro cigarettes, for instance, has over 20 different formulations around the world to suit local preferences. While Unilever's Timotei cosmetic brand is a success internationally, with its blonde model as a symbol of natural purity, it is the exception in the corporation's portfolio; other global brands, such as Impulse body spray, have different promotional executions in different countries, even though they all convey the same theme. The usual approach is embodied by the common phrase, "Think globally, act locally."

This undisputed fact underlines the academic challenge to Professor Levitt. Another major marketing commentator, Philip Kotler, argued that markets are becoming more fragmented, not less.[3] Standardization in his view will soon prove to be a red herring, as bland global brands prove vulnerable to local niche brands with higher added value for specific local wants, which the global brands ignore. In an article summarizing this debate, Susan Douglas and Yoram Wind conclude:

> The adoption of a strategy of universal standardization appears naive and oversimplistic. . . . Such an approach as a universal strategy in relation to all markets may not be desirable, and may lead to major strategic blunders. Furthermore, it implies a product orientation, and a product-driven strategy, rather than a strategy grounded in a systematic analysis of customer behavior and response patterns and market characteristics. . . . The design of an effective global marketing strategy does not necessarily entail the marketing of standardized products and global brands worldwide.[4]

So which is right—standardization or localization? The tough brand strategy decisions being encountered by many management teams are exemplified by two recent press reports on the activities of two branding giants, Unilever and Procter & Gamble.

> Unilever, the foods and detergents multinational, is entering into its first joint venture in Eastern Europe with the purchase of an 80 percent stake in Pollena Bydgoszcz, Poland's leading laundry detergents producer. Unilever said the new venture, to be re-named Lever Polska, was the first step in a long-term plan to enter other Polish consumer markets such as food and toiletry products. But Unilever has yet to decide whether to introduce any of its Western detergent brands—which include Persil, Surf, and Radion—into Poland. The market is currently served by local brands.[5]

> In the next three years Japan should replace West Germany as P&G's biggest foreign market. The key to cracking Japan: realizing that the company would have to fine-tune its "world products"—defined by P&G as the best you can buy anywhere—to the Japanese market. . . .
>
> P&G once truly believed its marketing prowess could ignore cultural differences. That attitude is changing. Says Arztz: "We need to develop the ability to deliver globally what we do well locally. We have to adapt to overseas markets."[6]

Examples of truly global brands (in the sense that all elements of the marketing mix are standard around the world) are in fact still rare, although powerful (e.g., the opening of McDonald's in Moscow). In recent years, Gillette has successfully launched a global world brand with its Sensor disposable razor, sold as a standardized product worldwide with standardized packaging. The global concept for the razor was researched across European markets following its success in the United States and it was concluded that consumers interpreted the images in exactly the same way. The images used were emotional ones, such as the link between father and son, and Gillette has since spent $50 million getting its message across Europe. It is now launching Sensor to such diverse markets as Japan and Iceland, using the same mass media campaign.

Is the Gillette Sensor approach the model of the future? Or is the more usual practice of local adaptation likely to be more successful? As usual, the truth is somewhere in between the two extremes. To understand how it should build its international brand portfolio, a company must be able to analyze the arguments in terms of several familiar marketing concepts.

The Elements of the Globalization Decision

All kinds of factors are mixed up in this argument: cultural trends, marketing, production economics, and more. They are too often employed without a real understanding of branding and how it relates to demand. The areas in which management must reach a view are many and complex.

Cultural Globalization versus Homogeneity of Demand

There is certainly a gradual merging of world cultures, brought about especially by communications technology and the growth of international travel. This need not result, however, in a homogeneity of demand—the fact that Japanese mothers change the diapers on their babies much more frequently than American mothers is for example unlikely to be changed by the gradual westernization of Japanese society.

On the other hand, there are certainly some universal drives that marketers can use to homogenize worldwide demand. People are remarkably alike in their need to be loved or the desire to be beautiful and healthy. Arguably, the most powerful global drive is that shared by the youth segment, given its propensity to identify with external images and role models. In all cases, it is vital to analyze how important cultural homogeneity is in brand preference, because it is clear that in some areas there *are* local variations in demand.

What Is Internationalism in Brand Terms?

Consumers will buy a global brand either because it is the cheapest (in which case its globalism is irrelevant) or because they subscribe to certain qualities that inevitably accompany that status: a big brand, a brand without "roots" in local production, a brand that supports (however implicitly) the ideas of cultural homogeneity. The most obviously successful global brands to date have been products like Coca-Cola, Levi's, or Marlboro where a particular image (the American way of life) has been part of the offering. Image-driven markets in which consumers can demonstrate their cosmopolitan outlook are a rich area for global brands such as Rolex, Gucci, or Lacoste. Another obvious area is new technology where a particular supplier has the reputation of being an innovator or expert, and where local suppliers are therefore regarded as laggards in quality terms—Kodak and Sony are obvious examples.

A global brand of course offers more than wide availability; its internationalism has to be part of the way it meets consumer wants. A company that understands this and employs it successfully as a strength is Benetton: The "United Colors of Benetton" concept takes all that is generally seen as good in the idea of a global village. This brand concept is also interesting in that it partly addresses the issue of the "new consumer," just starting to emerge in the more developed economies, who tends to show an antipathy toward all the forces represented by global brands, such as big business, mass markets, and cultural unity. If new consumerism spreads, the fragmentation of markets will accelerate, and there will be a swing toward local "heritage" brands.

The perception of the major Western global company brands in developing countries as symbols of a new era of material success is in any case already quite different from that in their home markets, where the perceptions of both familiarity and reliability feature much more strongly. It would indeed be remarkable for a single brand to incorporate the cultural diversity of the world, unless it were either representing globalism per se or appealing to some basic uniting human motivation.

The Difference Between Global Uniformity and Global Segments

In terms of brand preference in a given category, a German consumer may have more in common with Japanese and American counterparts than with another group of Germans. This does not mean that everybody in the world has similar preferences. This is one of the weak points in Levitt's argument. It is quite possible for there to be global segments at the same time that markets are fragmenting. If a product finds international demand, this does not mean that it is the only segment in the market and that the suitable strategy is one of standardization. An understanding of market structure is as important as ever in approaching global branding.

Levitt's assertions about homogeneity of demand fly in the face of all other trends in both marketing and production. In several industries, notably marketing services, financial services, and accounting and consultancy, there have been several attempts to create "one-stop shops." In all cases customers have fought against the offer of an exclusive relationship with suppliers across a range of services. They have chosen to maintain their power by having a range of suppliers, each specialists in a chosen field. Service conglomerates may well come to be viewed as the great business myth of the 1980s. Added to what is already known about the prevalence of repertoires and the relative rarity of exclusive brand loyalty in FMCG markets, this suggests that two of the factors behind the idea of globalization (the importance of size and the uniformity of demand) are exaggerated. The evidence points toward more fragmented markets. At the same time, these fragments or segments are becoming easier to identify, and easier to access across national boundaries.

Are There Economies of Scale, and Do Consumers Buy on Price?

Levitt's other argument for globalization is that it offers economies of scale that can be passed on to consumers. The common wisdom that higher volumes produce lower costs is less compelling than it used to be. Technological developments in flexible factory automation can give the same scale economies and allow products with much lower production volumes to compete with globally standardized products. This may make it possible for a small local supplier to be just as efficient without a global operation, and to offer products that match local needs. Flexible automation also allows for product modifications in the later stages of production, offering a wider variety of model versions adapted to local markets. In service markets, all available evidence points to a lack of economies of scale.

The positioning of a brand on price is in many ways a precarious strategy. Consumers who buy on price are usually not brand loyal and may well switch when the inevitable competition emerges. A low-price positioning strategy is also notoriously vulnerable to attack from changing technology. There is the additional risk that a standardized product at a low price may in fact be underpriced and underdesigned for a country that is relatively economically developed, but it may be overpriced and overdesigned for a less well developed country. It will end up serving neither market well.

Can a Standardized Approach Be Implemented in All Areas of the Marketing Mix?

Trade or government restrictions may hinder a uniform approach. Tariffs or quotas on the import of key materials, components, or other resources may, for example, affect production costs and thus hamper uniform pricing, or result in substitution of other components and modification in product design. Some products are legally required to contain a certain proportion of locally manufactured components. In Japan many products in the electronics and food category have to conform to product design and composition standards regulated by the relevant trade body; this may result in a product formulation different from that desired in other countries. There may be constraints and limitations in implementing advertising and promotional strategies worldwide, such as a ban on certain categories or regulations on content or the nature of claims. There may also be trade issues that cause conflict between countries where the retail scene is fragmented and those where distribution is concentrated into a relatively small number of major national chains that expect tailor-made promotions and negotiations over merchandising.

Internationalism: An Alternative to Globalism

A consideration of these factors will incline most managers to the view that the globalization of a brand is virtually impossible. This does not mean that the other extreme—local brand autonomy ("localization")—is any more desirable. The advantages of brands that claim to be global are obvious:

- Recognition on the part of the consumer who has traveled.
- Respect for success—any brand that is big will attract more trust on the part of some consumers, just as market leaders have an unfair advantage.
- Leverage with the distribution trade, an area where size certainly is a bargaining tool.
- The possible advantages already discussed of "internationalism" as a position, and possible economies of scale in numerous areas.

A management team will also probably be disposed toward some form of globalization for two very good reasons. First, it widens the target market geographically; as every company has a need to continue to grow, this opportunity will be welcome. Second, a globalization strategy may be less risky than the alternative, which will involve innovation rather than simply building on existing strength, and it may offer fewer potential economies of scale, not least in management time.

Standardization goes against all the value-adding instincts of the experienced marketer. However, while it may appear an unadventurous strategy, it does in fact demand extra courage. There are many ways in which the position could be threatened, such as local variations in demand or local triggers for change in the market, and while international positions may well be advantageous in a shrinking world, some form of targeting will also be vital.

The advantages claimed for global brands in fact accrue from internationalism rather than from the standardized globalism of Levitt's argument. The benefits of internationalization, without the risks of standardization, are the objective of the "Think globally, act locally" approach (sometimes called "global marketing"). This assumes that the basic position of a brand is the same worldwide, but that the execution is subject to local demands. (See the Johnnie Walker Scotch case study on pages 236–42.) The consumer picks up the internationalism of the brand, the trade respects its global status, and yet at the same time the brand is made relevant to local markets. This is now the approach employed by United Distillers, the world's largest liquor company, for all its brands. Although its status- and image-conscious market offers considerable scope for internationalization, the company is adamant that local execution is essential for maximization of brand power.

The key to this balancing act is a clear understanding of the brand management process. The earlier steps (understanding the brand and formulating its strategy or position) can be centralized, and the output is a global strategy. The implementation of the strategy (the marketing mix) can be varied to some extent between different parts of the world. Conflicting requirements for central and local management will need negotiating, but the outcome is more likely to maintain brand integrity and market relevance simultaneously.

Once again, central branding principles hold the key. The basic distinction between brand and product is vital. The brand is a perception in the consumer's mind. So long as that is unaffected, the mechanical aspects of product differentiation may be varied, as may any element of the marketing mix. Even the personality of the brand may vary slightly, so long as the consumer take-out ("I buy Brand X because. . .") is consistent. To manage a brand internationally, a company must be confident that it understands the essence of its brand. In this case, the essence will be the core value that translates internationally.

Text continues on page 242, after the case study.

"Think Globally, Act Locally"

Johnnie Walker Black Label Scotch

• • • • •

Johnnie Walker is the world's largest Scotch brand. In its Red Label and Black Label guises it has historically enjoyed a dominant position in many world markets. However, in recent years the brand has come under strong competition and its rate of growth has slowed and even declined in some areas.

In 1987 the Johnnie Walker brand became part of United Distillers, the spirits arm of the Guinness group. Johnnie Walker was by far the strongest in a stable of strong spirits brands and the new management of United Distillers were determined to revitalize it.

An internal review revealed that neither distribution problems nor relative pricing could account for Johnnie Walker's problems. A major project to research consumer perceptions and knowledge of the brand, with a view to developing future positioning and advertising strategies, was undertaken. This included both the Red Label and Black Label brands, though this case study concentrates on Black Label.

Establishing the "Essence"

Initial research focused on ten key markets worldwide, with fairly explicit objectives:

- Determine current perceptions of the Johnnie Walker brand and competing brands.
- Elicit the core values that make up the "essence" of the brand.
- Determine how far the core values translate across different markets.
- Elicit the extent to which Black Label has brand values distinct from those of its Red Label stablemate.

Research was conducted mainly through group discussions. It was felt that some of the strongest imagery concerning Scotch whiskey generally and

Black Label as a brand could lie at almost subconscious levels; group discussion is one of the best ways of allowing deeply held perceptions to emerge.

Two techniques were found to be particularly useful:

- **"Brand party" technique:** This asks people to imagine that all the whiskey brands they know are attending a party and to describe how they might behave—quiet, noisy, shy, popular, and so on. Using this technique, Black Label emerged as a respected figure with sophisticated tastes. He would be pictured, for example, in serious conversation about business or current affairs with Dimple or Chivas Regal. The brand also reflected some of the classic deluxe sector imagery current in each market—for example, sociable and playboyish in Thailand, aristocratic and British in Spain.
- **"Words and pictures" technique:** This gives people a collection of images, words, and phrases from which to make a collage of the ones they associate with the brand.

In addition, people in all the research markets were shown "theme boards" with pictures covering a number of possible advertising themes, such as Scottishness, romance, internationalism, and blackness. As a guide to potential communication and advertising strategies, these provided a vein of potential imagery.

The initial research provided some key conclusions on which future strategies would be based:

- Consumers across different markets held a clear and coherent perception of the Black Label brand.
- In many markets the brand was under threat from more active competitors, notably Chivas Regal.
- The brand needed to be firmly anchored in the premium Scotch whiskey sector by taking on more of the symbolism associated with the deluxe category and through a revitalization of its image.
- Black Label possessed a powerful latent imagery that would allow strong positioning against competitors.
- The consistency of the brand "essence" would allow a single *global* design brief for packaging.
- Different positions relative to competitors and different attitudes to Scotch whiskey in different markets required a *regional* approach to advertising.

Going Global on Packaging

The fact that the core values of the brand were consistent enough to allow a single packaging design worldwide was important. A high proportion of sales are through duty-free outlets, and customers need to be able to recognize the brand readily wherever they are shopping.

The design of both the carton and the bottle was considered, but this case concentrates on the bottle alone. The new bottle had a difficult task to fulfill. The existing one was believed to undersell the brand in two ways: by having less obvious visual appeal than some rivals and, more fundamentally, by holding the image back. However, both marketing department beliefs and the reaction of consumers who had been researched suggested that design changes should be subtle—the key features by which Black Label was recognized and loved had to remain untouched.

That meant that the designers had to work with the square-sided bottle, the black and gold coloring, the diagonal center label, and separate neck and foot labels. The only areas of difference were in the treatment of lettering and spacing, color tones (especially the gold), and the crest and "12-year-old" motif.

Five new bottle designs were tested in seven national markets. The main aim of the testing, apart from overall visual impact, was to find out the effects of the different elements of the design and to reduce them to one or two alternatives that appeared to create the effects desired for the brand. Two of the designs were thought to have sufficient promise to go forward, with amendments, for further testing.

Following design changes, the two new bottles and the existing one were tested in seven markets: Australia, France, Japan, Thailand, the United Kingdom, the United States, and Venezuela. These countries represented both differing cultures and differing lifestages of the brand. In the English-speaking countries the long history of Black Label made it the epitome of genuine, traditional, deluxe Scotch whiskey. In France it was seen as an elegant, modern confection similar to Chivas Regal. In the Far East the symbolism of black and gold was the most important property. In Venezuela the brand had associations of luxury and voluptuousness, again largely through the labelling.

Research uncovered two axes of importance to the brand:

Empty   ←——————→   Satisfying
Modern elegance   ←——→   Old-fashioned warmth

Figure 11.1 **Black Label: Matrix of Attributes**

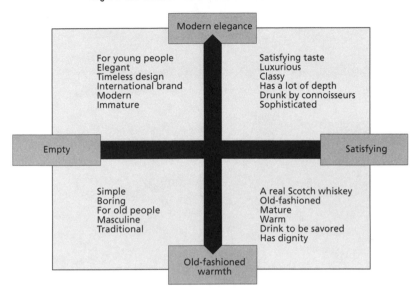

Source: Company data, 1988.

These can be combined in a matrix, with the attributes with the greatest influence in each quartile (see Figure 11.1 above).

Figure 11.2 (page 240) shows the positions of the test markets on the same matrix and illustrates the difficulties faced by the packaging. A single design was essential in an international market, yet the weaknesses to be corrected were diametrically opposed from one market to another. In some countries the brand had sunk into cozy old-fashionedness; in others it was smart and elegant but completely lacking in the warmth associated with brand loyalty. Venezuela, a highly successful market for Black Label, was in the most desirable position, with the brand being seen as elegant and modern, but not so much as to lose the elements of tradition and genuineness, and still retaining the satisfaction and product quality needed by a premium brand.

The testing of the three bottles showed that in terms of the matrix there was very little shift in terms of attributes in some countries, such as the United Kingdom, while in others, such as France, the shift caused by the new bottles was in the *wrong* direction, toward greater emptiness. What appeared to have happened was that the amendments made to the two

Figure 11.2 **Black Label: Matrix of Test Markets**

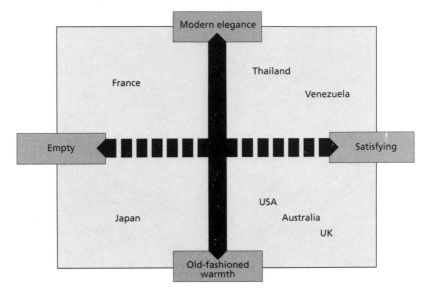

Source: Company data, 1988.

new bottles before retesting had gone too far. Two new designs for the foot label were therefore reworked. On one package the label was straight but with cleaner lettering and a softer, more luxurious gold. The other was similar, but with a curved label. This caused uneasiness that the brand might be moving too far from its roots. The changes to the straight label, though very subtle, were extremely effective in adding to the luxurious feel of the brand, and this was finally agreed as the new packaging.

Advertising—The Need for Local Heroes

Although research had confirmed the appropriateness of a universal packaging for Black Label, it also suggested that advertising communication would have to be locally, or at least regionally, directed. Separate advertising briefs were therefore prepared for the United Kingdom, the rest of Europe, Southeast Asia, Australia, Latin America, and North America.

These briefs all kept very close to the core values of the brand but differed in their description of the target audience, the desired user imagery, and the mood and tone of the advertising.

Both existing and planned advertising campaigns were evaluated in all the markets, usually by group discussion. As an example, it is worth looking at the development of a new advertising campaign in Southeast Asia.

Implementing the Global Strategy in Southeast Asia

The new advertising brief was given to a number of advertising agencies, and research to assess alternative campaign ideas against the communication requirements was carried out in Hong Kong, Singapore, and Thailand. Six campaigns were tested in qualitative groups of carefully selected male spirits drinkers. During each group, lasting about two hours, participants were shown visuals or storyboards of each campaign and invited to discuss them.

Of the six campaigns, most failed to achieve the communication balance needed. However, one did prove remarkably effective. This was called "Senses," and made a feature of evoking the look, touch, sound, and smell of the brand in a socially sophisticated setting. The story line was straightforward. A man at a cocktail party makes eye contact with a beautiful woman dressed in black. Shots of the man pouring a Black Label whiskey are intercut with evocative images of the woman touching her black stocking, playing a single black note on a piano, and so on. This concept delivered a communication concentrating on the special satisfactions of drinking Black Label set in a broader upmarket and appealing context. Unusually for liquor advertising, there was also a clear role for the brand, and the communication succeeded in evoking "appetite appeal" for the smell and taste of the brand.

Here was an idea obviously worthy of development. The Southeast Asia campaign looked a certain winner, though there were problems that were resolved only with local help. (Similar local input took place in all the markets.) Some older Thais, for example, reacted negatively to the campaign's emphasis on blackness. Black was felt to be dull, melancholy, and inappropriate. Thai colleagues attributed this to the local cultural associations with bad luck. While blackness could obviously not be abandoned, it was possible to make the black glossy-smart rather than funereal and to give more emphasis to the gold element in the brand's labeling.

A second problem was also a cultural faux pas. In the initial treatment of the cocktail party scene, the woman at one point adopts a pose in which her feet are higher than her head. In the Buddhist tradition this is very disturbing, since the head is regarded as special and not to be overshadowed, while feet are dirty and base.

CONCLUSION

Two key lessons emerge from the whole brand revitalization exercise at Johnnie Walker:

- A clear statement of core brand values, the "essence" of the brand, has to be agreed upon.
- Advertising development needs to be local even if the central strategy is a global one.

Text continued from page 235.

Strategic Options

The adoption of a global perspective, then, does not mean that a strategy of standardization should necessarily follow. It is quite possible to build a global brand position or image while having variation in the marketing mix. Nevertheless, this apparently "best of all worlds" solution has many pitfalls.

The first is the brand name. It is highly likely that any brand name that is pronounceable, inoffensive, and memorable in all languages will also be bland and unable to carry any special motivating significance. Perhaps the biggest single danger in trying to build any sort of international position is brand anonymity.

Deciding just when local variations become too varied is also difficult. If the brand property is a particular person, or a form of packaging, then even slight interference is likely to alter the all-important consumer perception. For this reason, "global" brands tend to place great importance on total uniformity in name, physical identity, and in many cases the promotion.

Figure 11.3 **Global Product Positioning Continuum**

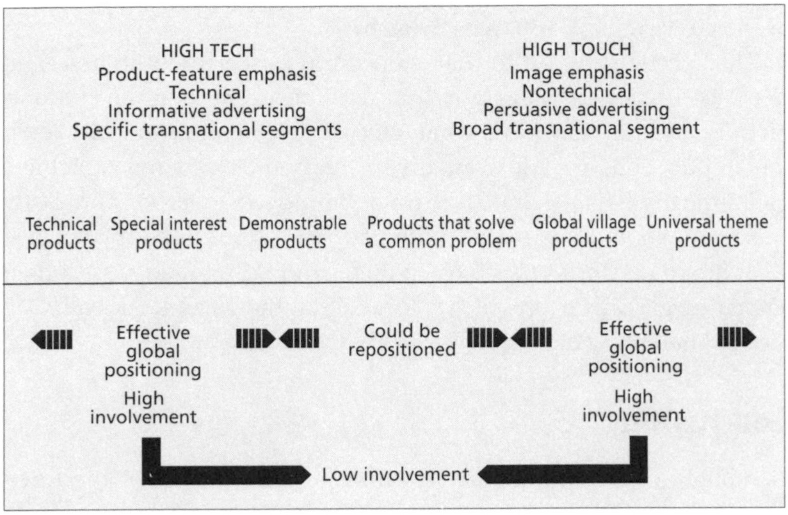

Source: Teresa Domzal and Lynette Unger, "Emerging Positioning Strategies in Global Marketing," *Journal of Consumer Marketing* 4, no. 4 (Fall 1987).

This is a graveyard for poorly managed brands. Globalization must not be seen simply as heavy spending behind a uniform identity. As in all areas of branding, managers of global brands will come to understand that the basic principles of a clear, differentiated, and motivating brand proposition that adds value to targeted customers must not be sacrificed in the rush toward the novelty of globalization. The key issues are, as always, understanding the market and identifying the brand proposition that most closely meets the need and the wants.

An interesting model that aims to decide which products are more suitable for global branding and standardized product imagery has been proposed by Domzal and Unger. Their continuum model categorizes brands into types based upon the level of involvement (see Figure 11.3 above).[7] They argue that two types of high involvement lend themselves to global positioning. The first, high tech, relates to products that have a strong emphasis on technical features, especially in new technologies, and where consumers worldwide share a common language; obvious areas are personal computers, video and stereo equipment, and cars. The second, high touch, refers to products that fulfill emotional needs, such as fragrance, fashion, and jewelry. It is possible to align these brands with universal human motivations, such as the desire to be beautiful (e.g., Chanel) or the desire to have fun (e.g., Swatch).

This model is useful in that it encourages selectivity in assessing markets ripe for globalization. It is also consistent with the evidence of those brands that have come closest to globalization. However, the implications that low involvement brands can never achieve global positions, and that they must be moved to either end of the spectrum, should be treated with caution. The logical approach to such brands is not to try to force them into false brand positions in search of globalism but to try to achieve the "Think globally, act locally" balancing act.

Conclusion

Genuinely global brands are few and far between. Even these few are increasingly vulnerable to local competition as markets fragment and consumers become more sophisticated in different ways in different regions. It is vital for companies to be selective in opting for global positions, and to test the brand rigorously against criteria for globalization.

Above all, a company must be clear about its objectives for pursuing an international brand strategy. Certain aspects of operations benefit from the consolidation that comes from a wider sphere. The "hard" end of operations, such as finance, distribution, production, or information systems, would possibly work better in a single international system than in a group of autonomous national units. In each area it may be possible to derive synergies from global approaches, and economies of scale. But branding is part of the "soft" end of a business; it deals with people's perceptions and can thus be categorized along with human resource management and corporate culture as an area where subtle local variations are likely to be significant (see Figure 11.4 on page 245).

While international branding is clearly feasible, the evidence points against standardization as an optimum route to this goal. The real management challenge is to balance the need for international consistency of strategic position with the need for maximum added value to segments of consumers wherever they may be.

Globalization is based upon certain assumptions about the future of marketing: Mass markets will become more important; big is

Figure 11.4 **Global Integration of Corporate Systems vs. Local Adaptation of Human Factors**

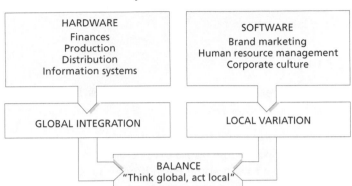

beautiful; regional variations in taste will disappear. For the most part, these would represent a reversal of recent trends. It will be a brave corporation that embraces these beliefs without the insurance policies of solid domestic markets and some local flexibility.

SUMMARY

The idea that the future of branding lies in globalization springs from a belief that all the world's markets are merging into one. This could be a reason to achieve economies of scale in costs or promotion, or be seen as a marketing imperative—as needs and wants converge, so brands should become simpler. In fact, in many cases markets are fragmenting, not converging, and mass global brands are less likely to succeed.

"Internationalization" is distinct from "globalization." It is quite possible for segments of a market to straddle national boundaries while markets are fragmenting. An international brand would be an appropriate response, but not a standardized brand for an international mass market. Internationalism is the basis for judging whether or not a brand is a suitable one for marketing in many countries. A truly international brand must offer more than multi-country distribution.

Genuinely global brands will be few and far between. The common solution of "Think globally, act locally" is the approach that is most likely to achieve a workable division between those aspects of an organization that can be standardized globally and those that are sensitive to local influences. Branding issues generally fall into the latter category.

CHECKLIST

The following criteria need to be applied in assessing the suitability of a brand for internationalization:

- Is there a genuine uniformity of demand?
- Is globalism part of the brand proposition?
- Does the brand meet some basic human need that transcends national cultures?
- Is it a specialist brand where the supplier is viewed as the most competent producer in the world?
- Is there an unsegmented mass global market?
- Are there economies of scale in any aspect of operations?
- Do customers buy on price?
- Can a global position be implemented across the marketing mix?

REFERENCES

1. *Wall Street Journal* (May 21, 1990), p. 12.

2. Theodore Levitt, "The Globalization of Markets," *Harvard Business Review* (May/June 1983), pp. 92–95.

3. Philip Kotler, "Global Standardization—Courting Danger," (Paper delivered at the American Marketing Association Conference, Washington D.C., 1985).

4. Susan P. Douglas and Yoram Wind, "The Myth of Globalization," *Columbia Journal of World Business* (Winter 1987), pp. 19–28.

5. *The Independent* (June 18, 1991), p. 25.

6. "P & G Rewrites the Marketing Rules," *Fortune* (November 6, 1989), p. 48.

7. Teresa Domzal and Lynette Unger, "Emerging Positioning Strategies in Global Marketing," *Journal of Consumer Marketing* 4, no. 4 (Fall 1987), pp. 23–40.

Glossary

Above the line Term for promotion activities that use mass media and are traditionally paid for by commission on usage; for normal purposes, the term means advertising.

Adstock The cumulative effect in the market of previous advertising, based on the fact that advertising may continue to have an effect on consumer perception for some time after it is shown. It is often calculated quantitatively in advertising models by applying a gradual decay rate to the rating points accumulated during campaigns.

Advertising-to-sales ratio (A/S) The expenditure on advertising expressed as a proportion of the total sales. Can be applied at brand, corporate, or industry level.

AIO (Attitudes, Interests and Opinions) Name for market research studies that categorize consumers into segments on the basis of these variables. Similar to lifestyle schemes.

A & P (Advertising and Promotion) Usually used to describe a department in a company or a budget.

Audience research Data on the number and categories of people who read, watch, or listen to various media. Used as the basis for measuring the number of people who are exposed to an advertisement.

Awareness The ability of a consumer to remember a particular brand or advertisement, either spontaneously or prompted. Widely used as a key indicator of marketing effectiveness.

Behavior Used in marketing to describe observable actions by consumers, quite distinct from the attitudes that lie behind the behaviors.

Below the line Term for promotional activities that are directed at targeted individuals or objectives, and are traditionally paid for by fee. The term is used for most nonadvertising promotions, such as sales promotions and direct mail.

Blind test A product test where consumers do not know the identity of the product(s), thus ensuring that they reach a judgment solely on the basis of a product's attributes without any influence from advertising, packaging, etc.

Brand The personality or identity of a product, range of products, or an organization, derived from consumer perception of both tangible and intangible attributes.

Brand equity The goodwill that exists in the market for a brand as a result of a period of brand presence and consumer experience.

Brand map A graphic representation of the relative positions of a number of brands in the market, mapped against the main dimensions of consumer perception in that market.

Brand property A specific brand attribute of a brand that is an identifier, widely associated by consumers with the brand; examples might be a logo, packaging, or a personality used in promotion.

Burst An advertising campaign where the advertisements are shown intensively over a short period of time.

Buying cycle The period of time between repeat purchases; for example, the buying cycle for sugar is much shorter than that for cars.

CATI (Computer Assisted Telephone Interviewing) Market research based on telephone interviews where results are fed into a computer for collation and analysis.

Cluster analysis A statistical technique that sorts a variety of brands or individuals into clusters of homogeneous groups, through analysis of their attributes.

Competitive advantage An aspect of a brand offering or an organization's operations that meets customer needs better than the alternatives in the market.

Concept Term widely used for the summary idea behind a brand or an advertising campaign, rather like USP or the proposition. Market research to test consumer reaction is therefore known as a "concept test."

Correspondence mapping A form of brand mapping showing the relative positions of brands within a market, or the relative importance of aspects of a brand to different segments of the market.

Cost-per-hundred (CPH) The cost of achieving 100 rating points during an advertising campaign.

Cost-per-thousand (CPT) The cost of advertising to 1,000 consumers through a given media; used to judge the relative cost-effectiveness of the media.

Coverage The percentage of the target market who have at least one opportunity to see an advertisement during a campaign.

DAGMAR (Defining Advertising Goals for Measured Advertising Results) A conceptual approach to advertising management, arguing that a specific communications objective can be set for any promotional activity, thus enabling expenditure to be evaluated.

Day-after-recall-test (DART) A method of evaluating advertisements based upon surveying consumers to see how many can recall an advertisement shown the previous day.

Depth A one-to-one market research interview, relatively unstructured in order to encourage exploratory discussion.

Drip An advertising campaign where the advertisements are shown at intervals over a longer period of time.

Dynamic difference model A method of evaluating advertising effectiveness by tracking the relationship between promotional expenditure and market share.

FMCG Fast moving consumer goods.

Focus group A market research discussion group of consumers, chaired by a researcher; usually used for qualitative research.

Frequency The number of times within a given period that a consumer has the opportunity to see an advertisement.

Gross Rating Points (GRPs) The total ratings achieved by an advertising campaign; that is, the sum of the ratings achieved by each individual exposure of the advertisement.

Hierarchy of effects A model of the consumer decision-making process, moving from unawareness of a brand to familiarity and preference.

Involvement The degree of care and trouble taken by a consumer in deciding which brand to buy.

Lifestyle A set of consumer behaviors uncovered by market research that are taken to indicate a particular set of social values and attitudes; used as a label for a segment.

Line extension The addition of a new variant to an already existing brand.

Marketing mix The areas of decision or activity through which a corporation markets its brands; usually used to indicate the simplified notion of the "four P's": product, price, promotion, and place (distribution).

Omnibus A form of market research where the same audience group is surveyed periodically, and various companies may buy into the survey with one or two questions.

OTS (Opportunity to see) One exposure of an advertisement to a consumer —the standard way of measuring promotional campaigns.

Panels Groups of consumers who keep a record of all their purchases; the results are then used by market researchers to identify consumption patterns.

Penetration The percentage of the target market who have bought a particular brand at least once.

Perceptual map Like brand mapping, a graphic representation of the relative positions of brands within a market. The positions are based upon consumer perceptions gathered through market research.

PIMS (Profit Impact of Market Strategy) An influential and ongoing research project into the factors driving profitability within and between markets.

Point vector mapping A form of brand mapping, in which a market or the different aspects of a brand are represented in terms of consumer perception.

Positioning The process of influencing a consumer's perception of a brand, implemented through the marketing mix.

Projective techniques Qualitative market research techniques used to investigate attitudes and perceptions not described by verbal answers. Methods include identifying brands as animals or cars, acting out brand personalities, etc.

Proposition A description of the appeal of a brand to its consumers; the reason why a consumer might prefer the brand.

Psychographics A research method of classifying consumers by their values and attitudes.

Recall The extent to which something can be remembered; often used as a measure of the effectiveness of advertising.

Repertoire The group of brands within a product category that a consumer regards as acceptable. In many markets exclusive brand loyalty is rare, and consumers switch within their repertoire.

Repertory grid A research technique that investigates the variables used by consumers to distinguish between brands within a market; sometimes referred to as a "Kelly" after the founder of the technique.

Retail audit   Surveys of sales taken at store level, widely used as the basis for market share calculations. Audits are run by sophisticated specialist companies.

Salient attribute   The aspect of a brand that is most noticeable to consumers and by which they tend to remember and judge the brand.

Segment   A subdivision of a market, consisting of a group of consumers with similar requirements of the product category, which are significantly different from the requirements of other consumers in the market.

Served market   The part of a market that a particular brand or company is targeting.

Share   The proportion of the overall sales in a market accounted for by a particular brand or company. It may be expressed as value share (when the calculations are based upon the expenditure in the market) or volume share (when the calculations are based upon the units sold in the market).

SOM (Share of market)

SOV (Share of voice)   The proportion of the overall advertising in a market that is accounted for by a particular brand or company.

Tracking study   Market research used to measure brand positions and the long-term effects of marketing activity. Usually consisting of a regularly repeated survey, a tracking study will measure awareness and attitudes, which can then be compared with the patterns of marketing activities.

Trial   The first purchase of a brand.

TVR (Television rating)   Expressed in points, a measurement of the weight of an advertising campaign. One TVR is 1% of the target population having one opportunity to see an advertisement.

U&A (Usage and Attitude)   The name given to a comprehensive research study of a market that includes both quantitative measures of consumer behavior and qualitative information on attitudes and consumer perceptions.

USP (Unique Selling Point or Proposition)   A phrase used to describe the characteristic about a brand that is unique and motivating to consumers and is thus its main appeal to the market.

Index